Teacher's Manual

HEALTH AND SAFETY FOR YOU

Sixth Edition

WEBSTER DIVISION

McGRAW-HILL BOOK COMPANY

New York   St. Louis   San Francisco
Auckland   Bogotá   Guatemala   Hamburg
Johannesburg   Lisbon   London   Madrid   Mexico
Montreal   New Delhi   Panama   Paris   San Juan
São Paulo   Singapore   Sydney   Tokyo   Toronto

THE AUTHORS

TED K. TSUMURA

teaches health at George Washington High School in Denver, Colorado. He holds a doctorate in Health Education and has 20 years of experience as a high school teacher. In 1976, he was named Colorado Teacher of the Year and was runner-up for the National Teacher of the Year award. He is also a member of the Advisory Board of the Colorado Department of Health Neonatal Screening for Genetic Disorders. He is a co-author of a textbook for high school biology students. He is past president of the Colorado Biology Teachers' Association.

LORRAINE HENKE JONES

is assistant professor of nursing at Ball State University in Indiana. Formerly, she was a teacher and health education specialist for Prince George's County Public Schools, Maryland. She holds a master's degree in both nursing and health education. She is also a member of Sigma Theta Tau (the national honor society of nursing) and Eta Sigma Gamma (the national professional health science honorary). She has written articles for health education and nursing journals. In addition, the American National Red Cross and the Agency for Instructional Television have published health and safety programs that she helped to write.

ISBN 0-07-065379-8

1 2 3 4 5 6 7 8 9 10 EDWEDW 92 91 90 89 88 87 86 85 84 83

TABLE OF CONTENTS

To Our Fellow Teachers:

ABOUT THE PUPIL EDITION

HEALTH AND SAFETY FOR YOU, sixth edition, is a practical text with a "wellness" approach for students of all abilities. Having taught health education in secondary schools, we wanted to aid both teachers and students. As you look over the special features of HEALTH AND SAFETY FOR YOU, we feel confident that you will be pleased with the unique set of learning features that allows this book to be used with classes of like ability and classes of mixed ability.

Trilevel Reading

The text is written to capture the interest of students at various levels of ability.

1. Photos, illustrations, and anatomical drawings are explained by captions using vocabulary words at or below grade level. Occasionally, a health-related term or technical term is used in a caption. Its meaning is explained in the easy-reference glossary.

2. The text section of the book is written at a reading level that the majority of secondary students comprehend with no difficulty.

3. An end-of-the-chapter feature, "Something to Think About," offers high-interest material written above grade level. This section is designed to motivate the average student and to meet the needs of the above average student.

Apply Your Knowledge and Extend Your Knowledge

Two groups of questions are presented at the end of each chapter. Questions in the "Apply Your Knowledge" group test mastery of basic concepts and health information. Questions in the "Extend Your Knowledge" group require both mastery and application of health concepts. Students are asked to use their acquired health knowledge to analyze complex situations, to discuss large-scale issues, or to initiate health-related projects.

Each question in "Apply Your Knowledge" and "Extend Your Knowledge" is keyed in the Teacher's Manual to the correct category of thinking according to Bloom's Taxonomy of Educational Objectives. (See page 42 for an explanation of Bloom's categories.) This categorization allows more sophisticated or less sophisticated questions to be directed or assigned to students of appropriate abilities.

Main Ideas and Key Words

The important concepts of a chapter are summarized in simple sentences at the end of that chapter. Health-related terms introduced or defined in the chapter are listed at the end of the chapter. Important health-related terms are defined again in the glossary. These learning aids are valuable for low-ability students, and they are also useful as study guides for students of average or higher abilities.

Basic-competency test questions and essay question

Each chapter test in the teacher's manual includes multiple-choice, true or false, matching, and short-answer questions. Each unit test includes a set of matching questions, a set of multiple-choice questions, and an essay question. The matching questions are basic-competency questions that test main concepts of the unit. Multiple-choice questions range from average to challenging in difficulty. The essay question in each unit test requires students to express individually what they have learned and to practice writing skills.

Full-color illustrations throughout

Students of all abilities are more easily motivated with visually attractive materials. We've taken special care to make this edition of HEALTH AND SAFETY FOR YOU a handsome book. New medical illustrations are included; new photos represent a balanced view of the lifestyles of men and women and people of different races. We want this text to "catch your students' eyes" each time they pick it up.

How will HEALTH AND SAFETY FOR YOU fit into your plans?

HEALTH AND SAFETY FOR YOU covers the core health topics commonly addressed in a secondary health survey course. This updated edition includes individual chapters on cancer, sexually transmitted diseases, coping with stress, genetics, and health-related careers. As a text-book, HEALTH AND SAFETY FOR YOU holds a definite point of view: an emphasis on prevention, a focus on the motivation of long-range and short-range positive health behaviors. Each unit and chapter can stand alone. While the book is intended to be used in sequence, it can be used effectively out of sequence to match various curricula. This helps in two ways:

1. HEALTH AND SAFETY FOR YOU can be used in any scheduling plan, for any length of time. There are enough units of material to cover a full school year. Or, you can select a single unit for a six-week marking period.

2. The flexibility of HEALTH AND SAFETY FOR YOU makes it easy to follow the guidelines or curricula of your own school district. If there is any content or activity included in the text which is outside your school's guidelines, you can appropriately exclude it. We encourage you to tailor your use of HEALTH AND SAFETY FOR YOU to the curriculum specifically written for students in your district.

ABOUT THE TEACHER'S MANUAL

HEALTH AND SAFETY FOR YOU is intended to support the curricula in your school district. Both text and teacher's manual are flexible in format to accommodate the considerable differences in communities across the nation. We urge you to tailor our materials to your local curriculum. Use only those activities that are appropriate to the needs of your community. Feel free to adapt or change our materials to suit your school district, your students, and your own teaching style.

As teachers, we wanted teaching aids that were more than just notes. We wanted
- activity suggestions with reproducible handout sheets;
- tests that could be reproduced and used as is, or that could serve as a source of suggestions for our own test questions;
- answers to end-of-chapter questions that also keyed level of difficulty;
- summaries of each chapter to refresh our memories.

All these aids are included in the teacher's manual. The pages are perforated for you to remove the tests or activities for reproducing. We're particularly pleased with the activities, since they are the ones we've used most successfully to reach and hold student interest.

We as authors are eager to know how you have used the book and the teacher's manual in your own classroom situations. If you have any suggestions or comments, please forward them to us through the Webster/McGraw-Hill sales representative in your area. Authors and publishers must rely on teacher feedback in order to make health education materials as pertinent and effective as we all want them to be.

TED K. TSUMURA AND LORRAINE HENKE JONES

REINFORCING BASIC SKILLS

Increasingly, the teaching and reinforcement of basic skills are the responsibilities of all teachers. The health education classroom provides an excellent setting for this contribution to the total education of each student. Because the study of health is so real, activities involving the reinforcement of functional reading and writing skills are often more readily accepted by students in the health course than in more traditional academic areas.

Following are some ways to integrate basic skills work into your lesson planning.

- *Overview the student text* to orient students to layout, organization, table of contents, headings, summaries, use of italics, glossary, and index. This process will help them see the book as a resource rather than a series of reading assignments.

- *Make the most of text reading.* Teacher intervention—a three-way interaction between student, teacher, and textbook—makes a big difference in student reading comprehension. Use the "Do you know?" questions at the beginning of each chapter to focus student reading. Have students use the text chapter summaries and encourage them to add other facts or concepts they see as important. Have students review the "Key Words" at the end of each chapter and encourage them to use the glossary as needed. "Apply Your Knowledge" questions may be answered orally in class or on paper as a homework assignment.

- *Encourage outside reading.* Because health and wellness are so much a part of our lives, there is an abundance of reading material available for student use. Newspaper and magazine articles are a good current-events supplement to the text and a good opportunity to teach students to critically evaluate what they read in the popular press. Research assignments provide the opportunity to teach students the use of the *Readers' Guide to Periodical Literature* and other reference materials in the library. An almanac, which will include a wide range of health-related topics (from accidents and aging to the World Health Organization and x-rays) is a good place for students to search for interesting facts and statistics.

- *Encourage writing.* Student writing assignments take time to correct, but repeated writing practice, supported by teacher feedback, is the basis of good writing. Correct all written work for grammar, spelling, structure, and clarity, as well as for content. The English department in your school may have a set of guidelines you can use as standards. There are many types of possible writing assignments in health. You might have students prepare written summaries of readings, field trips, films, guest-speaker presentations, or interviews. Students may prepare their reports individually and later share them with the class. Another area of possible assignments is letter writing. Health lends itself to letters to the editor, letters to members of congress, and letters of praise or complaint to product manufacturers. Here students are also practicing communication as it relates to civic responsibility. Health topics of special interest to adolescents make good subjects for articles for the school newspaper. This can be coordinated with the journalism instructor or newspaper advisor.

- *Provide opportunities for interpretation and use of numerical and written data.* This can begin with charts and graphs in the text. Some real-life examples include health-related job ads, hospital bills, insurance forms, and nutritional labeling on food packaging. Evaluating advertising to separate fact from puffery is another possibility.

CHAPTER 1 Health and Wellness

PERFORMANCE GOAL

After completing this chapter, students will know: how their bodies are changing, and what they can expect from their bodies in the future; what *health* and *wellness* mean; and what preventive health habits are and why everyone does not practice them. Most importantly, students will know how to take a personal health inventory.

SUGGESTED INCENTIVES

This chapter attempts to speak directly to the students in a highly personal and evaluative way. Open discussion will probably be very useful both in handling this chapter and in laying the groundwork for a study of the entire text. Discussion could first center on the difference between what the term *health* meant at the beginning of this century and what it means today. Then, a constructive personal review could bring out what preventive health actions the students or their parents did or did not take, and the reasons why. After this discussion, allow students time to take the health inventory. Those students who want to can then offer what they learned about themselves by taking the personal inventory. At this time, the weekly diary suggested as an "Extend Your Knowledge" activity could be started by the students. Stress the positive intention behind the diary—that everyone should take the responsibility for improving his or her own health.

CHAPTER SUMMARY

Today, health is considered to be a state of complete physical, mental, and social well-being. Simply being free from physical problems does not necessarily mean that a person possesses good health. More and more, mental and social well-being are also being taken into account. The noninfectious health problems people are suffering from today—heart attack, cancer, high blood pressure, and strokes—are now known to be influenced by mental and social health and a lifetime of daily health habits. In fact, it is almost impossible to separate mental and social health from physical health.

People who practice preventive health habits when they are young, and who continue to do so throughout their lives, have a better chance of avoiding or postponing illness and injury. But people will only take preventive health measures under certain conditions. Irwin M. Rosenstock, in "What Research in Motivation Suggests for Public Health" (*American Journal of Public Health*, March 1960), outlines the necessary conditions. First, people must see the health problem as one that has a good chance of affecting them. Second, they must believe that they would suffer serious consequences if the problem did affect them. Third, they must believe a course of action exists that they can take to reduce the threat. Fourth, they must think that this course of action is a reasonable one to follow. Mostly, it is lack of information, misinformation, or simply a poor attitude that makes a person not bother to practice preventive health measures.

There are probably as many excuses for not taking preventive health measures as there are people. One common excuse involves leaving the whole idea of "health" up to fate and thinking there is nothing that can be done to prevent disease and death. Another excuse comes from a belief that preventive health habits are too bothersome, difficult, or demanding. Taking health inventories often can serve as a good way to combat such excuses. It makes an individual recognize what particular personal health habits need to be, and can be, developed. Since excuses for not taking preventive health measures may be based on emotional reasons, Chapter 5, "Emotions and Mental Health," might be of some use in discussing this chapter with the class, especially the section on defense mechanisms.

CHAPTER 2 Basis of Movement

PERFORMANCE GOAL

After completing this chapter, students will know: that broken bones can bleed; how the arches of the foot protect the body; that muscles are made up of different colored fibers with different functions; and that heat is given off when muscles contract. Students will also know that a warm-up before physical activity is important to prevent muscle injury.

SUGGESTED INCENTIVES

This chapter attempts to encourage students to always do the proper amount and kind of exercise. This is accomplished by a careful explanation of the bones and muscles in the body, how they work, what can go wrong with them, and how they can be kept in excellent shape. It should be stressed that how much exercise a person should perform depends upon the condition of the heart and the person's general health as determined by regular physical examinations. But everyone should do some exercise. Warm-ups before sports and other recreational activities are especially important. As the title suggests, the information in this chapter is intended as a working foundation for the topics in Chapter 3, "Keeping Fit through Sports and Recreation." Students should be encouraged to refer to this chapter throughout the study of Chapter 3.

CHAPTER SUMMARY

Bones are living organs. They perform important jobs in the body, such as storing minerals, providing support, aiding movement, and protecting organs. The tissue inside bone, called bone marrow, produces red blood cells, three types of white blood cells, and platelets. Calcium and phosphate are two minerals that make bones hard and strong. Tough, fibrous tissues called ligaments hold the ends of bones together. This connection point between two bones is called a joint.

Bones need physical stimulation to be kept strong. In fact, the more bones are used, the stronger they become. Bones that are not used become weak through a process of decalcification, or loss of calcium.

Over 600 muscles move the different parts of the body. Muscle cells, also called muscle fibers, are long and can contract. Each muscle is surrounded by blood vessels, nerves, and connective tissue. Tendons are connective tissues that attach muscle to bone. It is the nerve attached to the muscle that, when stimulated, causes the muscle to contract. There are three types of muscles: voluntary, involuntary, and cardiac. Voluntary muscles are also called striated muscles or skeletal muscles. These muscles allow the body to move, and they can be controlled. Most involuntary muscles are smooth muscles. These muscles are in the stomach, the intestines, and other hollow tubes in the body. Their movements cannot consciously be controlled. The cardiac muscle is also known as the heart muscle. It looks like a striated muscle under a microscope, but it is really an involuntary muscle. This muscle permits circulation.

The color of muscle depends on myoglobin and on the amount of nerve stimulation to the fibers. Muscles are a mixture of red and white. Red muscle has more oxygen-supplying myoglobin and a nerve that is small in diameter. Therefore, it has a great amount of staying power and is always carrying impulses, but very slowly. White muscle has less myoglobin and a larger nerve. Therefore, it can exert greater force, but it lacks endurance and tires quickly.

At some point, everyone has experienced sore muscles. This is caused by a build-up of lactic acid and other irritating waste materials in the muscles when they are overused or have not been used regularly. Muscle soreness may be prevented by general warm-ups, and then by specific warm-ups appropriate to the sport or recreational activity one takes part in.

8

CHAPTER 3 Keeping Fit through Sports and Recreation

PERFORMANCE GOAL

After completing this chapter, students will know: why exercise is good for the heart and the muscles; whether or not they have good eye-hand coordination; how exercise affects blood pressure and pulse rate; that you should not wait until you are thirsty to drink water; and how to prevent sprains, dislocations, and shinsplints.

SUGGESTED INCENTIVES

Many of the myths about athletes and special diets and about women and sports can be aired during the study of this chapter. Students can also help one another test their physical fitness, and they can plan programs to increase their physical abilities. The importance of exercise should be stressed, along with the rules for exercising, such as knowing one's limitations, and not eating just before or after physical activity. Jogging is a popular form of exercise today, and students could form jogging groups together. They could also report to each other about any positive or negative exercise experience they might have had and how it happened.

CHAPTER SUMMARY

Exercise influences almost every body process. Running speeds the heartbeat, increases circulation, and raises blood pressure. When a person is at rest, approximately 1 gallon of blood per minute circulates through the heart. This is about two-thirds of the total blood supply. During vigorous exercise, this rate of circulation may increase about eight times. Breathing is deeper and more rapid during strenuous exercise, and nearly all lung space is used.

When a person eats shortly after exercising or exercises shortly after eating, there is a possibility that neither the digestive tract nor the skeletal muscles will receive enough blood to function satisfactorily. During training, exercise should be regular, with a gradual daily increase according to the person's physical capacities. Proper training results in stronger muscles, greater endurance, better coordination, a stronger heartbeat with a slower pulse, a slight rise in blood pressure during exercise, a quick return to the usual blood pressure after exercise, and good digestion and elimination.

There are several kinds of physical abilities. Flexibility means being able to move the joints of the body into and out of various positions easily. Coordination means that the entire body is working together smoothly. Equilibrium means being able to maintain balance. Agility is the ability to react quickly and surely. Speed is the measure of how fast body parts can move. Endurance is the ability of the body to withstand stress for long periods of time. And strength means to be able to lift, push, jump, or pull with powerful force of the muscles.

Most people need more exercise than they get. A good exercise program and proper diet help to prevent heart attacks and problems with blood circulation.

Many problems can occur during exercise if precautions are not taken. During exercise, the body usually perspires and can lose large amounts of water and salt. If these losses are not replaced, heat cramps, nausea, heat exhaustion, or heat stroke can happen. These problems can be prevented by drinking plenty of water before and during physical activity. Other problems are muscle lameness, which happens when muscles are overused; a pulled muscle, which is a torn tendon and may happen when proper warm-ups are not performed; and a charley horse, which comes from a hard blow to the front part of the thigh. Two major problems that can happen to the joints are sprains and dislocations. A sprain may be caused by too much stress being placed on a joint. A dislocation happens when enough force is applied to push the end of a bone out of its socket. Dislocations require a doctor's treatment at once. Most muscle injuries can be prevented with proper general and specific warm-ups. Warm-ups are needed even when muscles are toned and strong.

CHAPTER 4 Emotional Needs and Mature Personality

PERFORMANCE GOAL

After completing this chapter, students will know: how emotions can affect physical well-being; why conflict between parent and child usually increases during the teen years; how to develop self-confidence and maturity; and how to deal with sudden shifts in mood. Students will also know how to make good decisions and how to avoid misjudging the personalities of other people.

SUGGESTED INCENTIVES

A discussion exercise can be planned around such questions as: Which things in life can be changed? Which cannot be changed? Where do basic emotional needs come from? How can we change emotional reactions? Which emotional responses are taught? Who teaches them? Which emotional responses are learned by trial and error? Like Chapter 1, this chapter is highly personal, calling on the students to explore and evaluate themselves in light of the information provided. During discussion, students can see that many of their needs and emotions are shared by others in the class. Personality development can be linked directly to Chapter 1's definition of *health*.

CHAPTER SUMMARY

Emotional needs must be satisfied if a person is to enjoy life and feel a sense of security. Unmet emotional needs can make a person very unhappy or even emotionally sick. The specific emotional needs considered in this chapter are: the need for love—to give and receive attention, affection, admiration, and respect; the need for a sense of personal worth or autonomy—to make decisions, to achieve self-respect; the need for personal achievement—to accomplish something, to complete a job, to do something well; the need to create—to build, to paint, to write, to marry and have children; the need for role models in living—to admire and imitate great achievers; the need for a philosophy of life—to acquire a sense of values and to work out a way of living.

The family is one of the most important influences on personality. During adolescence, family relationships continue to influence the growing personality. Adolescents feel a strong inner drive for freedom and independence. The process of building a new relationship with one's parents during the teen years often leads to conflict and tension.

Maturity means full development. It is not necessarily characteristic of adulthood. People may be mature in some ways and not in others, or at some times and not at others. A person may be considered mature if she or he acts in a mature way most of the time. In order to develop maturity, teenagers must begin to understand their own feelings and moods. They must develop self-confidence. Teenagers must also begin to make responsible decisions, ones that cause the least possible harm to themselves and others. To make responsible decisions, they should use available resources, consult experienced advisers, explore all choices, and think about all possible consequences.

Looking at one's own personality, one should feel comfortable with oneself—able to deal with emotions, to endure disappointments, and to meet the demands of life. Looking at the personalities of others, one should consider background, aims, wants, and ways used to reach personal goals. Certain mistakes to avoid in judging others' personalities are: drawing a conclusion from only one event; placing too much importance on surface characteristics, such as appearance and clothes; using a "personality test" from a magazine or a newspaper; and labeling others as "types." Sterotyping is a very serious mistake when it involves a person's race, sex, religion, or nationality. A mature person accepts and is interested in the differences found in others. Students should remember that personality means the whole person in relation to his or her environment.

CHAPTER 5   Emotions and Mental Health

PERFORMANCE GOAL

After completing this chapter, students will know: how to handle hostile feelings; how fear can be a help at times; why a person might feel uncomfortable after doing something wrong; and why some people lie to themselves in trying to explain their failures. Most importantly, students will know how to do a self-check on their own mental health.

SUGGESTED INCENTIVES

To provide a better understanding of the emotions of anger and hostility, the students might put on several short plays. These plays could demonstrate how anger and hostility might be stirred up, and could show both good and bad ways of coping with these feelings. The dialogue under "Constructive Ways to Get Rid of Anger" in the chapter could be used as a starting point. Anger and hostility usually occur after a conflict or frustration because a person has not developed the capacity to react to frustration in other ways. Although anger and hostility are present in some degree in all people, the level can be kept low by learned reactions to conflict. The "acting-out" approach to this chapter may also be effectively used for "Coping with Stress" in Chapter 6.

CHAPTER SUMMARY

When the drive to satisfy an emotional need is blocked, a conflict occurs, and varying degrees of frustration are apt to result. The best way to deal with such frustration is to find other socially acceptable ways of satisfying the need. Other reactions to conflict and frustration may involve anger and hostility, anxiety and fear, or the use of defense mechanisms.

Defense mechanisms are ways of behaving and believing that protect a person who feels threatened. They are used in place of realistic methods of satisfying an emotional need. They sometimes enable people to live with themselves and preserve their sense of personal worth. But carried to extremes, defense mechanisms often lead to serious emotional illness. Rationalization is false reasoning used to preserve self-respect. Compensation is the process of making up for what a person feels he or she does not have or cannot do. Negativism involves refusal to do what is expected, or doing its opposite, because of a lack of confidence in one's ability. Identification is the process of identifying with a person who possesses characteristics the individual lacks. Daydreaming is the mechanism of substituting fantasy and dreams for realistic action. Escapism is the mechanism of completely avoiding whole situations or problems.

Like all emotions, anger and hostility can work either for or against a person. Uncontrolled anger and hostility may result in serious injury, delinquency, or crime. Controlled and put to use, anger and hostility may drive a person to work hard to achieve a goal, to right a wrong, to try to convince others by using reason. Small hostilities build up and accumulate even in normal people and must be drained off. Appropriate and socially acceptable ways of releasing hostility include talking to an understanding person about the angry feelings or participating in contests and competitive sports. Inappropriate and socially unacceptable ways include engaging in antisocial or criminal behavior, being excessively argumentative, and resisting reasonably constituted authority.

The list of eleven characteristics of a mentally healthy person should be studied in detail. Developing these characteristics is valuable in maintaining mental health. To help young people maintain good mental health, mature adults can assist them in making emotional adjustments.

CHAPTER 6   Living With Stress

PERFORMANCE GOAL

After completing this chapter, students will know: what a stress reaction is; when the body produces a stress response; whether or not stress can be harmful; what the common sysmptons of stress are; and how to cope with stress.

SUGGESTED INCENTIVES

In this century, when most of our illnesses are noninfectious diseases, the topic of stress and how to cope with it takes on tremendous importance. Use the "acting-out" approach described for Chapter 5 and the health inventory in Chapter 1. Focus on the stressful problems the students themselves would be most likely to experience, and ask them what physical problems might occur if these stressful situations were not dealt with. Effective coping with stress is a sign of mental and emotional maturity. But it is also something that people, including adults, are not able to do successfully all the time. Have students tell about some ways of coping with stress that have worked best for them.

CHAPTER SUMMARY

Stress is the effect of physical and mental demands made on the body. Stress may be a response to a crisis, such as physical danger, or to some unexpected news or request. It may also be a response to some everyday situation that you must experience again and again. Or it may simply be a response to change. Life changes are powerful stressors, and even a happy event can cause stress if a lot of change is needed. The Life Change Scale devised by Drs. Holmes and Rahe is a good indication of how stressful certain events might be for most people.

Sometimes stress may be harmful. The effects of unrelieved stress may take the form of stomach ache, headache, diarrhea, or indigestion. New research is also showing that stress over a long period of time causes damage and diseases of major body systems, especially the cardiovascular system, the digestive system, and the skeletal—muscular system. In addition, researchers have found that unrelieved stress can lower the body's resistance to ordinary infections, such as the common cold.

There are several ways of coping with stress to keep the stress level at the proper point. First, keep the body healthy by eating a well-balanced diet, getting enough sleep, and exercising regularly. A healthy body is better able to adapt to the normal stresses of everyday life, and it can better withstand the stresses caused by life changes. Second, know how to judge reality. Know when to change some situations and when to leave others alone. This includes what to try to change about other people and what to accept because it can't be changed. Fuming over situations and people will not change facts. Sometimes, removing oneself from situations one cannot easily handle is the best course of action. Third, try to spot stress and plan for it. Be prepared for stressful situations that are foreseeable. Sometimes, stress is hard to spot, and the stress symptoms, such as headaches, are felt before the cause becomes clear. Seek a doctor's advice for such symptons. Fourth, learn something about how to relax, and do things that are relaxing as part of your regular routine. Relaxation does not only mean play. It is necessary to health. Relaxing the muscles in the body slows down the body processes. Forcefully using the muscles in the body reduces built-up body tension. Both relaxation and exercise are good ways to obtain physical and mental relief.

Note: You may wish to include coverage of the supplementary material on suicide (pages 278 to 281) with the study of stress.

CHAPTER 7 Human Reproduction

PERFORMANCE GOAL

After completing this chapter, students will know: why some twins look alike and others do not; how some birth defects can be prevented; how cigarette smoking can affect an unborn baby; and what the function of the umbilical cord is.

SUGGESTED INCENTIVES

A visit to a prenatal clinic can be informative and can help students learn about the advice usually given to expectant mothers. If such a visit is not possible, a doctor (preferably an obstetrician) or a nurse might talk to the class about prenatal and postnatal care. A pediatrician could be helpful in providing the class with information on the growth and development of babies and children. The method and period of development of specific functions in individual organs in the fetus might be covered in the talk.

CHAPTER SUMMARY

Puberty is the period during which the ovaries in the female start to release ova, or egg cells, and the testes in the male start to produce sperm. Secondary sexual characteristics also begin to appear. In males, these characteristics are a deepening voice; hair on the face, under the arms, and in the genital area; and developed arm, leg, and chest muscles. The development of these male sexual characteristics is controlled by the hormone testosterone. In females, these characteristics are developing breasts, broadening hips; hair under the arms and in the genital area; and softer and smoother skin. The development of these female sexual characteristics is controlled by the hormone estrogen.

A human being starts as a single cell formed by the union of one ovum and one sperm. After the ovum and sperm join together, the fertilized ovum divides into two cells, and then these divide again, making four. Cell division continues, and cell differentiation takes place. Normally, a baby grows and develops within the uterus for about nine months. During this time, oxygen and nutrients pass from the mother's blood into the blood of the fetus through the placenta and umbilical cord. Waste products from the fetus pass into the mother's blood to be given off from her body. When the fetus is fully developed, the muscles in the walls of the uterus begin to contract, putting pressure on the baby inside. As the contractions become stronger, they force the baby down into the lower part of the uterus, causing the birth canal to stretch. The time from the start of the contractions until the baby is completely out of the birth canal is called labor.

Identical twins are born if one fertilized egg divides into two embryos soon after the union of egg and sperm. Fraternal twins are born if two ova are fertilized at about the same time.

It is important for a woman who is pregnant to receive prenatal care. An expectant mother should begin to follow a doctor's advice about diet, vitamins, and exercise as soon as possible. The quality of nutrition a woman gets during pregnancy can affect the fetus. A pregnant woman risks the health of her unborn baby any time she takes a drug without medical supervision. Women who are addicted to hard drugs, such as heroin, often give birth to babies who are addicted. Such babies may suffer withdrawal symptoms at birth. Nicotine and alcohol may also harm growing tissue. Research has found a very serious birth defect called fetal alcohol syndrome (FAS). Babies having FAS may be retarded, have heart defects, or suffer facial and other outer deformities. Recently, it has been found that even children whose mothers were light, so-called "social drinkers" during pregnancy are apt to suffer from fetal alcohol effect. Many of these children have lower mental and motor skills than normal children. They often suffer from growth and mental deficiencies. Hyperactivity and learning disabilities may also be caused by social drinking during pregnancy.

Pregnancy during the teen years is likely to present special emotional, physical, and financial problems.

CHAPTER 8   Family Life

PERFORMANCE GOAL

After completing this chapter, students will know: some ways to get along better in the family; what the advantages and disadvantages of going steady are; how to tell if a person is ready for marriage; what the different roles are in the family; and the different ways to plan for a family.

SUGGESTED INCENTIVES

Two important topics for discussion in this chapter are family planning and child abuse. If your school system's policies and curricula permit, the first topic might be addressed by a representative from the medical community or a family-planning agency, who could talk about the different methods of contraception and the advantages and disadvantages of each method. The representative could also talk about some of the problems he or she has witnessed among people who were not prepared for marriage or a family.

The second topic might best be handled by a social worker or a representative from Parents Anonymous. It should be treated in a compassionate way in order not to distress individuals in the class. Students could first discuss the "Something to Think About" at the end of the chapter, which stresses the fact that both parent and child need help.

CHAPTER SUMMARY

The family is the basic unit of society. There are many kinds of families. The members of a family affect one another emotionally, socially and economically. Within the family, each member plays several roles. Typical roles for a teenager include those of child, student, friend, member of a group or a team, babysitter, and newspaper deliverer. Each member of a family has responsibilities that fit her or his age, abilities, and relationships to others in the family. Parents and children have to support each other.

Family members can enjoy doing some things together, even though each member of the family may have different personal interests. For a young person, family life can be the training ground for learning how to communicate well and how to handle emotions. It is not realistic to hope for total harmony in the family. Some conflicts are likely to happen in any group of human beings. But if the people involved are willing to talk about the conflict and to listen to different points of view, many times the problem can be settled.

Dating is a normal part of getting to know members of the other sex. Young people mature at different ages and so are ready for dating at different times. Dating is often the first of the steps that eventually lead to marriage. Double dating, solo dating, and going steady enable young people to discover what qualities in a partner are most important to them, and what kind of person they might want to marry. Physical attraction to members of the other sex is usual, but love that leads to marriage should be based on acceptance of the total personality of the other partner.

Today statistics show that many marriages end in divorce or separation. Perhaps couples in these marriages did not determine their readiness for marriage by discussing such basic issues as these: acceptable ways of meeting physical and emotional needs; ways to realize individual potentials and to share the work and costs of maintaining a home; ability to afford things each thinks is important, and agreement on what these things are; desire for and ability to support a child; agreement on the same general goals in life.

Note: You may wish to include coverage of the supplementary material on death and dying (pages 282 to 283) with the study of family life.

CHAPTER 9   From Generation to Generation

PERFORMANCE GOAL

After completing this chapter, students will know: what the job of a medical geneticist is; and how genetic counseling is a form of preventive medicine; how some diseases that are genetic can be found before a child is born; what sickle-cell trait is and how it differs from sickle-cell anemia; why there are more color-blind males than females; and what happens when a person has too many chromosomes.

SUGGESTED INCENTIVES

Perhaps the easiest and most effective way to explain this chapter is to use the work-sheet activities at the back of this manual during the study of each genetic disease. Genetics always involves some mathematical probability that might appear too difficult for some students in the class. But slow, careful explanation, combined with actual practice at working out genetic problems, should dispel any fears the students might have.

Then, after students grasp the basic genetic concepts in the chapter, they might enjoy working out a "family pedigree" chart of their own families for eye color and hair color, and for the ability to roll the tongue, which is an inherited dominant characteristic. The genetic information obtained on the charts could be compiled for the whole class.

CHAPTER SUMMARY

Heredity is the process of passing on traits from parent to offspring by means of molecular structures called genes. Genes are segments of the large molecule DNA. Genes are arranged on paired structures called chromosomes. There are 46 chromosomes, or 23 pairs, inside all cells in the body except mature red blood cells without nuclei, and except sperm and egg cells, which have only 23 single chromosomes. Genes work in pairs to determine physical traits, with one gene usually being dominant over the other, recessive gene.

DNA (deoxyribonucleic acid) is the genetic material of the cell. The order in which any organism's DNA molecule is arranged is the genetic code of that organism. DNA causes the production of new cells and also tells each cell to make proteins for its growth and development. Proteins are made of amino acids arranged together in a particular order, depending on the protein. The arrangement of the DNA molecule decides the order in which the amino acids are arranged. And DNA contains the master plan for forming all protein in the body.

The sex of an organism is determined by the X and Y chromosomes. In humans, females have chromosomes XX and males have chromosomes XY.

The study of heredity is called genetics, a science that helps doctors understand many hereditary diseases, such as cystic fibrosis, Tay-Sachs disease, sickle-cell anemia, muscular dystrophy, glaucoma, and Huntington's disease.

Carriers are people who do not have a genetic disease, themselves, but who have the gene or chromosome that might cause their children to be born with the defect. Prenatal tests such as amniocentesis can be performed to find possible chromosome defects in fetuses.

With dominant inheritance, only one gene is needed to cause the trait to appear. With recessive inheritance, both genes are needed. With sexlinked inheritance, the defective gene is recessive and carried on the X chromosome. Since males have only one X chromosome, the defective gene can act dominantly in males without the other gene's being present to inhibit it.

Down's syndrome, or trisomy 21, is a genetic disease in which a baby is born with an extra chromosome. The older a woman is, the more likelihood there is of her having a child with Down's syndrome. Recently, geneticists have learned that the age of the father can also be a factor in the incidence of Down's syndrome.

CHAPTER 10 Environmental Hazards

PERFORMANCE GOAL

After completing this chapter, students will know: what the leading source of air pollution is; what causes a "killer smog"; the causes and effects of water pollution; whether or not a rock band is a kind of pollution; and what radiation can do to the human body. Most importantly, students will know that people are responsible for all kinds of pollution and should take certain measures to check environmental problems in their own communities.

SUGGESTED INCENTIVES

Preventive health measures to safeguard the environment can be taken by everyone. But such measures are often neglected, probably for the same excuses that personal preventive health measures are not taken. Open discussion can bring to light ways in which the students and people they know can specifically improve the environment. Included in the discussion should be a list of ways the students are harming the environment and wasting natural resources, and suggested ways to correct these problems. Then, students could check up on different factories and plants in their neighborhood and find out whether or not these industries are meeting federal pollution standards.

CHAPTER SUMMARY

Progress and the growing population have changed the environment and created many health hazards. Automobile exhaust and industrial wastes cause the greatest amount of air pollution. The five basic pollutants of air are carbon monoxide, sulphur oxide, nitrogen oxide, hydrocarbons, and small particles that float in the air. Individual people pollute the air when they smoke cigarettes, burn trash, and drive cars with poor exhaust systems. Air pollution may be a source of chronic bronchitis, of emphysema, and of lung cancer. Heart diseases, especially heart attacks, are found more often in places where there is a high level of carbon monoxide in the air. And automobile accidents happen more often in places where the air is polluted. To prevent air pollution, people should check car exhausts and home-heating systems regularly.

Today, huge increases in population, with many people living close together, have added to the water-pollution problem. Human and industrial wastes, in the form of sewage and chemicals that are spilled or washed into water systems, are the worst sources of water pollution. These substances are harmful to fish and other wildlife, may cause serious infectious diseases, and may destroy recreational areas.

Another type of pollution in the environment is noise pollution. Long exposure to noise pollution may cause a gradual hearing loss. Sudden noises of very high intensity, such as dynamite explosions, may also damage hearing. Noise may cause lack of sleep, may stop a person from relaxing or digesting food properly, or may raise the blood pressure and add to emotional problems. Noise pollution may be prevented by staying away from loud, ongoing noises and by covering the ears and wearing earplugs.

Radiation pollution is a more recent kind of environmental danger. Radiation is an invisible form of energy that comes from the splitting of atoms, the tiny, invisible particles that make up all matter. The most dangerous type of radiation is gamma rays. People who come into contact with small amounts of radiation over a long period of time may develop health problems such as leukemia, certain tumors, and genetic disorders. Scientists do not know exactly how much radiation the human body can stand.

The federal government has set up special safety precautions to be taken in handling, storing, and transporting radioactive substances. Government agencies measure the amount of radiation from nuclear weapons testing and atomic power plants. Medical technicians who work near X-ray machines wear lead shields or operate the machines from behind a protective device such as a wall of lead. Pregnant women should avoid exposure to X-rays, particularly during the first three months of pregnancy.

16

CHAPTER 11 Cancer

PERFORMANCE GOAL

After completing this chapter, students will know: what causes cancer; that many cancers can be prevented; what the seven warning signals of cancer are; how cancer is treated; how cancer can spread; and that the real responsibility for cancer prevention belongs to each person.

SUGGESTED INCENTIVES

This chapter could be coordinated with the study of Chapter 19, "Use of Tobacco." There is no way to treat the connection between tobacco smoking and cancer except bluntly and strongly. Students should be made aware that they incur the responsibility of destroying their own health by smoking. Students could also write to the Food and Drug Administration for a list of all chemicals, drugs, and foods that have been classified as carcinogens, and for the type of cancer each carcinogen is thought to cause. Throughout the chapter, it should be stressed that one out of every six people dies needlessly of cancer because that person failed to have regular physical check-ups.

CHAPTER SUMMARY

Cancer is often misunderstood, because some people think that all cancers are the same and that all cause death. Some types of cancer do grow and spread quickly and cause an early death. But others may be completely cured. In all types of cancer, there is uncontrolled and irregular growth of abnormal cells. This growth can take place in any tissue or organ of the body. The rate of growth and the spread of cancer cells often differ with each type of cancer.

A group of cells that grow together in a mass or lump is called a tumor. If the cells are normal and in an orderly pattern, the tumor is benign and grows inside a wall of tissue. A benign tumor does not spread and may be removed by surgery. If the cells in the tumor are not normal and grow irregularly, the tumor is malignant, may break out of tissue walls, and may spread to other parts of the body. The spreading of a disease such as cancer from one place in the body to another is called metastasis.

There is no single cause of cancer. Environmental factors or substances that cause cancer, such as asbestos, vinyl chloride, overexposure to the sun, radiation, and tobacco smoke, are called carcinogens. Biological factors include age and a "familial tendency" toward a certain type of cancer.

Some types of cancer, such as breast cancer, and lung cancer caused by tobacco smoking, can be prevented. The American Cancer Society has issued a list of the seven warning signals of cancer: a change in bowel or bladder habits; a sore that does not heal; any unusual bleeding or discharge; a thickening or lump in the breast or elsewhere; indigestion or difficulty in swallowing; an obvious change in a wart or mole; and a nagging cough or hoarseness. Early detection of cancer increases the chance of a cure.

Cancer may be treated by surgery, chemotherapy (in which the cancer is treated with powerful chemicals), and radiation therapy (in which radiation is aimed at cancer cells to kill them).

Sometimes, patients who have cancer and who feel hopeless turn to methods of treatment that are advocated by quacks and that have not been proven to work. They waste large amounts of money and valuable time on these worthless methods. This loss of time could lead to death.

Certain procedures are used to detect some of the more common types of cancer at an early stage. The first sign of bowel cancer may be trace amounts of blood in the bowel movements. Chemical tests can detect this blood. Screening tests have been developed to detect breast and uterine cancer. And an annual pelvic examination and Pap test can detect ovarian and uterine cancer. All of these tests can help to find cancer early, when a cure is still likely.

CHAPTER 12 Coordination and Control

PERFORMANCE GOAL

After completing this chapter, students will know: what a cerebral vascular accident is; how messages travel from the nerve cells to the brain; the differences between a reflex and a habit; what part of the brain makes memory possible; and how much rest is needed to keep the nervous system working properly.

SUGGESTED INCENTIVES

People need a working knowledge of the structure, function, disorders, and proper care of the nervous system in order to be healthy adults. Students could begin this chapter by testing their knee-jerk reflex. This reflex is easily demonstrated and does not involve pain or require elaborate equipment. The edge of a small, hardbound book can be used instead of a doctor's hammer. The students might compare their reflexes when they have their eyes open and when they have their eyes closed.

A trip to a nearby hospital to view a working electroencephalograph (EEG) might also accompany the study of brain activity.

CHAPTER SUMMARY

People react to their environment through the brain and nervous system, on which all human functions depend. Sensory nerves carry impulses from sense organs to the brain and spinal cord, which make up the central nervous system. If sensory impulses are blocked, sensation is lost. Motor nerve impulses from the central nervous system make muscles contract or relax and make glands secrete or stop secreting. If a motor nerve is cut, the connected muscles or glands are paralyzed.

A cell body plus threadlike projections called nerve fibers make up each nerve cell. Nerve impulses pass between nerve cells over fiber endings. Nerves are bundles of nerve fibers. They reach all tissues and organs.

The spinal cord contains cell bodies, associated nerve cells, and bundles of nerve fibers, all of which carry impulses to and from the brain. The brain is the largest collection of nerve cells in the body. The outermost, gray layers of brain cells are mostly cell bodies. Under these are white-covered nerve fibers. Because the brain contains billions of cells unique to human beings, people are able to reason and to understand complex relationships.

The large, upper portion of the brain, the cerebrum, contains nerve centers for memory, intelligence, and generalized concepts. Specialized areas of vision, hearing, smell, and taste are also located here. Other cerebral areas control various other bodily reactions. The cerebrum has two halves. Motor areas in the left half control the right side of the body, and motor areas in the right half control the left side of the body. Damage to one side of the cerebrum paralyzes the other side of the body.

Beneath the back part of the cerebrum is the cerebellum, which seems to coordinate muscles and maintain equilibrium. Two smaller portions of the brain, the midbrain and pons, connect the spinal cord and other parts of the brain. The medulla oblongata, tapering into the spinal cord, contains regulatory centers for breathing, heart action, and blood circulation.

A reflex is an involuntary reaction to stimuli. Habits are formed when impulses travel the same pathways many times. Habits differ from reflexes in that they are learned, and a person has some choice in their development.

Some disorders of the nervous system are epilepsy, or seizures; strokes, or cerebral accidents; meningitis, an inflammation of the membranes surrounding the brain and spinal cord; multiple sclerosis, in which the covering that surrounds the nerves is destroyed; and poliomyelitis, or paralysis caused by a virus.

To protect the nervous system, one should eat a well-balanced diet that includes enough Vitamin B, get plenty of rest and sleep, and avoid drugs and poisons.

CHAPTER 13 Eye and Ear Care

PERFORMANCE GOAL

After completing this chapter, students will know: that tears contain bactericide; the many advantages of contact lenses; why the eyes become tired, and how to rest them; that there is a pathway from the throat to the ears; what causes hearing problems; which hearing disorders can be corrected; and that the inner ear is also responsible for balance.

SUGGESTED INCENTIVES

A vision test and a color-blindness test for each student would be a useful activity that the school nurse might be able to help with. Female students could also determine whether they are carriers of the color-blindness trait by finding out if their fathers are color-blind. The feeling of pressure on the ears that may occur in an elevator can be related to ear structure. The reasons why it is important to discover hearing problems as early as possible should be stressed. Some students may wish to learn the manual alphabet and to demonstrate its use to the class.

CHAPTER SUMMARY

Head bones and eyelids protect the eye, a hollow ball about an inch in diameter. The transparent cornea, kept clean and moist by tear glands, covers the front of the eye. Muscles in the colored iris regulate the size of the pupil, an opening in the iris, thus regulating the amount of light that enters the eye. A transparent, oval-shaped lens behind the iris focuses light on the retina at the back of the eye. Nerve impulses go from the retina over the optic nerve to the vision center of the brain, which actually "sees."

In farsightedness, it is difficult to see near objects clearly because the retina is too close to the lens. Nearsightedness occurs when the distance between the lens and the retina is too great. Irregular eye surfaces bend light in varying degrees to cause astigmatism.

Crossed eyes, a form of strabismus, occur when one muscle of the three pairs that control the eyeball pulls too hard. Treatment involves exercise, glasses, or surgery.

A cataract results when injury, disease, or physical changes due to age cause the lens to become cloudy. Useful vision can be restored in most operable cases. More than one million Americans have glaucoma, damage to the optic nerve caused by blocking of the openings that equalize fluid pressure in the eyes.

The ability to read at 20 feet letters of a size most people can read at that distance is called 20/20 vision. The ability to read at 20 feet what most people can read at 40 feet is called 20/40 vision. The normal range is 20/15 to 20/30.

Eyes should be checked regularly by an ophthalmologist, a physician specializing in care and diseases of the eye. Opticians and optometrists are not physicians.

Sound waves, in the form of nerve impulses, reach the human brain through the ear and auditory nerve, becoming what we know as sound only in the brain. The outer ear directs sound waves to the eardrum through the ear canal. The middle ear, a small cavity in the skull, is separated from the ear canal by the eardrum and contains three bones, the hammer, anvil, and stirrup. Sound vibrations from the eardrum pass through these bones and through another membrane to the inner ear in the solid bone of the skull. The eustachian tube from the middle ear to the back of the nose and throat balances middle-ear air pressure. The inner ear contains the cochlea and the semicircular canals. The cochlea contains endings of the auditory nerve, which transmits nerve impulses to the brain. Fluid-pressure variations in the semicircular canals send impulses to the brain. These help maintain balance.

Two kinds of hearing disorders are conduction deafness, caused by a block to the passage of sound waves through the outer or middle ear, and central deafness, caused by damage to the auditory nerve that leads to the brain from the cochlea.

CHAPTER 14 Transport System

PERFORMANCE GOAL

After completing this chapter, students will know: what makes blood red; why high blood pressure is dangerous; the leading cause of death in the United States; how people can lower their chances of getting a heart attack; and how many times the heart beats in 24 hours.

SUGGESTED INCENTIVES

Perhaps the most useful health information one could know is one's own blood-pressure reading. The school nurse could demonstrate how a sphygmomanometer works and could take the blood pressure of several members of the class. Then students could measure their own pulse rates before and after exercise, as suggested in "Extend Your Knowledge" entry number 5. Finally, if equipment is available, students could do blood-typing tests on their own blood and could also determine whether or not they possess the Rh factor. But it should be emphasized that women with Rh-negative blood can receive medicines such as Rhogam after their first pregnancy to stop them from forming antibodies against the fetus's blood.

CHAPTER SUMMARY

Blood is a fluid tissue made up of plasma, red blood cells, white blood cells, and colorless cells called platelets. Blood carries all the things the body needs to live, including digested food from the digestive tract; oxygen from the lungs to all parts of the body; waste products from the body cells to the kidneys, lungs, and skin; and white blood cells to infected areas to fight infection.

Red cells are the oxygen carriers in blood. They carry oxygen by means of hemoglobin, the substance that also gives blood its red color. Red blood cells are always being formed in the bone marrow. White blood cells work to fight infection. They eat up disease organisms and take in polluted particles that stick to the lungs. White blood cells are also made in the bone marrow, but there are fewer white blood cells than red blood cells. Platelets help to form a clot that stops bleeding from a wound.

Anemia is a disease whereby the blood lacks either hemoglobin, red blood cells, or both. The body cells of an anemic person receive less oxygen, causing the person to tire quickly. One cause of anemia is a diet without iron. Leukemia is a disease in which the number of white blood cells has risen tremendously. Leukemia is considered a cancer of the blood. Hemophilia is a disease in which the blood clots very slowly or not at all. This is an inherited disease found mostly in males.

There are four blood types of human blood: A, B, AB, and O. Many people also have an Rh factor in their blood. The Rh factor sometimes becomes very important during pregnancy.

The heart is a pear-shaped, hollow organ made of muscle and divided into two sides, with two valves in each side. The upper part of each side is called the atrium and the lower part of each side is called the ventricle. The heart rests between beats. This resting time is called diastole. The contraction of the heart is called systole. The pulse rate is the number of times the heart beats each minute. Blood pressure is the pressure of blood against the walls of the arteries. Chronic high blood pressure, or hypertension, is abnormal and dangerous. It may result in clotting of blood and strokes if clots reach the brain. Heredity, overweight, and emotional tension are related to high blood pressure.

Some kinds of heart disease are rheumatic fever and coronary artery disease. Rheumatic heart disease is lifelong damage that develops from rheumatic fever. Coronary artery disease involves the vessels that carry blood to the heart. It may be atherosclerosis (narrowing of the arteries caused by deposits of fatty material or cholesterol) or arteriosclerosis (hardening of the walls of the arteries).

Taking care of the circulatory system includes getting enough exercise, choosing a proper diet low in cholesterol, maintaining normal blood pressure, and avoiding cigarette smoking.

CHAPTER 15 Respiration

PERFORMANCE GOAL

After completing this chapter, students will know: why they can hold their breath for only a few moments; how to stop hiccups; what causes asthma; how air pressure affects breathing; what emphysema is; and the pathway air follows from the nose to the lungs.

SUGGESTED INCENTIVES

The first four "Extend Your Knowledge" activities may be used during the study of this chapter. Activity 4 may be adapted to test the amount of air breathed in and out by a tobacco smoker and to compare it with that of a nonsmoker. Students could research the effects of smoking on respiration. If they can be obtained, pictures of damaged lungs could be shown to the class, to accompany the reports of some students on smoking and respiration. Breathing exercises to use total lung space could also be learned and practiced. Athletes, especially swimmers, could demonstrate specific breathing exercises associated with certain physical sports and activities.

CHAPTER SUMMARY

Air enters the body through the nose and passes into the pharynx, down through the larynx, and into the trachea. The trachea branches into two large tubes, the bronchi, which then divides into many smaller tubes, ending in tiny air sacs called alveoli that make up most of the lungs. The two lungs hang in the chest cavity. The chest cavity is completely enclosed. The walls of the chest cavity are made up of the ribs, the muscles between the ribs, and the breastbone. The floor of the chest cavity is formed by the diaphragm. During normal quiet breathing, adult lung capacity is one pint of air—only one-eighth of the amount the lungs can hold. The unused extra lung space is very important when injuries or disease are present, because the healthy parts of the lungs will carry on the needed air exchange while the injured parts heal.

Inhaling, or inspiration, is the process of taking air into the lungs. Exhaling, or expiration, is the process of forcing air out of the lungs. Respiration includes inspiration and expiration.

Breathing is controlled mostly by a nerve center in the brain called the respiratory center. This nerve center is affected by the amount of carbon dioxide in the blood. Too much carbon dioxide will cause the nerve center to send out strong breathing impulses to take in more oxygen. Hiccuping is caused by jerky movements of the diaphragm that end with a click caused by the sudden closing of the vocal cords. Hiccups can usually be controlled by holding the breath, sipping water, or trying hard to breathe slowly and regularly.

The higher one travels above sea level, the thinner the air, the lower the air pressure, and the less the amount of oxygen in the air. The human body can get used to small changes in the supply of oxygen. But when the body cells do not get enough oxygen, a feeling of light-headedness and stimulation occurs, followed by dizziness and confusion, and finally by unconsciousness. In air travel, all commercial airplanes and other high-flying craft are pressurized with airtight cabins, and air is pumped in to keep the level of air pressure high.

Some respiratory disorders are bronchitis, emphysema, asthma, and pneumonia. Bronchitis is swelling of the bronchi that often comes with a viral infection or from a long period of smoking. Emphysema is loss of elasticity of the alveoli, with symptoms of coughing and difficult breathing, because not enough oxygen can get to the blood. Asthma is swelling and irritation of the mucous membranes of the bronchi. The muscles of the walls of the bronchi contract, making the air passages narrower and keeping enough oxygen from getting through to the lungs. Pneumonia is an infection of the lung tissue that causes fluid to build up in the lungs.

CHAPTER 16 Skin and Hair: Your Protective Covering

PERFORMANCE GOAL

After completing this chapter, students will know: why pain is not felt when nails and hair are cut; how many meters of skin are needed to cover an adult's body; that skin is constantly being shed; that some people can get poison ivy without actually touching the plant; what regulates body temperature; and how to care for certain skin disorders, such as acne, athlete's foot, and boils.

SUGGESTED INCENTIVES

Healthy skin is an important topic for every teenager. How to care for skin properly, especially skin with acne problems, should be discussed thoroughly. Washing daily with soap and water should be strongly advised. Regular care of the hair should be stressed also, along with proper methods of brushing and shampooing. Students might want to share experiences with different skin and hair products that they use. They could analyze the advertising claims of several such products and consider some of the reasons why they choose the products—shape of the bottle, picture on the outside, effectiveness of commercial advertising, versus effectiveness of the product. Throughout this chapter, the importance of good health (diet, exercise, rest, and sleep) should be related to healthy looking skin and hair.

CHAPTER SUMMARY

The skin's two layers provide defense against bacteria and injury. The dermis, or true skin, contains blood vessels, nerves, sweat glands, oil glands, hair roots, and involuntary muscles that contract when they are cool. The epidermis, the thin outer layer that is continually shed and replaced, keeps body fluid in and water out. Pigment in the epidermis shuts out most of the ultraviolet rays that can damage skin. Dark-skinned people have more melanin in their skin than light-skinned people do. People who have no melanin in their skin at all are called albinos.

Several million sweat glands carry water, salt, and other wastes from the dermis to surface pores. A person perspires from a pint to more than a quart of waste liquid a day. In hot weather, the blood releases a great amount of heat through the skin. Perspiration also helps to cool the body. In cold weather, less blood reaches the skin, and heat is conserved.

Certain substances may irritate the skin and cause inflammation of the skin, or dermatitis. Several plants, such as poison ivy, poison oak, and poison sumac, cause contact dermatitis in many people. Allergic dermatitis is caused by a reaction to some substance the body is allergic to. Hives is a kind of allergic dermatitis in which small lumps appear on the skin. Other skin problems are boils, acne, and fungal infections, such as athlete's foot and ringworm. Ringworm causes itching and sores of the scalp. Athlete's foot begins with a slight itching, redness, and cracking of the skin between the toes. Both fungal infections should be treated by a doctor. Boils are skin infections that often begin in a hair root with an area of swelling and redness and a center of pus. This skin disease is infectious. Acne is most often skin infection caused by an oily secretion called sebum. The affected area should be washed often with soap and water.

Hair and nails are outgrowths of the epidermis layer of the skin. Each hair grows from a hair root in the dermis. Nails grow out of the skin beneath them and out of the cuticle, or nonliving epidermis surrounding the edges of fingernails and toenails. Hair and nails do not contain nerve endings. Brushing the hair increases circulation in the scalp, stops the buildup of dirt, and spreads the natural oil evenly over the hairs. Dandruff is made up of dead cells that come off the scalp when the scalp is too oily. Regular shampooing and brushing usually prevent dandruff. If not, a doctor should be seen for treatment.

CHAPTER 17   Regulators of Your Body

PERFORMANCE GOAL

After completing this chapter, students will know: how the endocrine glands are different from other glands; why the pituitary gland is sometimes called the "master gland"; what gland is the thermostat of body temperature and function; what diabetes is and how it can be controlled; and what the signs of a problem with the endocrine system are.

SUGGESTED INCENTIVES

As a helpful learning tool and study guide, the students could be given the following chart midway through the study of this chapter.

GLAND	LOCATION	HORMONE
Pituitary	in the skull	growth hormone
Thyroid	in the front of the neck	thyroxine
Parathyroid	in the neck	hormone to control use of calcium and phosphorus
Adrenal	in the trunk, near the kidneys	adrenaline
Islands of Langerhans	in the pancreas, near the stomach	insulin
Female gonads	ovaries, in lower abdomen	estrogen
Male gonads	testes, in outer pouch below abdomen	testosterone

CHAPTER SUMMARY

Hormones regulate many body processes, such as growing, keeping warm, metabolizing food, and regulating the development of the secondary sexual characteristics. Metabolism and growth depend upon balanced hormone production by the endocrine glands, located in the head, neck, and trunk. Because they pour secretions directly into the bloodstream, they are known as ductless glands.

The pituitary gland is located in the brain. It is called the "master gland" because of its regulating influence on other glands. One hormone made by the pituitary is ACTH (adrenocorticotrophic hormone), which causes the adrenal glands to produce their hormone. Another hormone made by the pituitary is the thyroid-stimulating hormone, which causes the thyroid to produce its hormones.

The thyroid is in the front part of the neck and produces the hormone thyroxine that influences metabolism in all body cells. The thyroid gland needs iodine to work properly. Without enough iodine, the thyroid enlarges to perform the extra work needed to produce thyroxine. This swelling in the neck is called a goiter. The four parathyroid glands behind the thyroid secrete hormones that control the calcium-phosphorus balance in the body.

Scattered through the pancreas are microscopic endocrine glands called Islands of Langerhans. They secrete insulin, the hormone necessary for the metabolism of sugar. Insufficient insulin is the cause of the disease called diabetes, the inability to use or store carbohydrates in the body. One sign of diabetes is an excessive amount of sugar in the blood and urine.

Lying above the kidneys are the two adrenal glands, each consisting of an inner part, the medulla, and an outer part, the cortex. When a person is angry or frightened, the inner part of each adrenal gland produces more of the hormone adrenaline. Adrenaline raises the blood pressure, decreases digestive activity, and increases muscle tone, thus preparing the body for emergency action.

The gonads, or sex glands, are the ovaries in the female and the testes in the male. The ovaries produce egg cells and the hormone estrogen. The testes produce sperm and the hormone testosterone. These hormones are produced in large amounts after puberty and account for sex differences in body structure, hair growth, and voice pitch.

The pineal gland, located in the center of the brain, regulates daily rhythms. The thymus gland, located in the upper chest, produces substances that help fight infections.

CHAPTER 18 Healthy Teeth

PERFORMANCE GOAL

After completing this chapter, students will know: why crooked teeth should be straightened; what the causes of bad breath are; how to use dental floss; how to prevent gum disease; how teeth develop; and what to do about an impacted wisdom tooth.

SUGGESTED INCENTIVES

Dental caries first appeared among the Innuits (Eskimos) when they copied the ways of Europeans. Students could investigate what the natural diet of the Innuits might have to do with resistance to dental caries. England has the highest per capita sugar consumption in the world. Students could also research the incidence of dental caries in that country. Throughout this chapter, it should be emphasized that taking care of the teeth is the responsibility of the individual. Brushing the teeth, using dental floss, and visiting the dentist regularly are important habits students should already have developed without constant reminding from parents. Also, a proper diet that does not include chewing gum is an effective way to take care of the teeth.

Volunteers from the class may wish to explain why they are wearing teeth braces, what their dentist hopes to accomplish by making them wear braces, and how long they have to wear them.

CHAPTER SUMMARY

Built for cutting, tearing, and crushing, teeth prepare food for digestion. Chewing breaks up food, preparing it for the action of saliva and other digestive juices. Saliva moistens the food and begins digestion. Chewing also stimulates circulation.

A tooth has three parts: the crown above the gums, the neck within the gums, and the roots in the jawbone. The inside of a tooth consists chiefly of bone tissue called dentine. Crown dentin is covered by enamel; root dentin, by cementum. A small internal pulp cavity contains nerves, blood vessels, and lymph vessels, which enter the tooth through the root canal. Cell metabolism occurs within the teeth, gums, and jawbone. The eight cutting teeth in front are the incisors. Next are four cuspids, or canines, for tearing food. The eight premolars and twelve molars crush and grind. There are ten primary teeth and sixteen permanent teeth in each jaw. All primary and some permanent teeth are formed before birth. Infection of the primary teeth may affect the permanent teeth beneath. Premature removal of primary teeth may cause crowded and irregular permanent teeth.

Dental caries (tooth decay) begins when food is left on the teeth. Acid formed by bacterial action on food, especially on starch and sugar, dissolves the enamel. Decay then spreads into the dentin and, if not checked, into the pulp cavity, the root canal, tissues around the teeth, and the jawbone. If the nerve is destroyed, all warning pain stops.

Malocclusion is poor bite caused by irregular teeth. Temporal mandibular joint (TMJ) problems can occur if correction is not made. TMJ can cause severe headaches in the facial and head areas. Malocclusion is treated by an orthodontist. Bacteria may travel down the pulp cavity and along the root canal of an infected tooth to form a root abscess. Bacteria or toxins from the abscess may spread infection throughout the body. Abscesses occasionally form around the roots of healthy teeth. Gingivitis is gum inflammation caused by lack of vitamin C, by improper use of toothbrush or dental floss, or by tartar on the necks of teeth. Trench mouth, a severe form of gingivitis, and pyorrhea, a gum infection usually accompanied by pus, require professional treatment. In most cases, routine care keeps gums in good condition.

Good oral hygiene is everyone's personal responsibility. Good diet helps maintain healthy teeth. Snacks that contain too much sugar should be avoided. Regular dental checkups and regular brushing and cleaning with dental floss help keep defects to a minimum. Fluoridated water and toothpaste should be used.

CHAPTER 19 Use of Tobacco

PERFORMANCE GOAL

After completing this chapter, students will know: why many smokers find it difficult to stop; what the substances in tobacco smoke are; the effects of smoking on the body; how "secondhand" smoke affects the nonsmoker; whether or not most people automatically gain weight when they quit smoking; and if there is such a thing as a "safer" cigarette.

SUGGESTED INCENTIVES

Lecturing students about the dangers of tobacco smoking probably will not change their behavior. But all the facts in this chapter, and more that can be obtained from the American Cancer Society and the American Heart Association, should be presented in a strong, straightforward manner. Smoking is clearly a serious problem and can become a harmful addiction. Students who smoke should explore the psychological reasons or social pressures that made them want to try their first cigarette or to continue smoking. Students who are allergic to tobacco smoke might explain how smoking harms nonsmokers. The class might then discuss the ways in which the smoking habit is glamorized in the media and mistakenly linked with maturity. The chapter will help students to counter this propaganda with facts. The use of snuff and chewing tobacco is increasing among adolescents. The feature on pages 239 and 240 focuses on the dangers of "smokeless" tobacco.

CHAPTER SUMMARY

Cigarette smoke contains nicotine, tars, and gases that are harmful to human tissue. It is impossible to smoke without the body's absorbing some of these poisons. Inhaled smoke leaves a greater residue of poisons in the system than smoke which is not inhaled. Filters vary in their effectiveness in screening out some of the poisons. No filter screens out all the poisons.

Cigarette smoking reduces appetite and the keenness of the senses of taste and smell. It constricts blood vessels and impairs circulation of the blood.

Smoking puts a strain on the heart and blood vessels. It also reduces blood flow through the lungs and causes the lungs to absorb less oxygen. There are more than twice as many deaths from coronary heart disease among cigarette smokers as among nonsmokers. Cigarette smoking is also responsible for one in every five cancer deaths. Smoking has been linked to cancer of the lung, larynx, pharynx, oral cavity, esophagus, pancreas, and bladder.

Heavy smokers often have chronic bronchitis and emphysema. Emphysema may begin with a slight difficulty in breathing at times. Later on, activity such as a short walk may result in breathlessness.

Involuntary smoking occurs when a nonsmoker unwillingly inhales smoke from a burning cigarette, cigar, or pipe. In a smoky environment, a nonsmoker breathes many of the same particles in tobacco smoke that a smoker inhales. The chemical components in smoke-filled surroundings come from mainstream and sidestream smoke. Mainstream smoke is the smoke inhaled and then exhaled by the smoker. Sidestream smoke is the smoke that goes directly into the air from the burning end of a cigarette, cigar, or pipe. Since sidestream smoke is not filtered in any way, many substances, including nicotine and carbon monoxide, are found in much higher concentrations in sidestream smoke than in mainstream smoke.

Studies have shown that a pregnant woman harms her unborn baby when she smokes cigarettes. Infants born to smoking mothers weigh less and are more likely to get diseases than infants born to nonsmoking mothers.

Some mistaken reasons for smoking are thinking that it relieves tiredness and eases nervous tension.

People who quit smoking have a better chance of living long and healthy lives than smokers do. If there is no disease present, as soon as someone stops smoking, the body begins to repair the damage that smoking caused. Many programs are now available to help people learn how to stop smoking. But the decision to stop is up to the individual.

CHAPTER 20 Use of Alcohol

PERFORMANCE GOAL

After completing this chapter, students will know: why people's behavior may change when they drink alcoholic beverages; how many calories there are in beer; how the blood alcohol level affects a person's ability to drive; why someone who passes out from drinking too much alcohol needs medical attention right away; and what the clues are that tell if a person has a drinking problem. Most importantly, the students will know enough information about the effects of alcohol on the body to make their own decisions whether or not to drink alcohol, and how much to drink.

SUGGESTED INCENTIVES

There is always the danger that the effect of teaching about alcohol might be weakened by what may seem to be a puritanical attitude on the part of the teacher or the authors. Resistance is sometimes neutralized by helping young people understand their emotional needs to be or to feel adult as soon as possible. Some may experiment with alcohol to assert their independence. Some think of drinking as a sign of maturity. It should be pointed out that drinking is not a mark of maturity, even in adults. Students should be directed to the more solid ways of achieving maturity described in Chapter 4. A committee interviewing project, in which selected adults are asked what they consider to be characteristics of maturity, is a good way for students to develop a better perspective on adulthood.

CHAPTER SUMMARY

Alcohol is a poison to living tissue if it is taken into the body in concentrated solutions. Some alcoholic beverages have a small amount of food value. But the alcohol, itself, has no known nutritional value.

Alcohol passes directly into the bloodstream from the digestive tract and probably affects all the organs of the body. Its greatest effect is on the brain. As a depressant rather than a stimulant, it dulls brain centers concerned with judgment, attention, memory, and self-control, sometimes causing socially offensive behavior. It also causes the body temperature to drop. The continued use of large quantities of alcohol may result in loss of appetite; indigestion; damage to heart, liver, and kidneys; and progressive disintegration of personality.

The incidence of diseases of the digestive system, cirrhosis of the liver, pancreatitis, heart disease, and psychiatric disorders is especially high among heavy drinkers. Alcohol outranks all other dangerous drugs in its total damaging effect on millions of people.

Alcohol weakens people's control over their nervous system and motor coordination. They do things more slowly and make more mistakes. Their critical judgment gets worse, but they feel more self-confident—a dangerous combination. Drinking, therefore, is a serious hazard to activities requiring quick reactions, good judgment, and good neuromuscular control. Driving after drinking is particularly dangerous. Over half of all fatal accidents are caused by drinking drivers, many of whom are social drinkers rather than alcoholics. Many accidents on the job, at home, and at play are a direct result of heavy drinking.

The misuse and abuse of alcohol have many serious social and economic effects. Many families are broken up when a parent is a heavy drinker or an alcoholic. Alcoholism in the family may result in separation, divorce, or inadequate homes for children. Many alcoholics can get help from an organization called Alcoholics Anonymous. Alateen is an organization for the children of alcoholics. It helps them cope with problems that come up in the home where one or both parents drink too much.

Whether or not to use alcoholic beverages is an important personal decision.

CHAPTER 21 Drugs: Use and Abuse

PERFORMANCE GOAL

After completing this chapter, students will know: why leftover prescription drugs should be thrown out; what the most widely used drug is; why certain drugs are likely to be abused; which commonly abused drugs are addictive; and how an unborn child can be affected by the drugs its mother takes.

SUGGESTED INCENTIVES

This chapter stresses the fact that the decision to take any drug is an important one—one that should be based on as much correct information as possible and made only after motivations and attitudes are honestly examined. It also points out that neither over-the-counter nor prescription drugs should be taken casually. Allow the students to air their personal feelings about drugs among themselves without fear of being "found out." Whatever drug a student may presently be taking, he or she should clearly understand the effects on health that the drug may have and the risks involved in taking it. With this chapter, the teacher has a good opportunity to cause students to think and consider the consequences of their actions.

CHAPTER SUMMARY

Many kinds of drugs may be bought without prescriptions. These drugs are sold over-the-counter and are sometimes called OTC drugs. Many different kinds of drugs are used to relieve pain. Analgesics, such as aspirin, allow people to be comfortable while they recover from an illness or injury. Anesthetics, such as novocaine or sodium pentothal, cause numbness or insensitivity to pain. Many other drugs, called psychoactive drugs, help people deal with stressful psychological problems. Tolerance means that a person's body becomes used to the effects of a drug that is taken regularly. Physical dependence, or addiction, means that a person must have regular doses of a drug. If a person who is physically dependent on a drug does not get the amount of the drug needed, the person may suffer withdrawal symptoms. Trembling, hallucinations, nausea, and vomiting are some symptoms of withdrawal. Sudden withdrawal from a drug may be fatal. Psychological dependence results from a mental or emotional need, not a physical one.

Some commonly abused drugs are depressants, narcotics, stimulants, and hallucinogens. Depressants slow down the activity of certain areas of the brain and spinal cord. These drugs cause muscles to relax and rates of breathing and heartbeat to slow down. Alcohol is the most widely used drug in this group, and barbiturates the second most widely used. Barbiturates slow down reaction time, produce drowsiness, and slur speech. They may reduce anxiety but they also decrease mental functioning and memory. The important narcotics are opium, heroin, morphine, and codeine. Morphine is an excellent pain reliever. Codeine is a weaker pain reliever used in prescription cough medicines. Heroin has the same effects as morphine but is twenty times more powerful. Methadone is a synthetic drug used as a substitute for heroin. Stimulants cause the heart to beat faster, the circulation and respiration to increase, and the blood pressure to rise. Caffeine is the most widely used stimulant in the United States. Amphetamines are synthetic stimulants. Hallucinogens are drugs that cause hallucinations or sense distortions. Some hallucinogens are mescaline, peyote, psilocybin, LSD, and PCP, or "angel dust." Marijuana does not neatly fit into any of the four drug categories and acts partly like a depressant and partly like a stimulant. Marijuana increases the heart rate and blood pressure and decreases the body temperature.

The National Institute of Drug Abuse cites some interesting facts about marijuana.

- Marijuana can cause vital-capacity decrease.
- Marijuana smoking produces 50 percent more polyaromatic hydrocarbon chemicals related to lung cancer than does cigarette smoking.
- Marijuana may cause fibrosis between the alveoli.
- Marijuana adversely affects motor skills, motor coordination, and visual perception.

CHAPTER 22 Sexually Transmitted Diseases

PERFORMANCE GOAL

After completing this chapter, students will know: how sexually transmitted diseases are spread; what the symptoms of gonorrhea, syphilis, and genital herpes are; how sexually transmitted diseases can be prevented; and how sexually transmitted diseases are treated. Most important, students will know where to get help if they suspect they have a sexually transmitted disease.

SUGGESTED INCENTIVES

It might be useful to make a chart of the diseases in this chapter for the students. Or, have them make the chart together, in class, in order to help them remember the most important facts about each disease. The chart could include the name of the disease, its cause, how it is spread, how it is prevented, and how its symptoms can be readily recognized. Then, "Extend Your Knowledge," entry 3, could be a useful class activity. It might be followed by an analysis of how many of those cases are teenagers and a discussion of how to prevent the spread of STDs among young people. This chapter should serve to clear up many wrong beliefs about STDs, especially how they are spread. If STDs are presented as "another communicable disease," the social stigma of having it can be reduced, and the fear, embarrassment, and shame associated with the disease can be eliminated. It is these feelings that prevent people from seeking fast treatment for these diseases.

CHAPTER SUMMARY

Gonorrhea and syphilis are the two sexually transmitted diseases that are causing epidemics all over the United States. Gonorrhea is the most common sexually transmitted disease. It is caused by rod-shaped bacteria called gonococci that show up in pairs. With gonorrhea, the male usually experiences pain and burning during urination, and possibly a puslike discharge from the penis. The female usually has no symptoms at all, but may have a vaginal discharge. After a while, male and female symptoms disappear, but the bacteria continue to live in the inner mucous membranes. If the infection is not treated by a doctor, serious problems, such as crippling arthritis or sterility, may develop. Syphilis is caused by spiral-shaped bacteria called spirochetes. The primary stage of the disease includes a painless open sore called a chancre. Then, if the patient is not treated, a skin rash and mouth sores may develop in the secondary stage. The rash and all other symptoms later disappear in the latent stage, while the spirochetes attack other parts of the body, such as the heart and brain. After many years, late syphilis, the final stage, may cause heart failure, mental illness, or blindness. A pregnant woman may pass on syphilis or gonorrhea to her newborn infant.

Genital herpes is caused by the herpes simplex II virus. The first symptom of genital herpes is pain in the genital area, followed by a skin lesion called a vesicle. Pregnant women may pass genital herpes to their newborn infants.

Gonorrhea, syphilis, and genital herpes are best prevented by not having sexual contact with infected people. There is no self-medication to treat these diseases. A toll-free referral service (800-227-8922) for treatment of STDs gives information on medical facilities in a person's area. There are also sexually spread diseases other than gonorrhea, syphilis, and genital herpes. Therefore, any sore, ulcer, or discharge involving the sexual organs should be diagnosed and treated by a doctor.

CHAPTER 23 The Common Cold and Other Miseries

PERFORMANCE GOAL

After completing this chapter, students will know: how the body defends itself against infections; how infections are spread to others; if there is a cure for the common cold; if hepatitis is contagious; and what the symptoms of infectious mononucleosis are.

SUGGESTED INCENTIVES

Growing colonies of bacteria is a good way to demonstrate the concept of "pathogens" and how they cause disease. The school biology teacher could help with this activity or could supply the class with the agar plates needed to grow the colonies. Prepare ten agar plates. Gently rub your fingers over one. Shake a cosmetic puff over one. Let a fly walk over one. Put a drop of clean, fresh milk in one. Put a drop of milk that has stood in an open container for some time in one. Students should then choose other ways, perhaps using classroom instruments, to contaminate the remaining five plates. Then place all the plates in an incubator or near a radiator for 24 to 48 hours. After this time, examine the colonies of bacteria that have grown. Most of the bacteria are harmless, but some may be harmful. Do not touch them. Ask the biology teacher to identify some of them for the class.

CHAPTER SUMMARY

The most common pathogens, or disease-causing microorganisms, are bacteria and viruses. Fungi (small, plantlike organisms) and protozoa (small, animallike organisms) may also cause disease. The diseases caused by pathogens are called infectious diseases. Some pathogens are spread directly from one person to another. For example, the mucus released in sneezing, speaking, or coughing can spread pathogens, and so can direct contact with saliva. Pathogens can also be spread indirectly, such as by handling the silverware or clothing of an infected person. Food may also carry pathogens, and so may water polluted by sewage, rats, houseflies, and mosquitoes.

After entering the human body, pathogens multiply but, at first, cause no symptoms of disease. This is the incubation period of the disease. Later, symptoms appear. The ability of the body to fight off infection is known as resistance. Resistance is decreased by poor nutrition, chronic illness, too much alcohol, smoking, emotional stress, and age. The body also has natural barriers to infection, such as healthy, unbroken skin; hair in the nose; cilia in the throat; and stomach acid. Certain blood cells and substances made in the blood help kill pathogens. Leukocytes (white blood cells) surround, kill, and digest invading organisms. Antibodies are protein substances that are made by white blood cells and that attack pathogens. Antitoxins are substances that neutralize harmful toxins produced by pathogens.

Some common infectious diseases include the cold, with symptoms of runny nose, sneezing, sore throat, and headache; the flu, with symptoms of fever, cough, weakness, and muscle aches; hepatitis, with symptoms of headache, nausea, vomiting, fever, pain in the abdomen, and jaundice; and mononucleosis, with symptoms of sore throat, chills, fever, weakness, and tiredness.

Each individual is responsible for disease prevention. Good personal hygiene, nutritional diet with enough fresh vitamins and proteins, and rest and exercise help keep up resistance against common infections. Getting medical advice early also stops problems from developing into more serious illnesses. Most bacterial infections may be treated with antibiotics, but most viruses cannot be killed by antibiotics. The prevention and control of infectious diseases have been major factors in creating longer, healthier lives.

CHAPTER 24 Immunizations

PERFORMANCE GOAL

After completing this chapter, students will know: how immunizations protect against infectious diseases; which diseases can be prevented by immunizations; why epidemics of diseases such as measles and polio still happen today; what the side effects of vaccines are; and what diseases the DPT vaccine protects against.

SUGGESTED INCENTIVES

The "Personal Health Record" activity can help students assimilate information learned in this chapter and may encourage them to take personal responsibility for their own immunization record. The students will probably have to consult with their parents about what childhood diseases they have or have not had. This should also serve to remind parents about the necessity of immunizing all children against communicable diseases—even those diseases that have been brought under control. Stress the fact that epidemics are still possible in this decade, and that certain contagious diseases, especially poliomyelitis, are even fatal in some cases.

CHAPTER SUMMARY

When harmful microorganisms cause infections in the body, white blood cells make protein substances called antibodies to fight the infection. Sometimes the same pathogens enter the body again. This time, white blood cells with a chemical "memory" rapidly produce more antibodies to kill the infection before it starts. This ability to produce antibodies against pathogens before they cause a disease is called active immunity. Active immunity may be natural immunity (present at birth), or acquired immunity (built up after a person has had the disease once).

Passive immunity lasts only a short time. It is acquired when a serum made from the blood of an actively immune person or animal is given to someone who has the disease. Toxoids are another type of vaccine, made from the poisonous waste products of disease-causing microorganisms. Tetanus toxoid is an example of this kind of vaccine.

Vaccines may have mild side effects that last only a short time. These side effects may include a slight fever, a sore arm, or a mild rash. The positive effects of vaccines are much greater than the risks of taking them. A combination DPT vaccine protects against diphtheria, a serious infectious illness with symptoms of sore throat and difficult breathing and swallowing; pertussis, or whooping cough; and tetanus, or lockjaw, a contagious disease that causes the muscles to lock in spasms.

Poliomyelitis is a contagious disease that often affects young children with lifelong paralysis. Polio is fatal in about one out of every ten cases. Measles begins with a cough, a fever, and a red rash. Sometimes added problems follow, such as pneumonia, blindness, or brain damage. Mumps has symptoms of fever and painful, swollen glands under the jawbone. In severe cases, mumps can cause brain damage or sterility. Rubella, or German measles, is most dangerous to pregnant women. A woman infected by rubella virus early in pregnancy has almost one chance in four of giving birth to a deformed baby.

After a ten-year immunization campaign launched by the World Health Organization, smallpox is the first disease to be completely eliminated by medical science. As a result, vaccines against smallpox are no longer needed.

CHAPTER 25 Nutritional Needs

PERFORMANCE GOAL

After completing this chapter, students will know: if the foods they eat are the ones they need; how to make "eating out" more nourishing; that large amounts of certain vitamins can be harmful; that water is a nutrient; why fiber is an important part of the diet, even though it cannot be fully digested; and that their basal metabolic rate tells how fast they use up the energy they get from food.

SUGGESTED INCENTIVES

Today, everyone eats "fast foods" and foods that may be considered "fads." Ask students to collect food-fad advertisements and bring them to class, along with any fad foods they may have at home or may buy occasionally, for example, artificially colored "cartoon" cereals. Discuss the merits of the advertising claims. Point out the devices each ad uses to convince people to buy the advertised product. Also, discuss the nutritional value of the food products the students bring to class.

Then review the menus offered by the school cafeteria. Analyze them in terms of the four basic food groups. Is each food group represented on the menus every day? Are any food groups over-represented? If so, would this encourage people to eat more of one food group than another? If the cafeteria menus are found to be imbalanced, this fact could be made known to the appropriate school officials.

CHAPTER SUMMARY

A meal may be judged in terms of nutrients and calories. An adequate diet must contain nutrients from the *four food groups:* the Milk Group, the Meat Group, the Vegetable-Fruit Group, and the Bread-Cereal Group.

Fats, carbohydrates, proteins, vitamins, and mineral salts are nutrients found in food. These nutrients provide raw materials and energy for building and repairing body tissues and for keeping body processes running smoothly. Digestion converts *protein* into amino acids. Animal protein sources—milk, cheese, eggs, fish, poultry, and meat—contain all the amino acids needed by the human body. They are known as complete proteins. Plant proteins, obtained from grains, nuts, beans, peas, and corn, are incomplete. For this reason, vegetarians who do not eat eggs and milk products need to combine incomplete proteins to get complete proteins. Protein is essential for growth and for tissue repair.

The starches and sugars in *carbohydrates* are quickly converted by the body into energy. Carbohydrates are contained in sugars and syrups, grain products, potatoes, and some other vegetables. *Fats* provide more energy per ounce than any of the other nutrients. Fats are found in milk products, eggs, some vegetables, nuts, and meat fats. Growth and the chemical processes of the body require minute quantities of *mineral salts:* calcium for bones and teeth, blood clotting, and muscle and nerve function; phosphorus for the formation of bones and teeth; fluorine for the prevention of tooth decay; and iodine for proper working of the thyroid gland.

Vitamins are important for the body to help speed up certain chemical processes. Necessary vitamins are vitamin A for the skin and eyes; vitamin D for bones and teeth; vitamin E to strengthen cell membranes of red blood cells; vitamin K to help the liver produce a protein needed for blood clotting; vitamin B for energy and growth; and vitamin C for energy and healthy gums.

Two other substances the body needs in the diet are water (eight glasses a day) and fibers (to aid in muscle contraction during elimination), even though fibers cannot be digested.

The basal metabolic rate tells how fast energy from food is being used up by the body. Energy is measured in calories. The number of calories in a nutrient tells how much energy is in the nutrient.

CHAPTER 26   Snacks and Special Diets

PERFORMANCE GOAL

After completing this chapter, students will know: that snacking can be an important part of the diet; how thin people can gain weight; how to lose weight safely; whether or not athletes need special diets; that in order for a vegetarian to remain healthy, the diet must be carefully planned; and that most fad diets are unbalanced in nutrients.

SUGGESTED INCENTIVES

This chapter dispels myths about special diets for athletes and fad diets or diet pills to lose weight. Remind students about the four basic food groups and about the nutrients and fibers needed in a balanced diet (see Chapter 25). Stress again that taking too much of some vitamins can be harmful, and that vitamin pills can never be a substitute for a proper diet. Let students keep a record of their daily snacks for one week. How many students eat cakes and pies or candy when they snack between meals? How many eat fruits and vegetables? Students could then think of ways in which teenagers and adults could be encouraged to eat more nutritious snacks. For example, more food machines in schools and work areas might contain cold fruits, vegetables, and yogurts.

CHAPTER SUMMARY

Snacking has become a social custom in the United States. For many people, it is part of their regular eating habits. But not all snacking foods are nutritious, and some snacks do not fit into the four basic food groups. They fit into a group called empty calories. Many people pick snacks according to how easy they are to get or to fix. So fruits and vegetables should be kept washed, sliced, and easy to get to.

Breakfast is an important meal. By morning, the body has digested dinner from the night before and has stored any extra carbohydrates in the liver. The need to renew the body's energy becomes important. If one does not eat a good breakfast, the body's energy level may drop as morning wears on.

Any diet, including one for the underweight, must have nutrients as well as calories. To gain weight, snacks should be eaten about two hours before the next meal. Snacking too close to mealtime raises the blood-sugar level, and this may lessen the appetite. To lose weight, food should be eaten only at mealtimes, and only fruits and vegetables eaten if snacks must be taken. A doctor should be consulted about any new diet. Diet pills are a risky way to lose weight.

Athletes do not need special amounts of vitamins, salt pills, or extra helpings of steak. Protein cannot be stored in the body in the same way as fats, and too much of certain vitamins may be harmful. For top performance during a game, it is best to eat at least three hours before the start of the game. Special drinks and candy bars eaten just before a game do not give extra energy because they must be digested. It takes several hours after digestion before the glucose is ready to be used by the cells. Nutrition experts say that an athlete should drink a total of about 12 ounces of noncarbonated soft drink, or fruit juice in small amounts, at frequent intervals during the event.

Vegetarian is a term that includes all those who do not eat meat. Most vegetarians will include eggs and milk in their diet. They are called lacto-ovo-vegetarians (lacto=milk/ovo=egg). Others use only dairy products, such as milk, cheese, and butter. They are known as lacto-vegetarians. The few who use only nuts, fruits, grains, and vegetables are called pure vegetarians.

CHAPTER 27   Nutrition, Labels, and the Consumer

PERFORMANCE GOAL

After completing this chapter, students will know: how to read nutrition information on packaged foods; if all the additives included in foods are necessary; that sugar is not one of the requirements in the diet; if health foods are really nutritious; and how additives are used to prevent food poisoning.

SUGGESTED INCENTIVES

The purpose of this chapter is to educate students to be intelligent, careful food shoppers. Perhaps the best way to accomplish this is to have the students "shop" for food after the information in the chapter has been presented and discussed. They could do this by keeping a list of what they would buy as they shop, rather than actually purchasing the products. Students could go shopping in pairs and decide upon which items to buy. Ask students to notice which items in the supermarket or grocery store have open dating and which do not. Then have each pair of students make a list of items that they disagreed about while shopping because of price, nutritional value, artificial ingredients, and sugar content. Let each pair of shoppers air their disagreements in class, and have other members of the class decide who made the better food choice, and why.

CHAPTER SUMMARY

The nutritional information on a package should include the serving sizes and the number of servings per container. Calories and nutrients are usually listed, along with ingredients. Some products also list information about sodium, cholesterol, and unsaturated fat.

The U.S. Recommended Daily Allowance (RDA) is the amount of each nutrient needed by most people in the United States. The daily needs for various nutrients differ according to sex, age, body size, and activity. Both age and sex are considered in each recommendation.

Any of the following terms may be used to indicate ingredients on a food product label: made from, prepared from, contains, and content. The first item in a list of ingredients is the largest item by weight in the product. The second item is the second largest by weight. Additives are usually given at the end of the list of ingredients. Additives are substances added to food in small amounts that are meant to improve the food in some way. Many kinds of additives are in foods to put back nutrients lost in preparation of the food, or to improve the food's taste. Preservatives are additives that keep bacteria, molds, and fungi from spoiling food. Antioxidants, such as vitamins C and E, attract oxygen and prevent stored foods from changing in color, taste, and smell. Two synthetic antioxidants are BHA and BHT. Acids and bases keep jams and jellies from hardening and put effervescence into soft drinks. Gelling agents, stabilizers, and emulsifiers keep oil and water mixed and ice cream "creamy." Taste enhancers, such as monosodium glutamate, enhance the flavors in certain foods. Coloring agents make foods look better. Improving agents include meat tenderizers and compounds for putting a glaze on baked goods.

Sugar has no nutritive value other than calories. People consume sugar only to satisfy their "sweet tooth." People who have high blood pressure should restrict the intake of salt in their diet.

Foods grown without the use of synthetic fertilizers, pesticides, or herbicides are called organic foods. Much that is sold as organic food is not organically grown. Supermarkets and grocery stores must display certification papers for foods they say have been organically grown.

Some foods, even with preservatives, spoil or lose their flavor in a short period of time. Open dating assures that foods on grocery shelves are safe to eat. Unit pricing is a method of showing the cost per unit of weight regardless of the size of the container or the weight of the contents. Unit prices are posted on supermarket shelves.

CHAPTER 28 Digestion and Elimination

PERFORMANCE GOAL

After completing this chapter, students will know: why the liver is considered to be a part of the digestive system; why the villi of the small intestine are important; how emotions can affect the digestive process; and where the major part of digestion occurs.

SUGGESTED INCENTIVES

The following chart may be a useful study guide for students:

SUMMARY OF DIGESTION PROCESSES

PLACE OF ACTION	FOOD	ENZYME OR AGENT	END-PRODUCT OF DIGESTION
Mouth	Starch	Ptyalin in saliva	Glucose
Stomach	Protein	Hydrochloric acid, pepsin, and rennin in gastric juice	Amino acids and protein fragments
Small intestine	Fats; Carbohydrates	Enzymes in intestinal and pancreatic juices	Glycerol and fatty acids; Glucose
Small intestine	Protein	Enzymes in intestinal and pancreatic juices	Amino acids

CHAPTER SUMMARY

Digestion, the process through which living organisms make use of food, begins in the mouth. Teeth break up food as the tongue pushes it into position for chewing. Glands near the mouth secrete saliva containing ptyalin, an enzyme that begins the digestion of starch by changing some of it to sugar. After the food has been chewed, it is swallowed. Swallowing starts with contractions of the muscles of the pharynx and the closing of the passage to the lungs. Once food is pushed from the pharynx to the esophagus, it is moved by peristaltic contractions in the esophagus to the stomach.

Gastric juices from stomach walls contain hydrochloric acid and the enzyme pepsin. The acid enables the pepsin to act on proteins, and it kills some of the microorganisms present in the stomach. Food in the stomach gradually passes into the small intestine. The stomach is empty within three or four hours after eating. Some glucose and alcohol get into the blood stream from the stomach, but little if any food does. The chief function of the stomach is storage. A person can live with the stomach removed because most digestion takes place in the small intestine. The upper part of the small intestine, the duodenum, is sometimes considered to be the most important part of the digestive tract.

Digestion of fats, carbohydrates, and proteins is completed in the small intestine by enzymes in the intestinal and pancreatic juices. After digestion, carbohydrates have been changed to simple sugars, fats to glycerol and fatty acids, and proteins to amino acids. Bile from the liver keeps fat in tiny droplets that can be digested by enzymes.

Pancreatic juice and insulin are secreted by the pancreas, which is located just below the stomach. Pancreatic juice, sent into the small intestine through the pancreatic duct, contains digestive enzymes that act on fats, carbohydrates, and proteins. The area of the lining of the small intestine is greatly increased by millions of tiny, fingerlike projections called villi. Nutrients are absorbed into the bloodstream through the villi. Each villus contains blood vessels and a lymph vessel. Digested fats enter the lymph vessel and pass through it to the bloodstream.

A function of the lower digestive tract is reabsorption of water from digested food. Peristalsis is slow in the large intestine, material passing through in twelve to twenty hours. Undigested food, dead cells from the intestinal lining, and bacteria found in the lower digestive tract make up feces.

Although digestion is under involuntary, autonomic nerve control, it may be influenced by a person's emotions. Strong emotion interferes with gland secretion and peristalsis.

CHAPTER 29 Personal Safety

PERFORMANCE GOAL

After completing this chapter, students will know: what causes the most deaths among people of high school age; why insurance companies charge higher rates for teenage drivers; why many accidents happen in the home; what the causes of automobile, motorcycle, and bicycle accidents are; and how to prevent accidents that happen in the home, at school or work, and in the water.

SUGGESTED INCENTIVES

This chapter is highlighted with boldly colored boxes that list the causes of automobile, motorcycle, and bicycle accidents. Students could make lists of ways to prevent the different kinds of vehicle accidents. Then students could give reasons why people might ignore these ways to prevent accidents. Remind students that wearing a safety belt while driving or riding in an automobile is a "preventive health measure" that many people ignore. Students could also find out the number, location, and type of accidents that happened in their school last year, and they could form committees to advertise ways to prevent such accidents.

CHAPTER SUMMARY

Accidents, rather than illnesses, are the chief cause of death among persons of high school age in the United States. In almost every case, the cause of accidents is carelessness. Automobile accidents cause more deaths in the United States than any other kind of accident. They are the chief cause of accidental death among young people.

There are four main causes of automobile accidents: the way a person drives, the condition of the driver, the condition of the car, and driving conditions, which include road conditions and weather. Dangerous driving includes speeding, being on the wrong side of the road, passing on a hill or curve, cutting in ahead of another car, failing to use proper signals, and tailgating. Dangerous drivers include those who are drunk, tired or inattentive to road and traffic conditions. Dangerous cars may have faulty brakes, worn tires, unsafe steering gear, poor lights, unclear windshields, or too many passengers. Dangerous driving conditions include bad weather, poor roads, darkness, glare, and heavy traffic.

A large number of motorcycles and mopeds are driven by young people. Because of the lack of protection to the body, the chances of a cyclist's being killed in an accident are five times greater than those of an automobile driver.

The American Red Cross has made a list of suggestions for water safety that appear in this chapter as "Rules for Safe Swimming." Rules to prevent accidents in the home are also given. Most home accidents happen because people tend to pay less attention to possible dangers in familiar surroundings.

Many work-related accidents also occur each year. These accidents are caused by the workers, themselves; by unsafe buildings, tools, and equipment; and by lack of proper safety equipment. Accidents in industry are not spread evenly through the day. Instead, they reach a peak between 10 and 11 A.M. and again between 3 and 4 P.M. Rest periods relieve tiredness and cut down the number of accidents.

CHAPTER 30 Basic First Aids

PERFORMANCE GOALS

After completing this chapter, students will know: what to do in an emergency; how to stop a wound from bleeding; how to help someone who has taken poison; what the differences are between first-degree, second-degree, and third-degree burns; how to help someone in shock; what to do for snake bites and convulsions; and what insect bites may be fatal.

SUGGESTED INCENTIVES

Before beginning this chapter, ask the students to draw up a list of items they would put in a home medicine cabinet. Then, after the chapter study is complete, ask them to make another list without referring to the first one. Compare the two lists to determine which additional items the students would put in a medicine cabinet after they have learned much more about first aid. The items that should be included in the second list are adhesive bandages, gauze bandage, adhesive tape, cotton balls, cotton swabs, tweezers, scissors, thermometer, aspirin, bicarbonate of soda, sling and splint, sunburn cream, laxative, alcohol, antiseptic, spirits of ammonia, activated charcoal, and antidiarrhea medicine.

CHAPTER SUMMARY

Certain conditions require immediate care, or first aid. These conditions include severe bleeding (hemorrhaging), failure to breathe, poisoning, extensive burns, and broken bones.

Bleeding may come from veins, capillaries, or arteries. If the bleeding is severe, pressure should be applied directly to the wound. If bleeding starts again after the pressure has been removed, pressure should be applied again until medical help is obtained.

Poisoning should be treated with an antidote, a substance that works against the poison. If the correct antidote is not known, give the person lots of liquid. Many labels give incorrect information. Call a poison control center for specific instructions. Activated charcoal, which soaks up poison, may be given in a glass of water if no immediate help can be reached.

Every injury causes some shock. A person in shock feels weak, faint, cold, and often nauseated. Shock may be brief and slight, or it may be prolonged, ending in death. Reassurance helps avoid shock in the patient. Keep the victim warm and lying on the back with the head low. Bleeding should be controlled.

A break in a bone is called a fracture. In a compound fracture, either the broken bone pushes through the skin, or a wound extends from the surface of the skin to the break in the bone. A dislocation is a bone that is out of place at the joint. It should be treated by a doctor.

Most burns are caused by heat, sunlight, electricity, or chemicals. These general rules govern first-aid treatment of burns: (a) Clothing should be cut from around the burned area. Material sticking to the skin should not be removed. (b) Blisters should not be opened. (c) Iodine, oily substances, soda, or salves should not be applied.

In a first-degree burn, the skin is reddened but not broken or blistered. Cold water is soothing, if applied immediately. A dressing of several layers of cotton cloth keeps the air out and reduces pain. In a second-degree burn, the skin is blistered and should be treated as an open wound. Treatment for shock is often necessary. Air should be kept out with several thicknesses of gauze or cotton dressing. In a third-degree burn, the skin is destroyed. Medical attention is essential. First aid consists mainly of treatment for shock and the application of dressings, as for second-degree burns.

Treatment for exposure to severe heat and cold, snakebite, electric shock, and convulsions is also covered in this chapter. Other everyday emergencies include bruises, nosebleeds, blisters, animal bites, and insect bites.

CHAPTER 31 Cardiopulmonary Resuscitation (CPR)

PERFORMANCE GOAL

After completing this chapter, students will know: what cardiopulmonary resuscitation is; what the early warning signals of a heart attack are; how to make the distress signal for choking; what a "cafe coronary" is; how to avoid choking; and what the Heimlich maneuver is.

SUGGESTED INCENTIVES

"Extend Your Knowledge," entry 5, deals with practical concerns about CPR that may be discussed with the students. Ask students how these concerns might be overcome in the face of an emergency. Then invite a member of the American Heart Association who is trained in performing CPR to visit the class. The visitor could demonstrate how CPR should be performed correctly and what mistakes to avoid while using the technique. Students could then practice giving the choking signal and performing the Heimlich maneuver (gently during practice, with the knowledge that it should be performed more forcefully under emergency conditions).

CHAPTER SUMMARY

CPR should be performed by a person who has completed a CPR course and who has passed the CPR tests of knowledge and performance. CPR courses are offered throughout the country by the American Heart Association and the American Red Cross. CPR combines artificial respiration with artificial circulation.

The most frequent cause of death is heart attack. Common early warning signs of heart attack are: pressure, squeezing, or pain in the center of the chest; sweating; nausea; shortness of breath; and a feeling of weakness. There are two phases of emergency care—basic life support and advanced life support. Basic life support includes providing CPR treatment. Advanced life support includes basic life support plus the kinds of care started by an ambulance paramedic, a nurse, or a doctor. Advanced life support can usually be obtained by calling a community's emergency medical services system (EMSS).

The CPR procedure is as simple as A-B-C: Airway—Breathing—Circulation. Before performing CPR, the victim's airway must be opened by placing the victim flat on the back. Then the head is tilted back, the nose pinched shut, and the rescuer's mouth is placed over the victim's mouth to give rescue breathing. If the victim's pulse is not present, artificial circulation is performed. If the victim has suffered a neck injury the airway must be opened without moving the victim's head.

Basic life support for infants and children is similar to that for adults, with a few important differences outlined in this chapter. Unless CPR is performed properly, artificial respiration and circulation are not effective. Complications, such as rib or breastbone fractures, may result from putting external pressure on a victim. But the alternative to CPR might be death.

Choking causes many accidental deaths. To avoid choking in children, keep small articles away from them, remove all bones and shells from food, and be sure toys do not have small parts that could be pulled off. To avoid choking in adults, eat slowly, keep dentures in good repair, and realize that alcohol decreases sensation in the mouth and lessens one's normal caution in eating.

A person gives the distress signal for choking by clutching the neck between the thumb and index finger. Sometimes choking is mistaken for a heart attack because not everyone knows about this signal. Dr. Heimlich developed a simple procedure called the Heimlich maneuver to save a choking victim. The Heimlich maneuver may be performed on a conscious victim. The American Heart Association recommends another maneuver if the victim is unconscious. Both are outlined in this chapter.

CHAPTER 32 Medical Care and Medicine Show

PERFORMANCE GOAL

After completing this chapter, students will know: when to call the family doctor; when to go to a medical specialist; how to talk with a doctor; how to spot a medical quack; what their own medical health histories should include; what an internist is; what the jobs of many medical specialists are; and some important warning signals of physical problems.

SUGGESTED INCENTIVES

The "Personal Health Record" activity is also very useful with this chapter. Students should review their health record, keeping in mind now that it is like a medical history. Students may organize a telephone survey of doctors in the community to ask the doctors when and how they might handle problems or give advice by telephone. Students could also check various magazines and newspapers for any advertisements of patent-medicine products that might sound "unreliable," and bring these ads to class for discussion. The claims that the ads use are worth noticing as a way of guarding against medical quackery.

CHAPTER SUMMARY

It is very important to know who can give you the very best medical care during emergencies. A doctor should have a license to practice medicine in the state where he or she works. Many family doctors are general practitioners. A person studying to become a general practitioner spends three or four years in college, four years in medical school, and up to three years as a resident. More and more doctors are also becoming specialists. Internists, or diagnosticians, are specialists. Other specialists and what they do are listed in this chapter.

There are many important warning signals that the body can give to indicate a doctor's treatment might be necessary. These are also listed in this chapter. When you visit a doctor, you should tell the doctor the following specifics about your problem: the major problem and how long you have had it; if you have ever had the problem before; if you have had problems with your eyes, nose, glands, heart, digestion, or lungs; whether or not you smoke cigarettes, drink alcohol, or take part in sports. After learning your medical history, the doctor may give you a complete physical examination that includes a chest X ray, blood count, and urinalysis. Regardless of the length or type of check-up, always ask questions when you do not understand the medical terms used by your doctor.

Psychiatrists and psychologists are specialists in the treatment of mental-health problems. Doctors of dental surgery (D.D.S.) are also important to one's health.

Years ago, there were more traveling medicine shows than medical doctors. These shows convinced people that aging and other illness could be cured with "elixirs." People, instead, were cured by the effect of having high expectations. In modern medicine, this is called the placebo effect. Many diseases are self-limited. Others are chronic, or ongoing. A person or organization selling a miracle cure may use the fact that some diseases are self-limiting to claim a cure. The American Medical Association suggests that people use common sense to protect themselves against these people or organizations. This is the best safeguard against medical quackery. A person or company that claims to have a special formula, guarantees a quick cure, complains about being mistreated by the medical profession, advertises through the mail or door-to-door, or encourages people to ignore medical advice should be reported to the local Better Business Bureau.

CHAPTER 33   Medical Consumer and Self-Care

PERFORMANCE GOAL

After completing this chapter, students will know: the difference between primary and secondary care; how much hospital care might cost; that self-care is preventive medicine; when tetanus shots are needed; what the doctor writes on a prescription; how to read labels on over-the-counter medical products; and that some medicines can be harmful.

SUGGESTED INCENTIVES

Ask students to bring to class any prescription drugs they or their parents may have at home for ordinary illnesses, such as colds or flu. Have students read the label on each prescription and determine the doctor's instructions by referring to the chart of special abbreviations in the chapter. Then ask students to bring to class any nonprescription drugs they may have at home and check to see if every product contains the information required by federal law on its label. Have students compare the "active ingredients" of two similar products, such as aspirin or cold medication, to determine if the products are really different. With this exercise students should become aware of the need to develop the habit of reading labels on over-the-counter products before they buy them.

CHAPTER SUMMARY

Self-care means knowing enough to be responsible for your own health. An informed consumer needs to know about the many kinds of health insurance. Medicare and Medicaid are government programs of health insurance. Medicare provides health care for elderly people; Medicaid, for people below a certain income level. Private health insurance plans are called voluntary insurance. Many people belong to group health insurance plans where they work. Others buy insurance policies on their own.

Different medical centers give different kinds of medical care. Primary medical care is treatment given by a doctor at a clinic, emergency room, or doctor's office. Secondary medical care is treatment given by specialists at a private or community hospital. Tertiary (third-level) medical care is treatment given by specialists at a hospital which is part of a university.

The following are different kinds of preventive medicine: regular immunizations, chest X rays, avoiding environmental dangers that can cause cancer, learning how to take blood pressure, and getting skin tests for diseases such as tuberculosis.

A prescription should have the following information: name of the medication, amount, dosage, date when it is no longer good or useful (the expiration date), time between doses, specific instructions, and the patient's name. A list of special abbreviations used by a doctor on a prescription is given in this chapter.

There are several kinds of over-the-counter drugs. Antiseptics are good for cleaning wounds and for killing bacteria. Decongestants are drugs used primarily to ease congestion. Cough syrups can help the body remove anything that is irritating the trachea. Cough syrups may be expectorants or antitussives. Aspirin may be used for arthritis, to lower fever, or to ease pain. Antacids decrease acid in the stomach. Over-the-counter drugs usually have an expiration date and should not be kept in the medicine cabinet beyond this time. They should also be kept tightly capped to prevent exposure to moisture, or to keep them sterile.

One government agency in Washington, D.C., which tests new and old products is the Food and Drug Administration (FDA). The FDA makes sure all products meet government health and safety standards. Drug manufacturers must first get permission to put a new drug on the market from the New Drug Section of the FDA. Scientists and organizations such as the FDA are constantly discovering new facts about the products people use. These discoveries are announced in newspapers and on radio and TV. People should keep informed about new scientific findings.

CHAPTER 34   Health in the United States

PERFORMANCE GOAL

After completing this chapter, students will know: that epidemics and plagues are still possible in the United States; what the term *public health* means; who is responsible for keeping water clean and fit to drink; what a "disease detective" is; and what services are provided by city, state, and national health departments.

SUGGESTED INCENTIVES

The "Resource Guide" at the end of this chapter can serve as a useful activity to broaden students' information about voluntary health agencies. Divide the list among the entire class, and have students write to the health agencies assigned to them for specific information. Students could then share the information they receive with the class.

CHAPTER SUMMARY

Public health means the health of all the people. The government, business and labor organizations, and voluntary health organizations help to fight disease and to improve health. Many services are provided by the city health department. A list of city services can be found in this chapter. The state health department has a similar job but usually deals with problems too large for local or city departments. The federal government is responsible for public health services that cross state boundaries. The United States Department of Health, Education, and Welfare was set up in 1953. It includes the Public Health Service, the Food and Drug Administration, the National Institute of Health, the Office of Education, the Vocational Rehabilitation Administration, the Occupational Safety and Health Administration, the Welfare Administration, and the Administration on the Aging.

The most important federal agency that takes care of public health is the Public Health Service. A list of the services this agency performs is given in this chapter. The Center for Disease Control (CDC) is a branch of the Public Health Service that is especially concerned with the control of communicable diseases. In 1977, the CDC helped to track down the carrier of the mysterious "Legionnaires' disease."

The American Heart Association, the Arthritis Foundation, the National Foundation-March of Dimes, and the National Association for Mental Health are examples of voluntary health agencies that also work for public health.

A special agency of the United Nations has as its goal the improvement of the physical and mental health of all the world's people. This agency is the World Health Organization (WHO). The goal of this organization can only be reached by worldwide cooperation. The major activities of WHO are these: to spread new health information; to stop the illegal traffic of narcotic drugs; to stop the spread of communicable diseases from one country to another; to give financial aid to countries that need help in controlling communicable diseases; to give emergency aid to countries dealing with epidemics; and to get all people to use good methods of fighting water, soil, food, and air pollution.

Today, health plays a large part in every community. Taxes support public health agencies that work to safeguard the health of all citizens. But still more information is needed about how to keep people healthy. Everyone should work with the governmental and voluntary organizations that have been set up to protect and improve health.

One example of how health agencies protect the health of citizens is the action of Dr. Frances O. Kelsey of the FDA. Because she was not thoroughly convinced of the safety of the drug thalidomide, which had been made in Germany and used in European countries, she did not give her approval of it. Therefore, it was not allowed to be sold in the United States.

ANSWERS

to Apply Your Knowledge and Extend Your Knowledge

In this section, answers are given to all the "Apply Your Knowledge" and "Extend Your Knowledge" questions that appear at the end of each chapter of the student text. For convenience, each question from the text is repeated here. Where appropriate, a resource address or other additional information is supplied so that students may be made aware of the latest relevant facts about health-related issues.

One additional useful teaching device is provided: Every question at the end of each chapter has been given a letter code that corresponds to a level of difficulty, or category of thinking, devised by Dr. Benjamin S. Bloom.* The following key explains each letter code and corresponding thought process:

A   KNOWLEDGE

The student recalls or recognizes information.

B   COMPREHENSION and INTERPRETATION

The student changes information into a different symbolic form or language and discovers relationships among facts, generalizations, definitions, values, and skills.

C   APPLICATION

The student solves a lifelike problem that requires the identification of the issue and the selection and use of appropriate generalizations and skills.

D   ANALYSIS

The student solves a problem in the light of conscious knowledge of the parts and forms of thinking.

E   SYNTHESIS

The student solves a problem that requires original, creative thinking.

F   EVALUATION

The student makes a judgment of good or bad, right or wrong, according to standards he or she designates.

---

* Benjamin S. Bloom, *Handbook on Formative and Summative Evaluation of Student Learning* (New York: McGraw-Hill, Inc., 1971).

CHAPTER 1 Health and Wellness

Apply your knowledge

No "Apply Your Knowledge" section was included in this chapter because the chapter was intended to be more of a personal health inventory for the students than simply a chapter for study.

Extend your knowledge

E
1. Discuss the following statement with your class: "Health determines the quality of your life." Is this statement always true?
Students should determine what factors affect the quality of life, and how good health and poor health affect a person's outlook.

F
2. Interview ten people about whether or not they practice the following preventive health measures:
   a. using a seat belt
   b. flossing the teeth
   c. being aware of the seven warning signals of cancer
   d. feeding the body the required daily nutrients
   e. having the blood pressure checked at least once each year.
   What can you conclude about the answers you were given? How many people practice most of the preventive measures?
   Answers will vary.

D
3. Keep a weekly diary as you use this health book. Include a list of the new health and safety habits you will add to those you already practice.
Results will vary.

CHAPTER 2   Basis of Movement

Apply your knowledge

A   1. Why is the skeleton called a living organ?

The bone is very much alive, with many blood vessels and living cells within it. Also, red blood cells, platelets, and white blood cells are produced within the bone.

A   2. Name the specific bones, or group of bones, that protect the heart, brain, lungs, spinal cord, and eyes.

Heart—sternum; lungs—ribs; brain—skull; spinal cord—vertebrae; eyes—facial and skull bones.

A   3. Give three reasons why calcium is important for your body.

Calcium is necessary for blood clotting, muscle contraction, and nerve conduction.

A   4. What is the function of synovial fluid? Where is it found?

The synovial fluid is found between the joints. It helps to lubricate the ends of the bones.

A   5. Explain the difference between a ligament and a tendon.

A ligament attaches bone to bone, while a tendon attaches muscle to bone.

B   6. List the four major kinds of joints and describe the movement of each.

The ball and socket is found in the shoulder and in the hips and rotates 360 degrees. The hinge joint is found in the fingers, knees, and the elbow and acts like a swinging door. The gliding joint is found in the vertebrae and allows bones to slide over each other. The pivot joint is found in the head and neck and allows the head to rotate.

B   7. Describe how cartilage is slowly replaced by bone.

Bone cells gradually invade the cartilage and calcium salts harden the tissue.

A   8. What is the advantage of having fontanels at birth?

The fontanels allow the soft bones to move so that the head can pass through the birth canal. Also, after birth the brain needs room to grow.

A   9. What are the major differences between the male and female skeletons?

Some of the differences are these: the female pelvis is wider and shallower, and the pubic arch is greater than 90 degrees; the opening of the female pelvis is nearly oval while that of the male is triangular.

B   10. Explain how flatfoot can happen.

Flatfoot can occur if the muscles and ligaments that support the arch are weak.

A   11. Are there any advantages to having arches in the foot?

There are no advantages for jumping high or landing gracefully, but arches seem to distribute the body weight equally over the foot.

A   12. Can all forms of arthritis be cured? Explain.

No. Arthritis cannot be cured, but there are drugs and physical therapy techniques that can reduce inflammation, ease pain, and help prevent crippling.

A   13. How would a sprinter's thigh muscle compare in size to a long-distance runner's?

The size of the thigh muscle of a sprinter is generally larger because of the power and strength required to push off and to force the body forward.

A   14. Name the three kinds of muscles. Where are they found? How are they controlled?

Striated or skeletal muscles are attached to the skeleton. They bring about voluntary contractions. Smooth muscles are found in blood vessels, the stomach, and in other parts of the digestive tract. The movements are involuntary. The cardiac muscle makes up the heart and its movement is involuntary.

A   15. Why is it important to strengthen both red and white muscles?

White muscle, although powerful, cannot continue to lift or exert a force because it lacks the endurance and fatugues quickly. Red muscle helps to maintain posture and allows graceful movement.

Extend your knowledge

B   1. Explain what would happen to your radius and ulna bones and the surrounding muscles if you had to wear a cast on the lower arm for several months.

If no exercise is permitted, there is a possibility that the muscle may slightly atrophy. Also, inactivity speeds up the demineralization and weakening of bones.

C   2. If you wanted to take part in an arm-wrestling contest, which muscle fiber—red or white—would you strengthen? What large muscle would you have to strengthen in order to be good at arm wrestling?

White muscle, biceps, brachioradialis, and brachialis.

A   3. Give examples of general and specific warm-ups for these sports: football, basketball, track, volleyball, wrestling, swimming, skiing, gymnasitcs, and soccer.

football—pushups, stretching, scrimmage, bumping shoulders
basketball—stretching, running in place, lay-ups, perimeter shots
track—stretching, running in place, running with more speed
volleyball—jumping jacks, running, bumping, serving
wrestling—stretching, pushups, jumping jacks, squat stance
swimming—stretching, diving, stroking
skiing—stretching, short movements with skis
gymnastics—stretching, slowly going through actual motions
soccer—stretching, hitting the ball with various parts of the body

C   4. Sheila was afraid that she would develop large, bulging muscles if she took part in active sports. What would you say to her if you were her coach?

Since you do not secrete large amounts of testosterone hormone, your white muscles will not hypertrophy and become massive.

A   5. The next time you yawn in a crowd or in class, check to see how many others copy you. Is yawning "catching"? Explain.

Yawning is one way of contracting the facial muscles. When the blood vessels are squeezed, circulation is improved.

CHAPTER 3   Keeping Fit through Sports and Recreation

Apply your knowledge

B   1. Look at page 36. Choose one activity that seems to call for most of the skills listed.
Ballet dance.

A   2. Using the same chart, list five sports that can help you increase your endurance.
Answers will vary. Badminton, ballet dance, basketball, bicycling, boxing, calisthenics, canoeing, figure skating, football, handball, hiking, hockey, jogging, jumproping, karate, lacrosse, mountain climbing, racquetball, bowling, skiing, soccer, swimming, tennis, track and field, and wrestling.

A   3. List some sports that call for a great deal of coordination.
Answers will vary. Tennis, table tennis, swimming, soccer, skiing, skate boarding, racquetball, lacrosse, karate, jumproping, hockey, handball, gymnastics, figure skating, fencing, swimming, calisthenics, boxing, basketball, baseball, ballet dance, and badminton.

A   4. Why should exercise be avoided just before and after eating?
During digestion, there is an increase in flow of blood to the digestive tract. This extra supply of blood cannot be moved quickly away from the muscles to the stomach and intestines. Also, since an additional supply of blood is needed in the walls of the digestive tract for a hour or two after eating, digestion is interrupted when blood is taken away to supply the skeletal muscles.

A   5. What are the effects of exercise? Why do you feel tired after exercise?
The effects of exercise include faster heart beat, breathing, and possibly fatigued muscles. The tiredness is due to build up of lactic acid in the muscles and reduction of energy in the cells.

B   6. What makes up a conditioning program?
Conditioning refers to a program of exercise, rest, and diet. The program is followed by athletes to establish and maintain good physical condition. The results of conditioning include good muscle tone, cardiovascular improvement, and generally good performance.

B   7. Explain the differences between muscle lameness and muscle cramps.
Muscle lameness occurs when there is tearing of tiny muscle fibers that have been forced to contract under a heavy load or force. A charley horse results from a hard blow to the front part of the thigh. The muscle, blood vessels, nerves, and other soft tissues are damaged.

B   8. How does a cold pack help a charley horse or a sprained ankle? Why should you prop up the injured area?
The cold will cause the blood vessels to become narrow. This lessens the bleeding. Raising the injured area lowers the blood flow through the arteries and increases the blood flow in the veins that lead away from the injury.

A   9. List some sports activities that call for a lot of flexibility.
Answers will vary. Badminton, ballet dance, calisthenics, diving, figure skating, frisbee, gymnastics, judo, karate, mountain climbing, raquetball, skateboarding, skiing, soccer, wrestling, and yoga.

B   10. Explain how shinsplints can be prevented.
Shinsplints can be prevented by gradually strengthening weak leg muscles. Avoid running on hard surfaces during warm-ups and early training. Make sure shoes fit properly, and wear an extra pair of socks for shock absorption. Learn the correct way of jogging. Always warm up adequately, even if muscles are toned and strong.

Extend your knowledge

C   1. Plan a physical activity program you would enjoy for the entire year.
Answers will vary.

A   2. Are large, tall people as agile as small, short people? Explain.
There are many tall people who are agile and many short people who are not agile. Agility depends greatly on conditioning. People are not born agile. They have to learn to be agile through practice and experience.

C   3. Take your pulse for one minute just before you get out of bed. Then sit up and take the pulse again. Next, stand and take the pulse. Explain why the pulse rates are different.
The changes are due to increased demand on the organs. Each organ requires nourishment, and as greater stress is placed on them, more oxygen is required.

B   4. Why are some people better coordinated than others?
Coordination involving the various parts of the body depends a great deal on conditioning. With practice, many people can learn to juggle, ride skateboards, and throw frisbees.

A   5. Make a list of all the physical activities you do that cause your pulse rate to reach 150 beats per minute or more. Take your pulse after each activity. Using the chart on page 30, rate your heart endurance on a scale ranging from fair to excellent.
Answers will vary.

B   6. Take the pulse of an athlete and a nonathlete in your class. Explain any difference in the pulse rate.
A person who is involved in sports and recreation will have an efficient heart. Since the cardiac muscles are stronger, they do not have to pump as often. The athlete will have the better muscle tone because exercising causes the muscle fibers to hypertrophy.

B   7. Invite one of the coaches to tell your class about the conditioning programs in your school.
There are many young women who do not participate in sports because of misconceptions about women in sports. If there are no women coaches in your school, check with a nearby college.

CHAPTER 4 Emotional Needs and Mature Personality

Apply your knowledge

A   1. List the five important emotional needs described in this chapter.
Love, a sense of personal worth, personal achievement, the need to create, and a philosophy of life.

A   2. Describe what can happen—both emotionally and physically—to a person whose emotional needs are not met.
Emotionally, a person may feel frustrated, lonely, or insecure. The person may feel a lack of purpose or a worthwhile place in life, and be very unhappy or even emotionally sick. Physically, the person can have aches, pains, or other physical problems.

A   3. What emotional need do teenagers satisfy by forming small, close groups?
Love.

B   4. Explain why it is important to have a positive self-concept.
Answers will vary. Points to be included are that, in gaining a positive self-concept, a person also learns to be independent and discovers his or her own identity.

A   5. List three methods you can use to find the activities in which you are most likely to experience personal achievement.
Aptitude tests, talking to counselors or other adults with special training, and trying new enjoyable activities.

A   6. What is maturity? Are all adults mature? What is mature behavior?
Maturity means full development. In general, maturity means having realistic goals, making wise decisions, practicing self-control, and accepting responsibility for personal behavior. All adults are not mature in their actions and attitudes. Mature behavior is behavior that is appropriate for a person's age and stage of development.

A   7. What are the physical and social reasons why teenagers sometimes experience rapid changes in feelings or moods?
One physical reason is that the hormones that are changing teenagers' physical structure are also affecting their feelings and attitudes. One social reason is that relationships teenagers develop with people around them are changing, especially the relationship with their parents, as they assume a new role.

B   8. How does taking risks increase self-confidence?
Self-confidence is often earned through experience. Taking risks to meet new people or to try new activities can result in success and in a feeling of self-confidence. Risk-taking that results in failure can serve to make a person try harder to be a better person.

A   9. List three good steps to follow in order to make a responsible decision.
Use available resources, explore the choices, and think about the results.

A   10. List four errors to avoid in rating the personalities of other people.
Drawing a conclusion from only one event, placing too much value on surface traits, using a "personality test" from a magazine or newspaper, and stereotyping.

Extend your knowledge

B   1. Describe three activities you participate in frequently. Explain how each one adds to your sense of personal achievement.

Answers will vary.

B   2. Think of three people who are famous for work in creative fields (dance, music, painting, writing, theater, or fashion design, for example). Write a brief description of each person and her or his work. Then think of three people you know about (preferably among your own friends, family, or acquaintances) who satisfy the need to create in ways that are not usually called "art." Describe the creative work of these people.

Answers will vary.

C   3. Review the list of factors that might affect a philosophy of life. How have these influences affected your values and goals? Describe at least three specific examples.

Various factors that affect a philosophy of life are family customs or standards, religion, ideas you have read, experiences you have been through, and personal beliefs.

C   4. Read a novel that describes a teenager growing up before the twentieth century. Report on the influences that helped shape that person's developing philosophy of life. Discuss the presence or absence of these influences in your life.

Examples of popular books that describe teenagers growing up before the twentieth century are Little Men *and* Little Women *by Louisa May Alcott,* The Adventures of Huckleberry Finn *and* Tom Sawyer *by Mark Twain,* Penrod *and* Penrod and Sam *by Booth Tarkington,* Little House in the Big Woods *and* Little House on the Prairie *by Laura Ingalls Wilder.*

D   5. Review the list of errors to avoid in rating others' personalities. Describe a situation from your own past in which you made one of these errors. Do you think other people ever make these kinds of errors in judging you? Give an example of the kind of misjudgment you think has been made or might be made about you.

Answers will vary.

CHAPTER 5 Emotions and Mental Health

Apply your knowledge

B 1. What are some good ways of getting rid of anger and hostility?
Answers will vary. Points to be included are talking about the problem with someone who is not involved, and working off the anger by engaging in a very demanding physical activity.

C 2. Describe how you might help a friend who is feeling very angry.
Answers will vary.

B 3. Name three fears or worries about the unknown with which you are familiar.
Answers will vary.

A 4. How can fear of the known be useful?
Fear can get you ready to act.

C 5. What can you do about situations that produce guilt feelings? Give an example.
Answers will vary. The point to be emphasized is to try to avoid situations that are likely to result in guilt feelings.

A 6. What is the purpose of a defense mechanism? How is it sometimes helpful? When can it cause a severe emotional disturbance?
The purpose of a defense mechanism is to help someone be relieved or avoid the pain of emotional conflict. It helps people "save face" in their own eyes and in the eyes of others. It can cause a severe emotional disturbance if the problems become too much to handle and the defenses break down.

B 7. Explain how compensation can have wanted and unwanted results.
Answers will vary. Points to be included are that compensation can have wanted results when successful actions are taken, and can have unwanted results when poor compensation is used and unacceptable behavior occurs.

A 8. What methods are used by therapists in treating emotional problems?
Individual therapy, psychoanalysis, drug therapy, electric shock treatment, and group therapy.

B 9. List the differences between a psychiatrist and a psychologist.
A psychiatrist is a physician holding a medical degree who has completed several years of treating mentally ill patients under the direction of a psychiatrist. A psychiatrist must pass tests to receive a license to practice in an office or a hospital. A psychologist is an individual who has a doctoral degree in psychology.

B 10. In your own words, describe a mentally healthy person.
Answers will vary.

Extend your knowledge

C 1. From your own experience, give an example of being blocked in reaching a goal. Then suggest a good way to reach it.
Answers will vary.

E 2. Write a brief story in which the main character uses rationalization to cover up a failure.
Answers will vary.

F   3. Find out how your community helps people with mental disorders. (Ask nurses, physicians, church workers, social workers, and so forth.) Do you think your community has enough resources for this health problem? Explain your answer.

Answers will vary.

F   4. Plan a debate between members of your class on this statement: "It is more important to treat some criminals for their mental illness than to imprison them." For the debate, find out how treatment of criminals has been improved and what further improvements are hoped for. Decide on your own point of view about the treatment of criminals and prepare to defend it.

Research source for the debate is the National Criminal Justice Reference Service, Box 6000, Rockville, Md. 20850.

C   5. Give a report on the role of occupational therapy in the treatment of mentally ill patients.

Occupational therapists provide patients with carefully prescribed occupations, such as needlework, weaving, metalworking, and furniture making. Patients maintain concentration because of their interest in what they are making. They gain self-confidence from finishing a product. Often a patient's renewed contact with reality is a result of occupational therapy. It is also important for patients who are recovering from a mental illness to engage in a worthwhile occupation, such as gardening, to acquire a sense of achievement or to provide a form of relaxation. A resource to obtain information about this topic is the American Occupational Therapy Association, 6000 Executive Boulevard, Suite 200, Rockville, Md. 20852.

CHAPTER 6 Living with Stress

Apply your knowledge

A   1. When might your body produce a stress reaction? Give specific examples.
In response to a crisis, to everyday situations, and to change. Examples will vary.

A   2. What happens when your body experiences a stress reaction and then cannot use the physical responses that result?
In a very short time, the body usually adjusts and returns to normal. If the demand made on the body by the stress was very strong, the person might later experience a physical reaction, such as indigestion or a headache.

A   3. When could a certain amount of stress be helpful and even necessary? Give specific examples.
To perform the daily tasks of life and in a crisis situation. Examples will vary.

B   4. What is distress?
Answers will vary. One point to be emphasized is that distress is the result of too much stress (physical or mental) on the body.

A   5. What are the common symptoms of stress?
Stomach ache, headache, diarrhea, indigestion, dry mouth, depression or irritability, lack of appetite or eating uncontrollably.

A   6. Name some life changes that might involve stress.
Answers will vary.

A   7. What are some possible effects of ongoing stress?
Heart attack, high blood pressure, migraine headache, ulcers, colitis, diabetes, backache, arthritis, being accident-prone, and increased likelihood of having more colds and minor illnesses.

A   8. Name some positive things you can do to cope with stress.
Answers will vary. Points to be included are to keep a healthy body, to know how to judge reality, to try to spot stress and plan for it, and to relax regularly.

C   9. How would a good public speaker use the "physical readiness" caused by stress?
Answers will vary.

A   10. How can relaxation help you to stay healthy?
When you relax the muscles in your body, you slow down the body's processes. When you use the muscles in your body forcefully, you reduce built-up body tension. Both of these forms of relaxation provide physical and mental relief and help prevent physical symptoms from building up.

Extend your knowledge

B   1. Rate the following life changes according to how stressful you think they might be for you:
       a. graduating from high school
       b. writing a term paper
       c. starting or breaking up a relationship
       d. putting a dent in the family car
       e. getting a part-time job
      Answers will vary.

C   2. Make a list of five healthy ways to relax that you have never tried before. Try out these new ways for one week. At the end of the week, report to the class about your experiences.

Answers will vary.

B   3. Find out about the work of Dr. Hans Selye, who did the original research on stress and who was responsible for the concept of the "stress syndrome."

Dr. Hans Selye was born in Vienna in 1907. He earned the M.D. and Ph.D. degrees in Europe, and the D.Sc. at McGill University in Montreal, Canada. He became director of the Institute of Experimental Medicine and Surgery at the University of Montreal in 1945. He is founder and president of the International Institute of Stress in Montreal. More information about Dr. Hans Selye is included in various encyclopedias.

B   4. Suicide is the third leading cause of death among young adults aged 15 to 24. Many people misunderstand suicide. For instance, find out if the following statement is true or false: "People who threaten to commit suicide never really do." Research how stress is related to suicide.

The statement, "People who threaten to commit suicide never really do," is false. In most instances, people who commit suicide give warnings verbally or through their actions that they are extremely unhappy or depressed. Anytime someone makes a statement about committing suicide, there is reason for concern, and an attempt should be made to determine how seriously the person meant the statement. Many of the same warning signs associated with stress are signs that a person is seriously depressed. Some of these signs are restlessness, inability to concentrate, a sense of uneasiness and impending doom, being accident prone, an unusual feeling of tiredness or the opposite, difficulty in sleeping, and wanting to be alone all the time.

B   5. What is biological feedback, or biofeedback? How does the current research in biofeedback relate to your knowledge of stress?

Biological feedback is the feeding back of information about certain body systems by the use of special monitoring devices. Scientists have learned that it is possible to change and control a body function based on information about how that system is operating. For example, the use of biofeedback can result in getting relief from such stress-related health problems as backaches, headaches, high blood pressure, and gastric ulcers.

CHAPTER 7 Human Reproduction

Apply your knowledge

B 1. Describe how sperm pass from the testes to the outside of the body.
By way of a wavelike movement, sperm pass from the epididymis (the back side of the testes) to an inner duct called the vas deferens. This duct connects with the urethra, which opens to the outside of the body. The sperm are carried to the outside of the body in secretions from special glands, namely the seminal vesicles, the prostate gland, and the Cowper's glands.

B 2. Describe menstruation.
Ten days to two weeks after ovulation, if there is no pregnancy, the blood vessels in the lining of the uterus (the endometrium) break down. The lining then comes away from the walls of the uterus. Along with the disintegrated ovum, the lining is passed out of the body through the vagina. Menstruation usually lasts from three to seven days.

A 3. What is fertilization? Where does it take place?
The union of an ovum and a sperm. It takes place in one of the Fallopian tubes.

B 4. Illness or a drug can affect the ovulation cycle. Explain why a change in the ovulation cycle would change the time when fertilization could take place.
Fertilization can happen only during the few days following ovulation.

B 5. What is meant by cell differentiation?
As the fertilized egg divides and multiplies, the cells become different in appearance. Each of the different types of cells group together and finally become, for example, the skeleton, the liver, the skin, or the muscles.

A 6. How does a fetus get oxygen, water, and other nutrients?
Through the umbilical cord, which is attached to the placenta of the uterus.

B 7. Describe the birth process.
A baby is usually born head first. The head, which is the largest and heaviest part of the fetus, moves to the lower part of the uterus many weeks before birth. The baby's head helps to dilate, or enlarge, the lower part of the uterus and the vagina. The umbilical cord connecting the baby to the placenta stays attached during birth and is cut soon after the baby is born. The baby is then ready to carry on life processes outside the mother's body.

B 8. What is the main difference between fraternal and identical twins?
A fraternal twin is one of two children born to a woman at the end of one pregnancy. The two fetuses were in the uterus at the same time, but each was in its own placenta and each developed from a separate fertilized ovum.

An identical twin is one of two children born to a woman at the end of one pregnancy. The two fetuses were in the uterus at the same time and share the same placenta. The two fetuses developed from one fertilized ovum that divided after fertilization.

B 9. Discuss the importance of prenatal care.
Points to be included are nutrition, exposure to diseases and drugs, use of cigarettes and alcohol, emotional problems and planning for the future.

C
10. What do you think an expectant mother should do when she has a headache?

Answers will vary. One point to be emphasized is that a pregnant woman should not take any drug, even aspirin, unless prescribed by a doctor.

Extend your knowledge

A
1. Look up the origin of the term Caesarean section. Report to the class.

The name of this operation refers to the belief that Julius Caesar was born in this manner.

B
2. If cell division is repeated 43 times between fertilization of an ovum and birth, what is the total number of cells in a newborn baby?

8,796,000,000,000 cells.

F
3. Investigate the services of a nearby prenatal clinic. How many patients does the clinic serve? How often are the patients supposed to visit the clinic? Do most of the patients follow the instructions they are given? Who pays the bills for those who cannot pay? Do you think the clinic provides adequate services? Why or why not?

Answers will vary.

B
4. Research the effects that cigarette smoking can have on an unborn baby. Report on effects other than those that are mentioned in this chapter.

Research centers provided below.

E
5. What is your opinion on the question of when a person should become a parent? Be sure to include what you think the parents should be able to provide for the child.

Answers will vary.

Up-to-date information about prenatal care and family planning can be obtained from the National Foundation March of Dimes, the U.S. Department of Health, Education, and Welfare National Clearinghouse for Family Planning Information, and the Planned Parenthood Federation of America, Inc. (Addresses for these organizations are located on page 405 of the student text.)

CHAPTER 8 Family Life

Apply your knowledge

B   1. Write about the family responsibilities of parents and children.
Parents are responsible for giving the kind of care that will help their child grow into a physically, emotionally, and socially healthy person. They should also be able and willing to help their child learn how to make good decisions. Children are responsible for showing respect toward their parents and other family members. They are also expected to do their share of work in maintaining the home.

E   2. What do you think the role of parents should be in the education of their children?
Answers will vary.

C   3. How do you think family members could prevent some of the conflicts that develop in family life?
Answers will vary. One point to bring up is the importance of communication between family members.

B   4. What are some advantages and disadvantages of going steady?
One advantage of going steady may be the security of always having a companion for social occasions. One disadvantage may be that it can limit one's chances of getting to know others.

F   5. What do you think the characteristics of a good dating partner are?
Answers will vary.

A   6. Explain why people who marry early are likely to have special problems.
Points to be included are that during the teen years a person's feelings and behavior are likely to be less steady than in later life, and that an early marriage usually means giving up comforts, conveniences, personal freedom, and sometimes educational opportunities. Early marriage also demands taking on responsibilities that most people are not emotionally or financially ready to accept.

C   7. When do you think a person is ready to get married?
Answers will vary.

C   8. What do you think are some of the advantages and disadvantages of being married?
Answers will vary.

A   9. Explain some of the advantages of family planning.
Points to be included are that family planning makes it possible for parents to give their children economic advantages as well as more individual attention. Family planning also helps to slow down population growth and the drain on vital resources, such as food and energy.

C   10. What would you say to a friend who had a serious family problem?
Answers will vary. One point to be emphasized is to encourage the friend to seek professional counseling.

Extend your knowledge

C   1. Investigate the services available in your community to help solve family problems. How many different kinds of services are available?
Answers will vary.

C

2. Compare the family life of two cultures. State your opinion on some aspects of each culture's family living patterns.

Examples of family living patterns that could be explored are rights and responsibilities of family members, dating patterns, care of aged family members, sexual standards, relationship with in-laws, and communication within the family.

F

3. What aspect of American family living patterns do you think would be most noticeable to an observer from another country?

Answers will vary.

D

4. Investigate the problem of family abuse. Explain how this kind of abuse can be prevented. What kinds of treatment are available for the abusive person? What ought to be done to protect the victim?

Answer may be found in the "Something to think about" on page 103.

E

5. Marriage requires many adjustments, especially during the first year. In which of the following areas do you believe the greatest number of adjustments are necessary?

(a) in-law relationships
(b) daily-living habits (the "little things")
(c) housekeeping and home-management tasks
(d) religious practices
(e) sexual relationship
(f) spare-time preferences
(g) outlook on life
(h) money management

Answers will vary.

CHAPTER 9 From Generation to Generation

Apply your knowledge

A   1. Which cells in your body do not have 46 chromosomes?
The sperm and egg cells, which have only 23.

A   2. What is the difference between genes and chromosomes?
Genes are very complex molecules. Thousands of different genes are neatly arranged on specific parts of paired structures called chromosomes.

A   3. Will all genetic defects be seen at the time of birth? Explain.
No, in some cases, such as sickle-cell anemia, Wilson's disease, and Huntington's disease, the symptoms may not appear until two to thirty years after birth.

A   4. How does DNA tell the cell to build protein?
The arrangement of the bases on the DNA specifically dictates the order that the amino acids should be in to make the protein the body needs.

B   5. Explain the job of a medical geneticist.
A medical geneticist beings counseling by examining the affected child and others in the family. With the aid of computers and a knowledge of mathematical probabilities, the medical geneticist helps the family understand all the facts concerning their particular problem.

B   6. Explain the steps in amniocentesis.
A small amount of the amniotic fluid is removed by passing a needle through the abdominal wall, the uterine wall, and into the amniotic cavity. The fluid containing the fetal cells is centrifuged and then cultured. By a special technique, the chromosomes are stopped at the proper stages of cell division, stained, and then photographed. The photograph is enlarged and the chromosomes are cut out like paper dolls and arranged according to size.

C   7. What color are the eyes of a person who has two genes for blue eyes?
Blue eyes.

A   8. What color are the eyes of a person with one gene for blue eyes and one gene for brown eyes?
Brown eyes.

A   9. Why are carrier tests important?
Carrier tests are important because the results of the test give the couple an opportunity to decide whether they should risk the chance of having a child. If neither of the parents are carriers, or if only one parent is a carrier, the couple will never have to worry about the disease appearing in any of their children.

A   10. What is the difference between sickle-cell trait and sickle-cell anemia?
Sickle-cell trait is not a disease. The person is a carrier of the sickle-cell trait but does not show the symptoms. Sickle-cell anemia occurs when both parents are carriers and contribute sickle-cell genes. The child, within six months after birth, will begin showing the symptoms of sickle-cell anemia.

A   11. List eight symptoms of sickle-cell anemia.
a. serious infections; b. tiredness; c. slow-healing ulcers; d. poor vision or blindness; e. strokes; f. requiring a blood transfusion; g. pain in many parts of the body due to sickled cells plugging small capillaries.

A   12. Is there an advantage for a person to have the sickle-cell trait? Explain.
There is strong evidence that a person who is a carrier is more resistant to malaria than a person who is not a carrier.

B   13. Explain recessive inheritance. Use Tay-Sachs disease as an example.
Recessive inheritance means that both parents of the affected child appear normal. However, by chance, they both carry the same defective gene. The child who receives the Tay-Sachs gene from both parents inherits the condition. When both parents are carriers of the Tay-Sachs gene, each of their children will have a 25 percent, or one-in-four chance, of inheriting the disease. Each child born to the couple will also have 25 percent chance of not inheriting the gene from either parent, and a 50 percent chance of receiving only one defective gene to become a carrier like the parents.

B   14. Explain dominant inheritance.
Dominant inheritance means that an affected child with polydactylism must have one parent with the same abnormality. The risk for a child with one parent having the gene for polydactylism is 50 percent. There is also a 50 percent chance that the child will not receive the abnormal gene. In a rare case, where one parent has two defective genes, all the children born will inherit the defective gene and be polydactyl.

B   15. Explain sex-linked inheritance. Use color blindness as an example.
In color blindness, the mother carries the defective gene on one of her X chromosomes. Since her other X chromosome is normal, she is "protected" from the disorder. Each son born to the couple has a 50 percent chance of inheriting the defective gene from the mother. If the son receives the defective gene on his X chromosome, he will automatically have the disorder because he does not have another X chromosome. His Y chromosome will not protect him.

A   16. What is the difference between a normal hemoglobin and a sickle-cell hemoglobin?
The normal hemoglobin is made up of approximately 560 amino acids joined together. The sickle-cell hemoglobin contains one incorrect amino acid. Instead of glutamic acid, the sickle-cell hemoglobin contains the amino acid valine. This one tiny error, caused by one mutated gene, causes the hemoglobin to become sickle-shaped.

A   17. Why is Down's syndrome more common in children of older mothers?
Eggs, or ova, are formed and present in the ovary of the female at the time of her birth. As the female grows older, so do her ova. Some geneticists theorize that the chromosomes are more likely to divide incorrectly in the older mother, producing a chromosome with an extra strand.

A   18. Name a disease that is caused by a person's lacking or not having enough of an enzyme.
Tay-Sachs disease.

B   19. Explain the problems caused by cystic fibrosis.
The disease affects the mucus and sweat glands of children. The mucus gland secretes a thick and sticky mucus rather than the free-flowing secretions. The thick mucus blocks various pathways of the body, such as the pancreas, trachea, and digestive tract. Breathing becomes difficult when the mucus clogs the air sacs.

B 20. Describe the makeup of the DNA molecule.
The DNA molecule is similar to a twisted ladder. The "rungs" of the ladder are made up of chemical compounds called bases. The bases are located along the ladder in a certain order. This order is the blueprint of heredity, or the genetic code or codon.

Extend your knowledge

B 1. Explain how your environment has affected your growth and development.
Answers will vary.

B 2. Make a list of traits you have inherited from your mother and father. Are there any traits that they have which did not appear in you? What trait seems to "run in the family"?
Answers will vary.

B 3. Construct a DNA molecule using gum drops or other materials.
Models will vary. Special instructions will probably be needed.

B 4. Construct a family pedigree chart to see how certain traits have been passed on to you.
Answers will vary.

A 5. Is there any sure way to tell the sex of an unborn child?
Yes, by performing an amniocentesis.

B 6. Contact your local medical center and interview a medical geneticist. Find out how many mothers have amniocentesis performed. What percent of the unborn babies are found to be normal.
Answers will vary. As a related activity, have the medical geneticist visit the school to supervise screening for sickle-cell trait and Tay-Sachs disease.

F 7. Explain the advantages and disadvantages of recombinant-DNA.
One advantage is that the technique may someday be used to correct genetically-related diseases. One disadvantage is that the technique will also give future geneticists the awesome power of affecting people's genetic makeup.

CHAPTER 10 Environmental Hazards

Apply your knowledge

A   1. What are the basic pollutants of air? Where do they come from?
The five basic pollutants of air are carbon monoxide, sulfur oxide, nitrogen oxide, hydrocarbons, and small particles that float in the air. Major sources of air pollutants are transportation vehicles (especially automobile exhausts), industry, and individuals.

A   2. What illnesses are connected with air pollution?
Chronic bronchitis, emphysema, lung cancer, and heart disease.

B   3. Describe some causes of water pollution.
Answers will vary. Human and industrial wastes are the major water pollutants. Examples of these are sewage, chemicals, oils, detergents, fertilizers, and pesticides.

B   4. How can water pollution be prevented?
Answers will vary. Points to be included are improved sewage treatment and avoidance of dumping industrial and human wastes into waterways.

A   5. Name some illnesses connected with polluted water.
Hepatitis, typhoid fever, and dysentery. Note: Diarrhea is a symptom of a disease but is not a disease.

A   6. Why do fish often starve for oxygen in a river used as a sewage dump?
The breakdown of sewage often takes oxygen from the water.

A   7. What are the sources of noise pollution in our environment?
Answers will vary. Examples are loud rock bands, motorcycles, some household appliances, industrial machines, and aircraft on takeoff.

A   8. How can noise pollution be prevented?
Know what noises are harmful to the ears and stay away from them whenever possible. If you must be near loud noises for a long period of time, wear earplugs or other devices to protect your hearing.

A   9. What are some radiation hazards in the environment?
Nuclear weapons, atomic power plants, X-ray machines, color television, and microwave ovens.

B   10. How has progress affected the natural resources of the environment?
Progress has damaged the natural resources of the environment and has created many environmental hazards.

Extend your knowledge

C   1. What happens to household wastes in your community? Find out how the sewage treatment facility works. What happens to garbage? Is there a recycling center?
Resources to obtain information include the local health department, the Department of Public Works, or the local sanitary commission, or write to the U.S. Environmental Protection Agency, Washington, D.C. 20460.

B   2. Invite a local health officer to your school to discuss the laws in your community which control the various forms of pollution.
Answers will vary.

B　　　3. Explain the statement "Environmental control is everybody's business."
Each individual's contribution to protecting or polluting the environment
is important.

B　　　4. Once, a polluted river caught fire. Explain how this could happen.
Oil spills are a common cause of water pollution. Oil spills can burn.

B　　　5. Write to the Environmental Protection Agency for material concerning the
latest pollution regulations.
Students should report findings to the class.

B　　　6. Black lung disease and asbestosis are occupational diseases. In what
occupations are these diseases a risk?
Miners and various types of factory workers have a higher incidence of black
lung disease and asbestosis.

CHAPTER 11 Cancer Prevention

Apply your knowledge

A   1. What is cancer?
Uncontrolled and irregular growth of abnormal cells.

A   2. How does cancer spread to other parts of the body?
Cancer cells may be carried to other parts of the body by the blood or lymph system. Cancer may also grow into the tissue next to it.

B   3. What is the difference between a benign tumor and a malignant tumor?
A benign tumor grows inside a wall of tissue and does not spread to other parts of the body. A malignant tumor (cancer) grows without limit and may spread to other parts of the body.

A   4. Name some things in the environment that may cause cancer.
Answers will vary. Examples are asbestos, tobacco smoke, and sun.

A   5. How can biological factors cause cancer?
Answers will vary. Examples include familial tendency, low resistance to a virus that may cause cancer, and age.

A   6. What can be done to prevent certain types of cancer?
Answers will vary. Emphasize avoiding cancer-causing substances, such as radiation and tobacco smoke.

A   7. List the seven warning signals of cancer.
A change in bowel or bladder habits; a sore that does not heal; any unusual bleeding or discharge; a thickening or lump in the breast or elsewhere; indigestion or difficulty in swallowing; an obvious change in a wart or mole; and a nagging cough or hoarseness.

A   8. What is a biopsy? When does a doctor suggest having one done?
An operation to remove a small amount of tissue from the body to look for abnormal cells under a microscope.

A   9. What are the three standard ways of treating cancer?
Surgery, chemotherapy, and radiation therapy.

A   10. Why does radiation kill cancer cells and not normal cells?
Cancer cells are more sensitive to radiation than normal cells.

Extend your knowledge

B   1. Contact the local office of the American Cancer Society and obtain information on the prevention and early detection of cancer.
Results will vary.

B   2. Invite a local doctor to discuss the current methods of detecting and treating cancer.
Results will vary.

B   3. Report on controversies in the treatment of cancer, such as the use of laetrile or of special diets.
Results will vary.

CHAPTER 12 Coordination and Control

Apply your knowledge

B   1. Explain how motor nerves are different from sensory nerves.

Sensory nerves carry information from sense receptors to the brain and spinal cord. Motor nerves carry impulses away from the brain and spinal cord to the muscles and glands. These impulses cause the muscles to contract or relax and the glands to secrete or to stop secreting their hormones.

A   2. How do nerve cells carry information?

The dendrites receive information from another cell, or from the environment, and transmit the impulses to the cell body. From the cell body, the impulses travel down the axon and the axon synapses with another nerve, muscle, or gland.

B   3. Explain how our reflexes protect us.

Reflexes are involuntary. You don't have to think about them. The nerve impulses that stimulate a reflex travel on a shorter pathway so you can protect yourself faster. One example is the touch reflex. Your hands will move quickly away from a hot stove even before the information reaches the brain.

A   4. List four diseases that affect the nervous system.

Epilepsy, meningitis, multiple sclerosis, and poliomyelitis.

B   5. If you are right-handed, which side of the brain is dominant? Explain why.

The left side of the brain is dominant because the motor fibers from the cerebrum cross over to the opposite side as they enter the spinal cord.

B   6. Give two examples of how our body structure protects the central nervous system.

The brain is protected by the skull, meninges, and cerebrospinal fluid, which all cushion the brain. The spinal cord is protected by the vertebrae, meninges, and cerebrospinal fluid.

B   7. Why is pain considered a warning?

The sensation of pain is very important in protecting your body from injury. It warns you to avoid those stimuli which may cause injury to the body.

B   8. Explain why constant tension and anxiety may be harmful to your nervous system.

Constant tension and anxiety may be harmful to your nervous system because the excess nerve impulses may cause fatigue and the nervous system may become overworked.

A   9. Describe the actions of each area of the brain.

The cerebrum is the large, upper part of the brain. It contains nerve centers concerned with memory, intelligence, and some of the generalized emotions, such as appreciation and beauty. Information is stored in the cerebrum. Specialized areas are concerned with the senses, such as vision, hearing, smell, and taste. The cerebellum is located beneath and behind the cerebrum. It coordinates muscle movements so that posture and balance can be maintained. The activities of the cerebellum are carried on below the level of consciousness. The medulla oblongata is the lowest portion of the brain. It tapers off into the spinal cord. It contains centers that regulate such vital functions as breathing, heart action, and blood circulation. The midbrain *and* pons *are the two smaller parts of the brain, which seem to function chiefly as connecting stations between the spinal cord and the various other areas of the brain.*

Extend your knowledge

C 1. How may a stroke be prevented?
A stroke may be prevented by keeping the blood pressure normal, cutting down or quitting smoking, getting plenty of rest, and not letting tension or anxiety build up.

A 2. Give some examples of drugs that may interfere with the activity of your nervous system.
Alcohol, amphetamines, barbiturates, narcotics, and hallucinogens can alter the nervous system.

C 3. Describe how a driver or passenger in a car may injure the central nervous system by not wearing a seat belt and not raising the headrest.
Without a seat belt, the body may be thrown violently against the front of the car (steering wheel, windshield, or top front of the car) or thrown out of the car.

B 4. List some common reflexes that occur among athletes during sports activities.
Some of the reflexes include a batter reflexively ducking a high and inside pitch, an ice skater extending her arms out to break her fall, and the slowing down of the heart beat as a diver enters the water.

CHAPTER 13 Eye and Ear Care

Apply your knowledge

A   1. What is the job of the ciliary muscles? How can you rest these muscles?
The ciliary muscles help to change the shape of the lenses for near vision. As long as the eyes are focused on a near object, the muscles will remain contracted. In order to rest the ciliary muscles, the eyes should focus on a distant object.

A   2. What is the job of the muscles on the surface of the sclera?
These muscles help to rotate the eyeballs in all directions. If the muscles are working correctly, both eyes converge when looking at an object.

A   3. List five structures that help to protect the eyes.
     a. fat deposits *act as padding;*
     b. brows *prevent perspiration from flowing into the eyes;*
     c. eyelashes *trap dust;*
     d. seven bones *of the face and skull surround the eye;*
     f. tears *contain lysozyme, a bactericide;*
     g. conjunctiva *is a thin layer of tissue that covers the eyelids and the cornea.*

B   4. Explain why tears are important. Trace the flow of tears from the tear gland.
Tears prevent the cornea from drying out. They are secreted by an almond-shaped tear gland and flow diagonally across to the nasal region. The tears flow out through tiny openings and enter the nasal lacrimal duct.

A   5. How does the lens change for near and far vision?
The lenses are attached to the suspensory ligament. When focused for far vision, the ciliary muscles are relaxed and the suspensory ligament pulls on the lenses and flattens them out. Then, when near vision is required, the muscles contract and the lenses return to their spherical shape.

A   6. What does 20/70 on a vision test mean?
The score 20/70 means that a person with myopia sees things at a distance of 20 feet that a normal-sighted person is able to see at a distance of 70 feet.

A   7. What is the shape of the eyeball in farsightedness? What is its shape in nearsightedness? How do lenses help to correct these defects?
A person who is farsighted generally has a short eyeball. The nearsighted person has an elongated eyeball. Lenses can bend the light at the proper angle so that the image will fall on the correct region of the retina.

B   8. Explain the work of an ophthalmologist, an optometrist, and an optician.
An ophthalmologist is a physician who is an eye specialist. The specialist can operate on the eye and prescribe medication as well as glasses. An optometrist is trained in making measurements and in fitting glasses. The optician grinds the lenses and makes the glasses.

A   9. How is myopia different from astigmatism?
Myopia is a condition in which the eyeballs are elongated. The clear image falls short of the retina. Astigmatism is a condition in which the cornea or lenses are irregularly shaped and refract the light, causing only a blurred image to strike the retina.

B 10. Explain what happens in glaucoma.
In glaucoma, the tiny openings that allow the fluid to pass out of the eyes and into the blood vessels are closed, causing the fluid pressure to build up. This pressure damages the optic nerve.

A 11. What is the major difference between a sty and conjunctivitis?
A sty is an infection of tiny glands located along the edge of the eyelids. Conjunctivitis is an inflammation of the thin tissue, called conjunctiva, that covers the upper and lower eyelids and the cornea. The inflammation is commonly called pinkeye.

B 12. Describe the path of sound waves from the time they enter the ear until they become nerve impulses that reach the brain.
The sound waves strike the eardrum and cause the malleus, incus, and stapes to vibrate. The vibration is sent into the oval window of the inner ear. This sets up waves of motion in the fluid of the cochlea. The movement causes the hair cells to be stimulated and the impulse passes over the auditory nerve to the brain.

A 13. How is the eustachian tube related to deafness?
If the eustachian tube becomes infected, the middle ear can fill with a thick pus-like fluid. If the infection is not treated promptly, there may be permanent damage to the hearing apparatus.

A 14. What is the job of the semicircular canals?
The semicircular canals are responsible for balance. There are three small canals lying at right angles to each other. Each canal is filled with fluid and contains nerve endings that connect with a branch of the auditory nerve.

A 15. What is the major difference between conductive loss and nerve loss?
Conductive loss is caused by damage or blockage to any part of the outer or middle ear structures. Nerve loss is caused by injury or damage to the tiny hair cells in the cochlea. Also, any damage to the auditory nerve leading to the brain causes nerve loss.

A 16. Explain how deaf people communicate.
Answers will vary. Examples include lipreading and sign language.

C 17. Discuss how you can prevent hearing problems.
Hearing problems can be prevented by immediate care of any infection in or around the ears, throat, or nose. Avoid swimming in polluted swimming areas and never insert anything into the ears.

Extend your knowledge

C 1. If the aqueous humor is not secreted in large enough amounts, what do you think happens to the eye?
The aqueous humor nourishes and moistens the crystalline lens. If the fluid level drops, the cornea, lens, and the iris may dry out.

E 2. If you had to choose between losing your vision or losing your hearing, which would you choose? Why?
Answers will vary.

B   3. Learn how to use Braille or the hand alphabet, and show your class how the method works.

There are many blind persons who are willing to share their feelings about blindness. Contact your local Ophthalmological Society or Prevention of Blindness Organization.

B   4. Obtain a decibel meter from your local health department. Check the decibel levels of sound in your school.

State health departments generally have decibel meters which can be borrowed.

C   5. An insect has entered your external auditory canal. What should you do?

Don't panic, and don't insert any object into the ear. If the insect does not back out, have your doctor remove it.

C   6. If your eustachian tube is blocked and you decide to go skiing, explain some of the problems you may have.

Since no air can be exchanged between the middle ear and the environment, the pressure within the ear will be greater and will cause the eardrum to push out. You will feel pressure and pain in the ear.

C   7. Stand on your toes, stretch out your arms in front of you, and then close your eyes. Can you stand in this position without moving for 30 seconds? Try it!

With practice, this exercise can be performed with a minimum of difficulty.

CHAPTER 14 Transport System

Apply your knowledge

A
1. What is the main job of plasma, red blood cells, white blood cells, and platelets?

Plasma is the fluid portion of the blood. It carries many blood proteins, water, hormones, nutrients, gases, and cells. The red blood cells contain hemoglobin and carry oxygen from the lungs to the body cells, and carbon dioxide from cells back to the lungs. White blood cells help to fight infection by leaving the blood vessels and moving into the body tissue where the bacteria have invaded the body. Platelets help to clot blood and stop the bleeding from a cut or wound.

A
2. What are blood types? Why is it important to know what your blood type is? What is the Rh factor?

The major human blood types are A, B, AB, and O. The importance of knowing your blood type is to prevent the chance of a wrong type of blood being given to you, which would be destroyed by your antibodies and would clot, thereby blocking vital pathways in the circulatory system. Rh factor is similar to the A, B, or AB factors. Approximately 85 percent of the people in the United States carry the Rh factor in their red blood cells.

B
3. Without looking at the diagram of the heart, make a sketch showing the four chanbers and the valves. Use arrows to show the direction of the blood flow through the heart. From which side is the blood pumped to the lungs? From which side is it pumped to the rest of the body?

The right side of the heart (right ventricle) pumps blood to the lungs through the pulmonary artery. The left side (left ventricle) pumps blood to the body through the aorta.

B
4. How do capillaries, veins, and arteries work together? In what direction does the blood flow through these vessels?

The arteries carry blood from the heart to the organs. They branch to form smaller arteries, and the smallest arteries, called arterioles, branch to form tiny capillaries. The capillaries are very important because nutrients, water, and gaseous materials pass through the capillary walls. The capillaries join to form small veins (venules), which join to form larger veins. The large superior and inferior vena cava return blood to the heart.

A
5. What are the dangers of high blood pressure?

If the pressure in the arteries increases beyond the normal range, the heart must work harder to pump the blood. Some of the smaller arteries may break. If the tiny vessels break in the brain, or a clot blocks off a larger vessel of the brain, a stroke may occur.

A
6. What are some of the causes of heart disease? How can they be avoided?

Infection from any part of the body can enter the blood stream and affect the heart. Diphtheria, scarlet fever, syphilis, and rubella are some of the diseases that can harm the heart.

A
7. What is rheumatic fever?

Rheumatic fever may develop two to six weeks after a throat infection from a type of bacteria called streptococcus. A person usually has fever and swelling in the bone joints. If swelling occurs in the heart muscle and in the heart valves, scars form, making the permanent damage called rheumatic heart disease.

A   8. Why is it important to discover high blood pressure in young adults?
Many types of heart diseases begin early in life. If high blood pressure is detected early, the person can avoid those risk factors that can increase the possibility of heart diseases later in life.

A   9. What foods may lead to circulatory disorders if you eat too much of them?
Cholesterol, other saturated fats, and salt may lead to circulatory disorders and should be reduced to prevent high blood pressure.

A   10. What happens to the arteries of a person who has arteriosclerosis?
Deposits of fat build up on the inside walls of the arteries, causing them to thicken and harden.

Extend your knowledge

C   1. Look at a drop of blood under the microscope. The next time you cut your finger, notice how long the blood takes to clot.
If the blood smear is prepared with Wright's stain, the white blood cells can be seen. Clotting time will vary from person to person.

C   2. Ask the Red Cross about the blood-donor service in your community. Who can give blood? How it is collected? How is it stored? What use is made of it?
Answers will vary.

C   3. Get a sheep, beef, or pig heart from the meat market. Find each atrium, ventricle, and valve. Squeeze water through the heart. Can you see the valves close? Point out the major parts of the heart.
Answers will vary.

C   4. Contact the local branch of the American Heart Association for pamphlets on preventing heart disease. What added information do these pamphlets contain? What other services does the American Heart Association provide?
Contact American Heart Association, 7320 Greenville Avenue, Dallas, Texas 75231. Many of the local heart associations have programs for cardiopulmonary resuscitation.

C   5. Check your pulse rate per minute by placing your second and third fingers over the artery at the base of your thumb and wrist joint. Now jump in place for two minutes. Check your pulse rate again. How does exercise affect your pulse rate?
Exercising will cause the heart muscle to contract more rapidly. Since more oxygen is required by the muscles of the body, blood flow will increase as cardiac output increases.

C   6. Record the pulse rate of a cigarette smoker before and immediately after a cigarette is smoked. How many extra times does that individual's heart beat because of cigarette smoking?
Answers will vary. Since nicotine in cigarettes is a vasoconstrictor, the heart will pump faster to compensate for the narrowed vessels.

CHAPTER 15   Respiration

Apply your knowledge

A   1. How does the body use oxygen?

The body uses oxygen to make energy. During oxidation, oxygen mixes with food or glucose. The oxygen available in the cells combines with hydrogen to release energy and to produce water.

A   2. Trace the passage of air from the nose to the alveoli. How is the air cleaned? What keeps the air passages from collapsing?

From the nose, the air passes back into the pharynx, down through the larynx, trachea, and bronchi, and finally to the microscopic alveoli. Air is cleaned, filtered, and warmed as it passes through the nostrils. Cilia and the mucus from the mucous membrane lining the respiratory tract take out most of the bacteria, dust, and other harmful particles. There are rings of cartilage that are part of the larynx, trachea, and bronchi that prevent the air passages from collapsing.

A   3. What is the difference between breathing and respiration? How is outer respiration different from inner respiration?

Breathing is the process of air entering and leaving the lungs. Respiration involves the exchange of gases at the cellular level. External respiration is the exchange of gases between air and blood in the lungs. Internal respiration is the exchange of gases between blood and cells throughout the body.

A   4. What muscles do we use in breathing? When these muscles contract, what happens to the size of the chest?

The most important muscle is the diaphragm. The diaphragm and the muscles located between the ribs contract to increase the size of the chest cavity.

B   5. How is breathing controlled? Why can you hold your breath for only a few moments? Why is a mixture of oxygen and carbon dioxide given to a person who is suffocating? What would happen if only pure oxygen were given?

The respiratory center controls breathing but is affected by the amount of carbon dioxide in the blood. The increase in carbon dioxide when a person holds his or her breath stimulates the respiratory center to send impulses to the muscles for contraction. The mixture of gases provides the cells with the needed oxygen and the carbon dioxide stimulates the respiratory center. If only pure oxygen were given, the level of carbon dioxide in the blood would be too low to stimulate breathing.

A   6. What happens when you hiccup, when you yawn, and when you cough?

Hiccuping is caused by jerky movements of the diaphragm. The quick intake of air and the closing of the epiglottis causes the sound. Yawning is a deep inspiration followed by a short expiration. It is assumed that the level of oxygen is low in the bloodstream and the yawning helps to circulate the blood (muscle contraction forces the sluggish blood in veins to return to the heart). Coughing starts with some irritation in the pharynx, trachea, or bronchi. Air is taken in and forced out at a rate of 800 kilometers per hour.

B   7. What changes happen to air pressure at increasing heights above sea level? How does a person's body adjust to living at a high altitude?

Air pressure decreases as altitude increases. Many people feel light-headed and dizzy from not enough oxygen. The body adjusts to high altitudes by breathing more quickly for a time. The heart also beats faster than normal, and red blood cells increase in number so that more oxygen can be carried to various parts of the body.

A   8. What are common causes of asthma? Why does a person who has asthma find it hard to breath?

Asthma can be triggered by allergy to dust, molds, pollen, feathers, and certain foods. The mucous membranes of the bronchi become irritated and swell, and the opening of the tubes become narrowed. The muscles of the walls of the bronchi contract, making the air passages even narrower. Also, the excessive mucus forming on the membrane decreases the passage to the lungs.

A   9. What is bronchitis?

Bronchitis is inflammation of the bronchi. It can be caused by viral infection, prolonged cigarette smoking, or other upper respiratory problems.

A   10. What is emphysema?

Emphysema is a condition in which the alveoli lose their elasticity, become enlarged, and eventually lose their function. Carbon dioxide cannot be forced out of the lungs; therefore, less oxygen enters the alveoli and the patient gasps for breath. Infections and irritations of the lungs, cigarette smoking, and air pollution are all thought to be the likely causes of emphysema.

Extend your knowledge

B   1. Obtain the lungs of a sheep or a pig from the meat market. Find the trachea and bronchi. Put a glass tube into the trachea and try to blow up the lungs. Why do the lungs feel spongy?

The spongy texture of the lungs is due to the many thousands of tiny alveoli which contain small amounts of air.

B   2. Look at a model or dissection of the lungs of a small mammal. Find the ribs and the muscles between the ribs, the diaphragm, and the pleura.

Answers will vary.

C   3. Experiment with your own breathing. How slowly can you breathe? How fast can you breathe? (Be careful not to make yourself dizzy!) What happens when you cough? Keep your ribs still, and use your diaphragm for breathing. Keep your diaphragm still, and use your ribs for breathing.

Answers will vary. Discuss the advantages of rib breathing over diaphragm breathing.

B   4. Ask a physical education instructor or a biology teacher to demonstrate the use of a spirometer. For a few members of the class, find the amount of air they breathe out in a forced expiration. Find the amount they breathe out after a forced expiration and a forced inspiration.

Results will vary.

E   5. Report on the special systems that provide air for space travelers and for people who live underwater for days or for weeks.

Air embolisms occur when divers inhale air at great pressure and then rise to lower pressures without exhaling. The expanded air travels through alveoli and bubbles into the bloodstream. The air bubbles block the normal flow of blood to the brain. Nitrogen can also dissolve in the diver's body. If the diver rises too rapidly, pressure is released too fast, causing the nitrogen gas to bubble before it can be exhaled.

CHAPTER 16 Skin and Hair: Your Protective Covering

Apply your knowledge

A   1. How is the dermis different from the epidermis?

The epidermis is the outer layer of the skin. It is a thin layer of cells that grows and pushes to the outer surface of the skin. The cells that reach the surface are no longer alive. The dermis is the under layer of skin that gives the skin its strength and elasticity. It is thicker and contains a network of connective and fatty tissues, blood vessels, nerves, hair roots, and sweat and oil glands.

A   2. What are the four general functions of the skin?

(A) Protection: the skin is the first line of defense. It keeps bacteria out, acts as a cushion for bumps, and covers delicate interior tissue. The melanin pigments prevent ultraviolet light from injuring the soft underlying tissue. (B) Regulation of body temperature: the blood vessels in the dermis layer enlarge to increase blood flow. Redness is a sign that heat has been carried by the blood to the surface of the body and is escaping through the skin. Also, as perspiration is released through the pores, it evaporates from the skin surface. This reaction helps the body to cool down. (C) Sensation: there are many receptors in the skin, such as those for cold, heat, and pain. They warn the body of possible dangers. (D) Expression: blushing, smiling, and frowning are some of the changes that appear on the face. People respond to these expressions and may even offer compliments on how healthy a person's skin looks.

A   3. How does the process of perspiration help regulate your body temperature?

Perspiration cools the body down and helps keep the body from overheating.

A   4. Give some examples of contact dermatitis.

People sensitive to certain plants may develop rashes or inflammation. Also, some people may react to contact with chemicals, clothing, or cosmetics.

A   5. What is the proper way to get a suntan? How can you keep from getting a sunburn?

At first, limit the amount of exposure to the sun. Then slowly add more time in the sunlight. A brief exposure of 20 minutes each day will let a suntan develop within two to three weeks. The harmful ultraviolet rays in sunlight are most intense at noon. Avoid the "peak burning" hours. Severe sunburn is less likely before 10:00 AM or after 2:00 PM (standard time). Sunscreens used 15 minutes before going out in the sun will help to reduce the penetration of the sun's rays.

A   6. How can athlete's foot be prevented?

Feet should be washed carefully with soap and dried thoroughly, especially between the toes. Always use your own towels. Avoid wearing another person's shoes. Wear shoes that allow some air to circulate. And seek immediate medical care if you suspect you have athlete's foot.

A   7. How do pimples and blackheads form? Describe what can be done to help prevent the development of acne.

Generally, when bacteria enters the pores of the skin and the pores become clogged, there is a chance that some infection will develop. To prevent acne, clean the area of the skin that is infected with soap and water every morning, night, and after school. Dry the skin with a towel. Avoid greasy creams and oily preparations. Eat a well-balanced diet and avoid foods that seem to make acne worse. Get enough exercise and rest. Short exposure to sunlight helps dry the pores and prevents build up of oily material.

A   8. What determines the color of your hair? Why do some older people have gray hair?

The amount of pigment in the hair cells determines the color of hair. As a person gets older, the amount of pigment decreases so the hair color gets lighter.

A   9. Name some common skin problems that can usually be prevented with good personal habits.

Dandruff, acne, pimples, dry and oily skins.

A   10. When are moles harmful?

Moles are harmful when they are cancerous. If a mole gets larger, changes color, or is constantly irritated, it may be harmful and should be checked by a doctor.

Extend your knowledge

C   1. Explain why you must drink more fluids on a hot summer day than on a cold winter day.

More fluid is lost through the skin as the body perspires.

C   2. Make a list of cosmetics that claim to help your skin. Do you think they are all needed for proper skin care?

Answers will vary.

A   3. Which skin disorders are likely to be transferred to others if special precautions are not taken?

Athlete's foot and ringworm.

CHAPTER 17 Regulators of Your Body

Apply your knowledge

A   1. Name the glands that make up the endocrine system.
The endocrine glands include the pituitary, thyroid, parathyroid, thymus, adrenal, testes, and ovaries.

A   2. Which gland is sometimes called the "master" gland? Why?
The pituitary gland is considered the master gland because it secretes hormones that control other endocrine glands.

A   3. What is another name for an enlarged thyroid gland? What causes an enlarged thyroid to develop?
An enlarged thyroid gland is also called a goiter. Iodine is essential in the production of thyroxine. If insufficient iodine is absorbed by the body, the thyroid gland must work harder and thus, will become enlarged.

B   4. Explain what cretinism is. How has this disorder been controlled?
Cretinism is caused by too little thyroxine. A person suffering from this disease grows slowly, the skin becomes thick, and the hair is dry and dull. It can lead to physical and mental retardation. When iodized salt is included in the diet and early treatment with thyroxine is given, cretinism can be controlled.

B   5. Explain how producing too much or too little insulin can cause disorders.
Insulin is needed by the cells so that they can absorb glucose. If not enough insulin is available, the cells cannot produce energy. The glucose level increases in the blood and much of it is excreted in the urine. Too much insulin can cause hypoglycemia, or low blood sugar. This condition results from glucose being removed from the blood too quickly or from too little glucose being secreted into the blood.

B   6. Which hormone helps to prepare the body for action or stress? How?
Adrenaline, the hormone from the adrenal gland, prepares the body for the fight or flight reaction by making the heart beat faster, by increasing muscle tone, and by slowing down digestion.

A   7. What hormones are produced in the ovaries? Which are produced in the testes?
Ovaries secrete estrogen and testes secrete testosterone.

A   8. What gland secretes the hormone cortisone? What does cortisone do in the body?
The cortex, or outer part of the adrenal gland, produces cortisone. Cortisone decreases swelling and helps the body react to stress. It also controls the use of salts, fats, and glucose in the body.

A   9. Which gland in the body secretes hormones that are needed to help use calcium and phosphorus?
The parathyroid gland.

A   10. List the functions of the pituitary gland.
The pituitary gland functions as the master gland. It influences the other glands and produces the hormones that control growth. It is thought to control the temperature of the body.

Extend your knowledge

B 1. Locate the endocrine glands on a chart of the human body or on an anatomical model.

Anatomical charts generally provide a better view of the endocrine glands than anatomical models.

E 2. Do some research on the discovery of insulin by Banting and Best. Report your findings to the class.

Answers will vary. Recently, several scientists have been able to insert the human genetic code for insulin into bacteria to induce them to produce that hormone.

B 3. Ask a pharmacist which hormones are now synthetically made by drug companies.

Synthetic hormones are available to help people whose glands to not work in the normal way. In addition to synthetic hormones, animal hormones can be extracted and used in humans. For example extracts from the pancreas of cattle have enabled diabetics to live normal lives.

D 4. Collect articles in newspapers and magazines about research on hormones and on the endocrine glands. Report your findings to your class.

Take advanced students to a local medical library to review current journals on hormone research.

B 5. Describe the blood tests that are used to find out whether or not the glands are working normally.

Since the circulatory system is responsible for carrying endocrine secretions, the level of hormones in the blood can be examined and compared to the norm. If a patient's hormone level is abnormal, the patient is further examined for disorders.

CHAPTER 18   Healthy Teeth

Apply your knowledge

B
1. Draw a picture of a tooth. Label the crown, neck, roots, dentin, enamel, pulp cavity, pulp, and root canal.
See the figure on page 222.

A
2. What is the function of teeth?
Teeth help prepare food for digestion.

A
3. Diet is important in the formation of teeth and in stopping tooth decay. Which foods should be included in the diet? Which foods should be eaten in small amounts? Which foods make good between-meal snacks?
In order to maintain strong teeth, foods that have vitamin D, calcium, phosphorus, and other minerals are needed. Foods such as candy, cake, cookies, pie, and sweet drinks should be eaten in small amounts. Raw fruits, celery, carrot sticks, and unsweetened drinks or milk are good between-meal snacks.

A
4. What is plaque and how can you remove it?
Plaque is a sticky, colorless layer of bacteria. To remove plaque, brush teeth regularly.

A
5. How is sodium fluoride used to stop tooth decay?
Sodium fluoride can be added to drinking water or the dentist may apply it to the teeth during a checkup. Sodium fluoride can also be added to tooth-pastes or made into tablets or drops to be used at home. Fluorides make the teeth harder and more resistant to decay.

A
6. Why is it important to have cavities filled while they are small? How often should you go to a dentist?
Filling cavities when they are small will stop the decay from spreading down into the pulp. The dentist should be visited once every six months.

A
7. Discuss ways to stop malocclusion.
Proper care of teeth, which includes filling cavities, replacing lost primary teeth, or putting in retainers that keep the spaces between teeth open until the permanent teeth grow in, will help prevent malocclusion. Also, an ortho-dontist can apply braces that gently move the teeth into place.

A
8. Describe the way the mouth looks if a person has gingivitis.
The gums become bright red, soft, and very swollen.

A
9. Why is care of the gums important? In what ways can you keep your gums healthy?
Teeth cannot be fully healthy without healthy gums. Gums can be kept healthy by regular brushing, a well-balanced diet, and regular dental checkups.

E
10. Imagine that you have just sat down in the dentist's chair. List some of the things you expect the dentist to do to your teeth.
The dentist will clean the teeth, take X rays, and check for cavities.

Extend your knowledge

C
1. If sodium fluoride is added to drinking water in your community, find out when this practice was started. What was the rate of dental caries before fluoridation? How much sodium fluoride is being used in the

water? What, if any, results have been found so far? Make a report to the class.

The local state department of health may have the information regarding sodium fluoride.

B   2. Visit a dentist's office or dental clinic. Ask the dentist to explain the use of some of the instruments and the X-ray machine. Ask to be shown X-ray photos of the following: primary teeth, with the permanent teeth ready to push through; dead teeth; root abscesses; and dental caries.

During your regular checkup it is important to ask questions regarding your teeth.

B   3. Discuss the advantages and disadvantages of electric toothbrushes, dental floss, and water irrigators.

With frequent brushing and flossing, water irrigators and electric toothbrushes are really not necessary.

C   4. Compare all the ingredients of five different mouthwashes sold in stores. Which ones contain sugar? How much sugar do they contain? If all the ingredients are not listed, write to the manufacturer and ask for a list.

Answers will vary.

CHAPTER 19   Use of Tobacco

Apply your knowledge

A   1. Why does the carbon monoxide in tobacco smoke cause shortness of breath in smokers?

Carbon monoxide reduces the oxygen-carrying capacity of the blood.

A   2. What is the effect of smoking on the mouth and teeth?

Smoking causes unpleasant mouth conditions, such as bad breath and brown stains on the teeth. It also irritates the mouth and can cause cancer of the lips, tongue, and other parts of the oral cavity.

A   3. What effect does tobacco smoking have on the temperature of the fingers and toes, on the heart rate, and on the blood pressure?

The temperature of the fingers and toes is lowered. The heart rate and blood pressure are increased.

A   4. What are some of the symptoms of mild nicotine poisoning?

Dizziness, faintness, rapid pulse, clammy skin, and sometimes nausea, vomiting, and diarrhea.

A   5. What effects do tobacco tars have on the body?

Tars are responsible for loss of smell, bad breath, and the brown stains on the teeth and fingers of smokers. Tars can cause cancer of the respiratory tract, bronchitis, emphysema, and other diseases of the respiratory tract.

B   6. Explain the difference between mainstream smoke and sidestream smoke.

Many harmful substances are found in much higher concentrations in sidestream smoke than in mainstream smoke because sidestream smoke is not filtered in any way.

A   7. Does tobacco relieve tiredness? Explain.

Smoking may result in a temporary relief of tiredness because of the release of sugar to the blood. After a brief time, however, fuel is gone and the tiredness is greater than before.

B   8. List the facts unfavorable to smoking.

Smoking results in many accidents, diseases, added health-care expenses, and lost work output. A smoker coughs a lot, has bad breath, and stained teeth and fingers. The smoker's circulatory and respiratory systems are damaged, and the smoker has a shorter life expectancy than does a non-smoker. Smoking has a harmful effect on unborn babies of smokers, on young children, and on people who have chronic heart or lung disease. Many other people experience physical discomfort when exposed to a smoke filled environment.

B   9. What are some of the smoking regulations in your community?

Answers will vary. The local Lung Association may be of help in increasing your knowledge in this area. Students should be encouraged to obtain their information first-hand by surveying shopping areas, restaurants, public meeting places, doctors' offices, and so forth.

D   10. What do you think the smoking regulations should be in:

(a) hospitals

(b) restaurants

(c) transportation facilities (airplanes, buses, trains)
(d) high schools?
Answers will vary. Encourage the students to be as objective as possible in their responses.

Extend your knowledge

B
1. Investigate the smoking regulations that have been established in some cities and states. Which city or state do you think has the best smoking policy? Give your reasons.
The teaching suggestion for Unit Six Activity, "The Cigarette Habit," provides the answer to this question.

B
2. Studies have shown that smoking affects the way in which the body uses many different drugs. Report on the results of some of these studies.
Studies show that smoking affects the body's ability to utilize vitamin C. Smokers who drink alcohol increase their risk of developing esophageal and laryngeal cancers; and smokers require greater amounts of pain-relieving and anxiety-reducing drugs than do nonsmokers in order for these drugs to be effective. Women smokers who use oral contraceptives greatly increase their risk of having a fatal heart attack.

F
3. Throughout the country, recently, individuals have been bringing lawsuits to secure a smoke-free environment, and courts have been upholding their rights. Investigate some of these cases. Are you in agreement with the courts' rulings? Give your reasons.
The most publicized case is that of Shimp v. New Jersey Bell Telephone Company. *Donna Shimp, a New Jersey Bell Telephone Company employee, brought a suit before the state superior court to have cigarette smoking banned in her office. The court's December 1976 decision upheld her right to a smoke-free working environment. Because of the high interest in her two-year court battle, Shimp wrote a book entitled* How to Protect Your Health at Work.

A
4. What is the history of the use of tobacco in the United States? What are some of the early laws pertaining to smoking?
Columbus saw Indians smoking tobacco by using a pipe. The highly profitable tobacco trade, which originated in the United States, is thought to have begun in 1613 when John Rolfe sent the first shipment of Virginia tobacco from Jamestown to England. (Rolfe later married the famous Indian Princess Pocahontas.) Over the years, many tobacco products have been used in the United States, including cigars, cigarettes, chewing tobacco, pipe tobacco, and snuff. Cigarette smoking became popular during World War I, and during World War II, cigarettes were in such demand that a shortage existed in the United States and other countries.

Laws existed in early New England which forbade smoking because it was a nonproductive pastime. About 1896 antispitting ordinances, precipitated by the tobacco-chewing habit, began appearing in cities around the country. In 1965, the United States government passed a law requiring a health warning on every pack and box of cigarettes sold in the country. And in 1970, a law was passed banning cigarette advertising from radio and television.

F   5. The social trend in America today is not to tolerate tobacco smoking in indoor environments. Predict the acceptance of tobacco smoking twenty years from now. State the reasons for your predictions.

An article entitled, "The Spitting Image of Smoking," which originally appeared in the American Lung Association Bulletin, *March 1976, volume 62, no. 2, points out the interesting parallel between the successful campaign against public spitting and the campaign against public smoking. Both campaigns came about as a result of an increased awareness of health hazards related to the habits, both have been strongly supported by the American Lung Association (formerly the National Tuberculosis Association), both campaigns have generated strong supporters and strong critics, and both campaigns have been directed toward the rights of others not to be injured by another person's habit. As stated in the article, "The final victory against spitting did not come all at once, or even in one generation. But sometime after the peak involvement of TB associations in the 1920's, the custom lost its grip and succumbed." Copies of this article are available from the Group Against Smoker's Pollution (GASP), two founding members of which coauthored the article. (Address for this organization is located at the end of Chapter 34 of the student text.)*

Resources to obtain information to help answer these questions include the U.S. Department of Health, Education, and Welfare Office on Smoking and Health, the American Lung Association, the American Heart Association, the American Cancer Society, and the Group Against Smoker's Pollution. (Addresses for these organizations are located at the end of Chapter 34 of the student text.)

CHAPTER 20   Use of Alcohol

Apply your knowledge

B   1. List four reasons why a person may drink alcoholic beverages. For
            each reason, give another action that might serve the same purpose.
   Answers will vary.

A   2. Alcohol is a depressant. Explain what this means.
   *Alcohol dulls the nerve centers of the brain that are concerned with judg-
   ment, attention, memory, and self-control.*

A   3. Why does a certain amount of alcohol taken in over a long period of
            time have less effect on a person than the same amount of alcohol
            taken in during a short period?
   *Alcohol is metabolized very quickly in the body. At the end of several
   hours, most of the alcohol in a drink has been metabolized.*

A   4. What are the effects of alcohol on the nervous system?
   *Alcohol dulls the nerve centers of the brain. Drinking large amounts of
   alcohol at one time may lead to paralysis of many nerve centers in the brain.
   Finally, the nerve centers that control the action of the heart and lungs
   may become paralyzed.*

A   5. List some ways in which drinking too much alcohol affects a person
            physically.
   *Muscular incoordination, flushed face, indigestion and loss of appetite,
   and damage to the heart, liver, and kidneys.*

A   6. What is meant by *blood alcohol level*?
   *Blood alcohol level is the amount of alcohol in a person's blood. It is
   usually expressed in terms of percent.*

A   7. What are some reasons for getting medical help for a person who loses
            consciousness from drinking too much? What are some things you can
            do before help arrives?
   *Medical help should be obtained for a person who loses consciousness from
   drinking because the person could die from alcohol poisoning, or from the
   effects of combining alcohol with another drug, or from choking to death
   on the person's own vomit. Before help arrives, make sure the person can
   breathe freely by keeping the tongue away from the air passages and by
   removing any food or gum from the mouth. If necessary, give mouth-to-
   mouth resuscitation.*

A   8. What are some signs that a person may have an alcohol problem?
   *Some signs that a person may have an alcohol problem are these: drinking
   in order to get to work or to perform a job; being intoxicated while driving
   a motor vehicle; doing something under the influence of alcohol that one
   would not do without alcohol; becoming injured seriously enough to need
   medical attention as a result of using alcohol; coming into contact with the
   law because of using alcohol; being intoxicated four times in a year.*

B   9. What do you think is meant by the statement: "Alcohol is sometimes
            used as a form of self-medication"?

*Answers will vary. Students' answers should indicate that alcohol is some-
times used to relieve physical or emotional discomfort.*

C
10. What advice would you give to someone whose parent was a problem
drinker? Be as specific as possible about factual information that
could help the drinker's child.

*Answers will vary. A point to be emphasized is that the drinker's child
should be encouraged to seek professional counseling.*

Extend your knowledge

B
1. Find out what laws your state has to control the sale of alcohol.

*To obtain information concerning this topic, students could contact the
public relations person or department of the local police, local government,
or local Alcohol Control Board.*

B
2. Find out how many automobile accidents happened in your state last
year. What age group was most often involved? How many accidents
involved someone who had been drinking?

*Research sources include the state police and the U.S. Department of Trans-
portation, National Highway Traffic Safety Administration. (Address is
located at the end of Chapter 34 of the student text.) Students might
also research the effects of changes in state or local laws related to
alcohol on the number of accidents involving alcohol.*

F
3. What is your definition of the responsible use of alcohol? What is the
irresponsible use of alcohol?

Answers will vary.

F
4. What resources exist in your community to help the problem drinker and
the drinker's family? Do you think your community has enough resources? Do you think these resources are well-publicized? Can you think
of any other means of publicizing them?

*Resources that may exist in the community include Alcoholics Anonymous,
Al-Anon, Alateen, Veterans Administration Services, a local branch of the
National Council on Alcoholism, Inc., local Community Mental Health Serv-
ices, Health Department Addiction/Alcoholism Clinic, local Community
Drug Abuse Treatment Clinic, and facilities or Hotline for Child Abuse and
Neglected and Battered Wives. Also, many places of employment now offer
an alcohol-related employee assistance program.*

CHAPTER 21   Drugs: Use and Abuse

Apply your knowledge

A   1. Name three things people can do to improve their use of prescription and OTC drugs.
1. Follow recommended dosages carefully. 2. Do not take drugs that have been prescribed for someone else. 3. Do not take a combination of drugs without a doctor's approval.

A   2. Describe the function of vaccines and antibiotics.
Vaccines help the body to fight germs that can cause disease. Antibiotics fight infections that have already developed in the body.

A   3. Explain some of the ways in which a social environment can influence drug use and abuse.
Peer-group pressure may influence a person to experiment with drugs.

A   4. What is the difference between physical and psychological drug dependence?
Physical dependence means that if the drug is taken away, or if not enough is taken, a physical reaction, such as convulsions, nausea, and fever will occur. Psychological dependence means that an abuser will try to duplicate the intense high by increasing the amount of the drug. Anxiety and depression are common.

B   5. Compare the general effect of depressants and stimulants on the human body.
Depressants slow down certain body activities: the heart beats slower, breathing is slower, and the muscles relax. Stimulants speed up the body's processes: circulation and respiration increase, and blood pressure rises.

A   6. Define the term *psychoactive drugs*. Describe some of their effects.
Psychoactive drugs affect a person's behavior or mood. Some types make a person seem depressed. Other types act as a stimulant.

A   7. What is tolerance? What effect does tolerance have on a drug user?
Tolerance is the condition in which a person's body becomes used to the effects of a drug that is being taken regularly. A person who has developed a high level of tolerance needs to take larger and larger doses of a drug in order for the drug to have an effect.

A   8. Why should pregnant women avoid taking drugs?
Pregnant women should avoid taking drugs because drugs can pass through the placenta to the fetus. Since the fetus's body is smaller, the drug effect is greater. Abnormal growth can occur.

B   9. Why is the Drug Regulation Reform Act of 1978 important to consumers?
The act is important because it requires that all patients be given more information about drugs prescribed to them. Drug packages now contain simplified information about the dangerous side effects and benefits of the drugs.

A   10. What are the medical uses for morphine, cocaine, and amphetamines?
Morphine is used as a painkiller. Cocaine, when pure, is used as a local anesthetic for eye, ear, nose, and throat surgery. Amphetamines are used to treat depression, overweight, excessive sleeping, and overactive children.

A   11. What can happen when barbiturates and alcohol are used together?
Barbiturates and alcohol, when used together, act as an extra-strength depressant which slows the functions of the brain and nervous system down to a dangerously low level. Sometimes, breathing may stop completely.

A   12. What is methadone? What are some of its uses?
Methadone is a synthetic drug. It is used as a substitute for heroin in many drug programs. It is also used as a painkiller.

A   13. What are the physical and psychological effects of cocaine?
Psychologically, cocaine causes a quick, intense feeling of well-being, and frequent users experience a psychological dependence. Physically, cocaine speeds up the heart rate, and raises both body temperature and blood pressure.

A   14. What may be some of the dangers of using marijuana?
Marijuana may cause distorted perception and reflexes, particularly dangerous effects when driving a car.

A   15. Why should leftover prescription drugs be thrown out?
The chemicals in drugs may change over a period of time.

Extend your knowledge

C   1. Make a survey of the people in your school. Determine which drugs are most commonly abused, and to what extent.
Answers will vary.

C   2. Write a report on the abuse of volatile chemicals, such as glue, aerosol, and paint thinner. Find out what effects these chemicals have and what dangers they present.
Airplane glue, household cements, and solvents such as paint thinners, lighter fluids, and nail polish remover come under the heading of volatile chemicals. These chemicals are easily obtained and abused by young people. Generally, the chemicals are inhaled until the person feels dizzy and begins to hallucinate.

E   3. Role-play a situation in which a group of friends is urging one person to try a new drug. Take turns trying to resist the arguments of the peer group. Find some humorous and some serious ways of saying "no."
Situations acted out will vary.

F   4. How would you feel if you found out that your younger brother or sister was using marijuana regularly? What would you say to him or her?
Answers will vary.

C   5. Collect as many current articles on drugs and drug abuse as possible. Try to evaluate the opinions of the author and the accuracy of reporting in each one. Then write a monthly article for your school newspaper or publish a newsletter to inform other students.
Guide the students toward unbiased sources of drug information.

D   6. Visit one or more drug rehabilitation centers. Interview some staff members and some former drug abusers.
Situations will vary.

CHAPTER 22 Sexually Transmitted Diseases

Apply your knowledge

A   1. How are sexually transmitted diseases spread from one person to another?
Sexual contact.

A   2. What are the symptoms of gonorrhea? Does every person with a gonorrhea infection have symptoms?
The male usually has pain and burning when he urinates. These may also be a puslike discharge from the penis. The female may have a vaginal discharge, but often she has no symptoms at all. After a while, both male and female symptoms may disappear, but the person continues to be a carrier of the infection.

A   3. How does a physician find out if a person has gonorrhea?
Samples of fluid from the cervix, the vagina, or the urethra are examined in the laboratory. Gonorrhea organisms in the fluid can be seen under a microscope or grown in a culture bottle.

A   4. How does a physician find out if a person has syphilis?
A doctor may take a blood test or may examine a sore under a microscope.

A   5. What are the four stages of syphilis?
Primary stage, secondary stage, latent stage, and late syphilis.

C   6. How can STDs be prevented?
Answers will vary. A point to be emphasized is that sexual contact with anyone who may be infected with an STD should be avoided.

A   7. Why should a person with an STD tell a sexual partner?
So that the partner can also be examined.

A   8. If gonorrhea is left untreated, what other serious problems may develop?
Crippling arthritis and sterility may develop. Also, a pregnant woman may pass the infection to her newborn infant, sometimes causing blindness.

A   9. Why can't a person get syphilis from towels or toilet seats?
Because the bacteria that cause syphilis cannot live outside the body.

A   10. Why do doctors often give pregnant women a blood test for syphilis?
Because a pregnant woman may pass the syphilis infection to her unborn baby, resulting in deformities in the newborn.

Extend your knowledge

B   1. Make a list of the similarities and differences between gonorrhea and syphilis. Could a person be infected with both diseases at the same time?
Similarities of gonorrhea and syphilis include: they are both communicable diseases spread by sexual contact; the victims often do not know they are infected; the victims often spread the disease without knowing it; the symptoms may disappear without treatment; both infections can be treated successfully with antibiotics; and both diseases can result in serious compli-

cations if the victims do not receive proper treatment. Gonorrhea and syphilis differ in that they are caused by different bacteria; the symptoms of the diseases are not the same; and the diseases have different complications. A person could be infected with both diseases at the same time.

A
2. Explain why it is possible for a person to have gonorrhea or syphilis, especially latent syphilis, without knowing it.

The victim does not show definite signs or symptoms of having a serious disease.

B
3. Visit your local health clinic and obtain information on the number of cases of STDs in your city, county, or state.

Answers will vary.

E
4. What ideas do you have on how to prevent STD among teenagers?

Answers will vary. The purpose of this question is to provide an opportunity for students to consider seriously the problem of STD among teenagers. Hopefully, the students will develop a responsible code of conduct for themselves and think of ways to motivate other teenagers to do the same.

Apply your knowledge

A
1. What are some common types of pathogens that may cause infectious diseases?
Bacteria, viruses, fungi, and protozoa.

B
2. Why does it help to know the incubation periods of common diseases?
Answers will vary. Points to be included are that this information can sometimes help keep you from getting a disease by avoiding people who may be in the incubation period of an infectious disease, or by obtaining an immunization to the disease. In cases where you are unable to avoid getting the disease, you can recognize the symptoms of the disease more readily and obtain prompt treatment.

A
3. How does your body protect itself against infection?
The skin provides a barrier; hairs in the nose and cilia in the throat help screen out pathogens from the air; stomach acid destroys some pathogens after they enter the body; and certain blood cells and substances made in the blood help kill some pathogens.

A
4. How do white blood cells kill invading organisms?
The white blood cells surround kill, and digest invading organisms.

A
5. You have just breathed in a pathogen that causes the flu. What happens to that pathogen once it is inside your body?
The pathogen multiplies, spreads to nearby tissues, and then is carried by the blood and lymph to all parts of the body.

A
6. How does the common cold or the influenza virus spread from one person to another?
The virus is spread in the mucus released when an infected person sneezes, speaks, or coughs, or is spread from direct contact with the saliva.

A
7. What is the difference between viruses and bacteria?
Viruses are smaller than bacteria and cannot be seen under an ordinary microscope.

A
8. How can you avoid contact with the hepatitis virus?
Avoid close contact with an infected person; do not share cups and utensils; and practice good personal hygiene, such as washing your hands before eating and after using the toilet.

A
9. Name some common infectious diseases that teenagers may get. How can these diseases be prevented?
The common cold, influenza, hepatitis, and mononucleosis.

A
10. Name some of the factors that affect a person's ability to resist disease.
Practicing good personal hygiene, eating a nutritious diet, and getting enough rest and exercise.

Extend your knowledge

B
1. Invite a doctor or public health official to talk to your class about the prevention of infectious diseases in your community.
Situations will vary.

B   2. Find out what influenza epidemics have occurred in the United States
       in the past twenty years.
    *Recent worldwide epidemics (called pandemics) that have occurred are the
    Asian flu of 1957 and the Hong Kong flu of 1968. Epidemics of influenza
    type A usually appear in the U.S. at intervals of 2 to 3 years. Epidemics of in-
    fluenza type B usually appear at intervals of not less than 4 to 6 years. A
    major exception occurred in 1968 when the pandemic of influenza type A
    (Hong Kong strain) followed one year after a major type A epidemic. Re-
    sources to obtain information to answer this question include the local
    health department and the American Public Health Association, 1015
    Eighteenth Street NW, Washington, DC 20036.*

B   3. Explain what is meant by "an ounce of prevention is worth a pound
       of cure."
    *Basic everyday prevention can ward off many illnesses, even some serious
    ones.*

B   4. Under a microscope, examine slides of different microorganisms, such as
       bacteria, that may cause disease.
    Situations will vary.

CHAPTER 24   Immunizations

Apply your knowledge

B   1. What is the difference between passive and active immunity?
Active immunity is the ability to form antibodies against pathogens before they can cause disease. Active immunity lasts a long time. A person with passive immunity does not make antibodies but acquires them in some other way. Passive immunity lasts only a short time.

B   2. Why should people be immunized even against diseases that are not common?
The pathogens that cause these diseases are still in the environment. By becoming immunized, people can protect themselves, their family, and their community from many serious diseases.

A   3. What is a vaccine?
Weakened pathogens or substances made by pathogens that cause the body to make antibodies. Vaccines can be given by mouth or by injection.

A   4. Name seven diseases that may be prevented by immunizations.
diptheria, measles, polio, whooping cough, mumps, tetanus, rubella.

B   5. Explain why epidemics of disease, such as measles, polio, and diptheria, still happen today.
Many people do not become immunized against these diseases because they do not know that the pathogens that cause them are still in the environment.

Extend your knowledge

B   1. Invite a local health official to your school to discuss the increase or decrease of preventable diseases in your state.
Situations will vary.

C   2. Plan an immunization schedule for a child from birth to age 16.
Answers will vary.

B   3. Ask your parents to list the childhood diseases that they had as children. Are you protected from getting these diseases?
Answers will vary.

CHAPTER 25   Nutritional Needs

Apply your knowledge

A   1. What is the major difference between food and nutrients?

Foods are anything that enter the mouth. But nutrients are vital to the body. They provide energy, build new cells, and maintain body processes.

A   2. Should you let your appetite choose the foods you eat?

No. If you let your appetite tell you what to eat every day, your body's needs for nutrients will not be met.

A   3. Why is it important to have variety in your diet?

Eating one kind of food may not give your body the proper nutrients.

A   4. What can proteins do for your body that fats and carbohydrates cannot?

Protein is needed to build and to replace all the cells in the body.

A   5. Which food group will give you the best selection of amino acids that your body needs?

The meat and the milk group.

A   6. Which nutrient is a fast source of energy?

Carbohydrates.

A   7. List three reasons why fats are important in your diet.

Fats are needed for padding, protection, storage, and energy. They also add flavor to foods, and help absorb vitamins from the intestine.

A   8. What is the function of iron in your body?

Iron is a mineral in hemoglobin whose function is to attract oxygen.

A   9. How can iron-deficiency anemia be corrected?

By eating good sources of iron, such as organ meats, beans, shell fish.

A   10. If you had niacin deficiency, what symptoms would you have?

Lack of niacin in the diet can cause dry, red patches on the skin.

Extend your knowledge

A   1. Why must foods from all four basic food groups be eaten every day in order to maintain good health?

Eating food from all four basic food groups every day develops good eating habits so that when all four basic food groups cannot be eaten for several days, the health of the body will not decline in that time.

2. Using the chart on page 291, find out the percentage of vitamin C intake if only a deluxe cheeseburger and a glass of milk are eaten during a meal.

7 mg

C   3. Suppose that you had a cheeseburger and a glass of milk for lunch. Using the chart on page 291, figure out what other nutrients you would need to fulfill the recommended dietary allowance for that day.

Protein: 3 to 7 g for females; 3 to 13 g for males. Vitamin A: 338 IU for females; 538 IU for males. Vitamin C: enough. Calories: 1446-1646 for females; 2046-2246 for males. Calcium: 902 mg for both males and females. Iron: 13.7 mg for both males and females.

C   4. Assume that farmers eat more fibrous types of food than people living in cities. How would you test the theory that "farmers have less cancer of the colon than city people"?

Contact local public health officials to see how many people died from cancer of the colon in one year who also lived on the farm.

CHAPTER 26 Snacks and Special Diets

Apply your knowledge

A
1. Why are jams, candy, and carbonated beverages not included in the four basic food groups?
Because they are considered empty calories. They are high in carbohydrates but low in other nutrients.

B
2. Examine the chart on page 304 and find out which snack is the best source of these nutrients: vitamin C, calcium, vitamin A, and riboflavin.
Vitamin C can be found in orange juice; calcium can be found in malted milk; vitamin A can be found in raw carrots; and riboflavin can be found in malted milk.

A
3. Why is breakfast an important meal?
Breakfast literally means "breaking of the fast." By morning, the body has digested the dinner from the night before and has stored extra carbohydrates in the liver. Most of the stored energy, however, is used during sleep. If breakfast is not eaten, there may not be enough energy for the morning hours.

A
4. What is the best way to gain weight if you are underweight?
No one single method or food can help you to gain weight. Gaining weight takes time, and a variety of food is required. Breakfast, snacks, and exercises play an important role in gaining weight.

B
5. Discuss several ways to avoid becoming overweight.
When snacking, eat fruits or vegetables, not high caloric foods. Eat only when at the dinner table at mealtime and avoid seconds. Don't gulp down food, and rest between small bites.

B
6. Using the chart on page 308, find out about how many calories you will lose if you: jog for 20 minutes; jump rope for 15 minutes.
200, 165.

A
7. Why are diet pills dangerous?
Diet pills are dangerous because they speed up the food through the digestive tract so fast that it cannot be absorbed. The pills add to the output of urine and can cause a great loss of water and needed salts. The metabolic rate is also speeded up.

B
8. What would happen if an athlete ate a large steak just before game time?
Eating steak just before game time is not a good idea since it takes several hours before complete digestion can occur. No energy would be available from the meat. Also, protein is not a very good source of energy. In fact, more energy is required to digest the protein.

A
9. Should athletes eat energy foods just before a game? Should they drink any fluids during a game? Why or why not?
Eating energy foods just before a competition will not help. Eating large amounts of glucose, cubes of sugar, hard candy, and dextrose pills will cause the intestinal tract to draw extra fluids from the body tissue. During a game, an athlete should replace the fluids that are lost. Performance is poor when the body is dehydrated. See discussion on heat cramps and heat stroke.

A
10. What is the difference between pure vegetarians and lacto-ovo-vegetarians?
The lacto-ovo-vegetarian does not eat meat but does eat eggs and drink milk. The pure vegetarian will not eat meat or eggs, or drink milk.

Extend your knowledge

E   1. Peanut-a-la-celery is a nutritious snack. It is made of peanut butter spread on celery sticks. Invent another nutritious snack. Prepare it and eat it. Calculate the nutrients and describe the taste.
Answers will vary.

A   2. Discuss some current diet fads, including the pros and cons of each diet.
Liquid protein is considered unsafe. Low carbohydrate diet causes fatigue, increase of cholesterol in the blood, dehydration, dizziness, and kidney problems.

B   3. You know that a low carbohydrate diet is dangerous. What would a high carbohydrate diet do to your body?
Carbohydrates in excess are stored as adipose tissue in the body. The danger of this diet would be obesity.

C   4. If you were to take in 600 extra calories per week for 1 year, how many pounds would you gain during that time?
Approximately 8.8 pounds.

C   5. Find out what five or six members of the class ate for breakfast. Suggest lunches, dinners, and snacks that, along with these breakfasts, would make an adequate diet for the whole day.
Answers will vary.

D   6. Gather information about the diets of people in some other countries. Compare the foods of the "have" and "have not" countries to determine their protein, carbohydrate, fat, mineral, and vitamin intakes.
Answer will vary.

C   7. If you were to open a weight-reducing clinic, what steps would you take to help an obese person lose weight?
Obtain an examination by a physician for the patient, develop a personal diet, encourage the patient, provide follow-up meetings, and continue contact with the patient.

CHAPTER 27 Nutrition, Labels, and the Consumer

Apply your knowledge

A   1. Refer to the picture on page 318 and answer the following questions: (a) Is this food a good source of calcium? Why or why not? (b) How many people will this container serve? (c) How large a serving will each person receive? (d) Can you classify this food into the four basic food groups? Which groups are represented? (e) Is there a great difference in vitamin C content when prepared with milk instead of water?

(a) yes, if the product is prepared with milk; (b) two people; (c) 10 ounces; (d) fruit and vegetable, milk (if prepared with milk), bread and cereal; (e) no.

C   2. Check your cupboard for any food items that contain sugar. List them. Did you find any without sugar? Would you add sugar to those foods? Why or why not?

Answer will vary.

A   3. Why was monosodium glutamate dropped from baby food?

Because it is not a necessary ingredient in foods, and the U.S. National Research Council thinks that babies should eat bland foods for as long as they can before being taught to crave flavor-enhanced foods.

A   4. What are antioxidants? Are they necessary in your foods? Why or why not?

Antioxidants prevent foods from changing color. If antioxidants were not added, the color, taste, and smell of some foods would change.

A   5. How can nitrites be both helpful and harmful?

Nitrites are additives that prevent the deadly botulinum toxin from growing in hot dogs, bacon, and sausage. Unfortunately, nitrites are also capable of forming nitrosamines, a cancer-producing agent.

A   6. Does your body need sugar? Explain.

The starch you eat is broken down into simple sugar. The simple sugar is used for energy. Processed sugar has no nutritive value other than calories.

A   7. Why are some people interested in health foods?

Some people think products labeled "health food" can actually improve their health.

A   8. Why might canning food at home be dangerous?

Because unless you are careful and thorough during the canning process, bacteria, molds, and fungi may spoil the food.

Extend your knowledge

A   1. Check several soup cans to see what percentage of your U.S. RDAs are given for the various nutrients.

Answers will vary.

B   2. Refer to the picture on page 319 to find out how much protein you would get from the sample breakfast.

Bread-5g, peanut butter-9g, milk-9g, cereal-6g. Total: 29g of protein.

B   3. Explain how our eating habits would be affected if there were no preservatives.

Without preservatives, very few of the food items on grocery shelves would last over a week. We would eat less convenience foods, and would be forced to include more fresh foods in our diet. Also, we would have to be very careful of spoilage.

C 4. Next time you are at the supermarket, check to see if most of the items on the shelves have open dating. Make a list of those that are not dated and find out why they are not. Assign teams of students to specific markets.

Findings will vary.

C 5. Find out who prepares the menus at your school. Check to see how foods are purchased and prepared for large numbers of students.

Assign a student who may be interested in journalism or one who may be on the school newspaper staff. Have the student publish the article.

D 6. How might your family's shopping habits change if all mass media influences were absent?

Answers will vary.

B 7. Eat two samples of the same kind of food, one with additives and one without. Compare the tastes.

Have students bring a variety of foods with and without preservatives.

C 8. Go to the supermarket and watch people shop. List poor shopping habits that you can discuss in class later on. Explain why such habits are poor ones.

Answers will vary. Some of the observations may be: buying dented can products, not reading labels, not checking dates on milk, not comparing prices, not comparing generic packages with labeled packages.

CHAPTER 28   Digestion and Elimination

Apply your knowledge

A   1. Put the following words into the order that they appear in your system: uvula, rectum, pharynx, duodenum, stomach, esophagus, tongue, large intestine.

Tongue, uvula, pharynx, esophagus, stomach, duodenum, large intestine, and rectum.

A   2. List three functions of the tongue.

Tasting, chewing, and swallowing.

A   3. What is the function of the enzyme found in saliva?

The enzyme amylase breaks down starch to maltose.

A   4. What happens to food in the mouth? In the stomach? In the small intestine?

Food in the mouth is masticated and made into a bolus. Starch is partially broken down. The stomach mixes the food with the gastric juices. In the presence of hydrochloric acid, protein is partially broken down, and the food eventually takes on a soupy appearance. The soupy substance called chyme enters the first part of the small intestine, called the duodenum. Enzymes are secreted to break down starches, fats, and proteins. The remainder of the small intestine helps to absorb the nutrients.

B   5. How do emotions affect digestion? Describe a school lunch scene that would be good for digestion.

Emotions such as fear, anger, resentment, or excitement can cause changes in peristalsis and in secretion of glands in the digestive system. The answer will vary for the second part of this question.

A   6. What are common causes of constipation and diarrhea?

Constipation results when too much water is removed from the large intestine. Also, diets lacking fibers can cause less movement of the large intestine. Diarrhea is caused by nervous upset or by microorganisms in the food. Excessive fibers can also cause diarrhea.

A   7. List two functions of hydrochloric acid in the digestive system.

Hydrochloric acid kills bacteria in the stomach, softens fibers, and allows pepsin to change to pepsinogen, which partially breaks down protein.

A   8. Why is it unwise to make a habit of taking laxatives?

Laxatives make the muscles of the large intestine weak. Eventually, the person may become dependent on stronger doses to produce a bowel movement. The muscles may become overworked and suffer some damage.

A   9. How can diarrhea be dangerous?

Excessive diarrhea can cause dehydration.

A   10. How does gastric juice help in the digestive process?

Gastric juice contains digestive enzymes and acids.

A   11. How can constipation be prevented?

Constipation can be prevented by exercising, drinking plenty of fluids, and including fibers in the diet.

A   12. How does flatus (gas) form in the digestive system?
Gas forms when air is swallowed. Also, bacteria in the large intestine can form gases such as hydrogen and methane.

B   13. Explain the work of the kidneys.
Wastes containing nitrogen and minerals salts are excreted through the kidneys.

A   14. How are intestinal infections and infestations spread?
By improper washing of hands before eating, cooking, or serving food.

A   15. Describe the symptoms of appendicitis.
The first symptom is pain, followed by nausea, vomiting, constipation, fever, and soreness in the lower abdomen.

A   16. What should a person with appendicitis symptoms do until a doctor is reached? What kinds of treatment are dangerous?
A person should remain quiet and eat nothing. Dangerous treatments include using a laxative, hot water bag, or electric heating pad.

A   17. Name the two types of secretions from the pancreas.
Insulin and pancreatic juice.

A   18. What are the functions of the liver and of bile?
The liver plays a crucial role in the process of digestion. The liver secretes bile which aids in the digestion of fats.

A   19. What is the function of the ureters?
The ureters carry the filtered waste from the kidney to the bladder.

A   20. How could a person function without a stomach?
No food is absorbed directly into the bloodstream from the stomach. Consequently, a person can function without a stomach by eating frequent, small meals.

Extend your knowledge

B   1. Explain which organs of the digestive system are absolutely needed for life.
Some students might mention that the entire digestive system is not needed since total intravenous feeding can provide up to 4000 calories, and sufficient nutrients, per day. The duodenum is essential because it must chemically digest all the foods to their basic components. The ileum is important for absorption of the nutrients. The stomach, portions of the large intestine, gall bladder, and the portion of the pancreas that secretes pancreatic juices are not essential. However, the person would have to change his diet if these organs were removed.

C   2. Allow a dog or cat to lick your hand. How does it feel? What causes the roughness? Explain the purpose of the texture of the tongue.
The raspy texture is due to the papillae on the tongue, which are prominent in animals that lap their food.

B   3. Make a list of things in your own environment that may affect your digestion.
Clean and decorative table setting, congenial friends, food prepared appetizingly.

C   4. Visit the nearest medical center and find out how a dialysis (kidney) machine works.

CAT scanner is also recommended.

C   5. Ask a radiologist to show you X rays of a stomach and intestines. Explain how these X rays are made.

Assign students to other equipment and instruments as well.

E   6. Study how thinking about foods affects you. Does thinking about certain foods cause you to salivate? Which foods make your salivary glands secrete the most saliva?

Answers will vary.

E   7. Smell some foods. Does smelling or thinking about foods cause more saliva to flow?

Answers will vary.

E   8. Hold your nose and look at some food. Does looking at foods affect your salivary glands? Does being hungry make a difference?

Answers will vary.

E   9. It is fun to do some experiments with taste and smell. Blindfold yourself. While holding your nose, bite into a slice of an apple, an onion, and a potato, one at a time. Were you able to tell the difference between these foods?

Be sure to precut the items into similar sizes. Try other foods for texture and odor.

D   10. Find the taste buds for sweet, sour, bitter, and salty on your tongue. *Use dill pickle juice, quinine solution, sucrose, and salt to determine the taste areas on the tongue.*

CHAPTER 29 Personal Safety

Apply your knowledge

A   1. State the main causes of death among young people.
Automobile, motorcycle, water, and home accidents.

B   2. Name four driving conditions you would consider very dangerous.
Answers will vary.

B   3. Watch pedestrians and automobile drivers for 30 minutes or longer. Make lists of the things they do that are related to safety.
Answers will vary.

B   4. Study the driving rules of your state and city. Ask the police to explain any rules that you do not understand or do not agree with.
Answers will vary. Discuss rules students do not understand.

E   5. Why do you think young drivers are involved in more automobile accidents than older drivers? What do you think could be done to lower the high accident rate among young drivers?
Answers will vary.

A   6. List three rules that are very important in preventing water accidents.
Answers will vary.

B   7. List some safety measures for stopping accidents in the home that could apply to your own home.
Answers will vary.

A   8. What are some safeguards that should be taken when working around machinery?
Turn off a machine before adjusting, repairing, or cleaning it; use proper safety guards and eye protectors; and do not operate powerful machinery without training.

C   9. Collect newspaper articles about accidents. Discuss how some of these accidents could have been prevented.
Answers will vary.

B   10. What general rule is most important in preventing accidents?
Answers will vary. One point to be emphasized is the importance of knowing and following safety rules.

Extend your knowledge

E   1. Imagine that a state official placed you in charge of lowering the number of injuries and deaths that occur in the high-school-age population in your state. Describe your plan for doing this. What percent of deaths and injuries do you think would be prevented if your plan were followed?
Students' plans of action should include gathering as many facts as possible related to the injuries and deaths, determining the most frequent and significant contributing factors (carelessness, not following safety rules, driving while under the influence of alcohol), and recommending ways to prevent behavior that is likely to result in an injury or death. A detailed analysis of accidents that occur throughout the country is available from the National Safety Council. The address for this organization is located at the end of Chapter 34 in the student text.

D 2. Write a report or lead a class discussion on the topic of high school driver education courses. Include such facts as these: why some states require high schools to offer driver education courses; why other states are in the process of ending these courses; the cost of such courses, and who you think should pay for them. Be sure to state your point of view and the reasons for it.

Some states require high schools to offer driver education courses to insure that all teenagers have an equal opportunity to learn how to drive safely, and to reduce the number of serious injuries and fatalities in the high-school-age population. Some states, however, are in the process of ending these courses because of the high cost of such courses and the lack of definitive evidence that they contribute significantly to reducing fatalities.

D 3. Find out the number, location, and type of accidents that happened in your school last year. Explain how some of these accidents could have been prevented. Have any safety measures been added as a result of these accidents? If so, have these safety measures helped to lower the number of accidents? Why or why not?

Answers will vary.

D 4. Find out whether or not your community has enough bicycle paths and special lanes for bicyclists on heavily traveled roads. What person or group in your community is responsible for carrying out bicycle safety measures? What needs to be done to improve bicycle safety on the road?

In general, many concerned civic groups are attempting to have their local government provide special lanes for bicyclists or improve roads so that surface conditions where bicyclists must ride are free of hazardous items such as raised sewer grates, potholes, and rocks, all of which can easily "throw" even a skilled driver.

B 5. Give a report on federal regulations that set safety standards for automobiles.

Resources to obtain information to help answer these questions include the National Safety Council, the U.S. Consumer Product Safety Commission, the National Clearinghouse for Alcohol Information, and the U.S. Department of Transportation National Highway Traffic Safety Administration. (Addresses for these organizations are located at the end of Chapter 34 in the student text.)

CHAPTER 30 Basic First Aids

Apply your knowledge

C   1. Is there any emergency situation in which you would hesitate to give first aid? Why, or why not?

Answers will vary.

A   2. Describe how to control bleeding.

Place a clean cloth over the wound and press down firmly. If no cloth is available, press your hand directly on the wound. If bleeding starts again when you release the pressure, keep pressing until medical help arrives. In addition to applying pressure to the wound, raise the injured part of the body, if no bones are broken. Also to help stop bleeding, you can apply pressure to the artery leading to the wound and, as a last resort, a tourniquet can be used.

A   3. Why is a tourniquet dangerous to use?

It cuts off the supply of blood to the tissues of the limb. If it is left on too long (more than 20 minutes) those tissues may suffer permanent damage.

C   4. What is the location and telephone number of the closest poison center? Where in your home would be a good place to keep this information?

Answers will vary.

A   5. If a poisoning victim is conscious, how can you help? How can you help an unconscious victim?

Conscious victim: dilute the poison with drinking water or milk; try to identify poison. Unconscious victim: give CPR or artificial respiration if needed; do not give liquids or induce vomiting. Call physician in both cases.

A   6. Explain how you can help prevent shock.

Keep the patient warm. Put a blanket over and under the victim.

B   7. What is the difference between a closed fracture and an open fracture?

In a closed fracture, the skin is not broken. In an open fracture, the broken bone comes through the skin, or a wound reaches from the surface of the skin to the break in the bone.

B   8. How can you tell whether or not a person is suffering from heatstroke or from heat exhaustion? What is the treatment for each?

In heatstroke, the skin is hot and dry, the pulse is fast and strong, and unconsciousness and convulsions may follow. In heat exhaustion, the skin is cold and clammy, breathing is shallow, the pulse is weak, and the victim may faint. To treat heatstroke, move the victim to a cool place and apply wet cloths or ice to the victim's skin. To treat heat exhaustion, move the victim to a cool place and give the person salt water to sip.

F   9. Find out where the first-aid kits are in your school. Look in the gymnasium, science laboratories, and shops. Do you think your school has enough first-aid supplies?

Answers will vary.

C   10. Collect newspaper clippings about accidents. Discuss the first aid that should be given in each case.

Answers will vary.

Extend your knowledge

E   1. If your were teaching a first-aid course, what advice would you give to the students to help keep them from panicking in an emergency situation?

The purpose of this question is to provide an opportunity for the students to give attention to the importance of keeping calm in an emergency situation. Examples of ways to help keep calm are to take deep breaths as you move about and carry out emergency procedures, or to keep repeating to yourself over and over again, "Keep Calm. Keep Calm." Students may be quite creative in deciding what would keep them from panicking in an emergency situation.

F   2. Are there disaster centers in your community? What supplies are provided in them? Where else in the community are there supplies for first aid? Do you think your community is adequately prepared for the emergencies that are likely to occur?

Answers will vary.

B   3. Ask your local Red Cross about classes in first aid and how to qualify for a first-aid certificate.

Answers will vary.

F   4. Investigate the policies of an ambulance service in your community. What are the policies regarding the following:
(a) required training for the ambulance drivers?
(b) use of warning devices such as lights or siren? (Give situations in which the devices are used, and tell when they are not used.)
(c) transporting minors when a legal guardian is not available to give consent?
Do you agree with all of the policies? Why, or why not?

The required training for ambulance drivers varies greatly from community to community. Some require several weeks of training, others several months, and still others much longer. In general, the longer the training period, the more prepared the ambulance personnel are to handle serious medical problems. Warning devices are usually used when transporting a patient who has a life-threatening condition, such as cardiac arrest or severe bleeding. It is usually recommended that warning lights or sirens not be used and that speed limits be followed when transporting a victim who has a nonlife-threatening condition, such as a fracture or minor burns. Transporting minors when a legal guardian is not available to give consent is usually avoided unless the victim has a life-threatening condition.

B   5. Fire departments often have information on preventing fires. Does the fire department in your community offer this service? Find out the rules for fire safety.

Rules for fire safety include having a smoke detector in the home, having a family emergency escape plan, avoiding smoking in bed, not discarding smoldering cigarette butts in wastebaskets, keeping matches out of the hands of young children, and, if outdoors, making sure matches and tobacco products (cigars, cigarettes) are completely cold before tossing them away.

CHAPTER 31 Cardiopulmonary Resuscitation (CPR)

Apply your knowledge

A   1. Name six unexpected events that could result in a sudden death.
Answers will vary. Events that could result in a sudden death include heart attack, choking, drowning, poisoning, suffocation, electrocution, and smoke inhalation.

B   2. In your own words, explain how CPR saves a person's life.
Answers will vary. Students' answers should indicate that CPR provides artificial respiration and artificial circulation.

A   3. List four early warning signs of a heart attack.
Answers will vary. Early warning signs include chest pain, sweating, nausea, shortness of breath, and a feeling of weakness.

B   4. Explain the difference between basic life support and advanced life support.
Providing basic life support means being able to recognize a blocked airway, the absence of breathing, and the absence of a heartbeat or pulse, and providing CPR. Advance life support includes providing basic life support and the use of medical equipment and other techniques to keep the patient alive.

F   5. Do you think your community has an effective emergency medical services (EMS) system? Why, or why not?
Answers will vary.

A   6. State four preventive measures that should be used with children to avoid choking.
Answers will vary. Following are examples of preventive measures. Keep small articles that could be swallowed out of the reach of infants and small children. Encourage children to stay seated and calm while eating. Remove all bones and shells from foods before giving them to a small child. Don't give nuts, candy containing nuts, or unchopped pieces of meat to small children. Be certain that toys do not contain small parts that could be chewed or pulled off.

A   7. Describe the distress signal for choking.
Clutching the neck between the thumb and index finger.

A   8. What is a "café coronary"?
A fatal choking accident that happens in a restaurant and is mistaken for a heart attack.

A   9. Suppose you were in a restaurant and someone eating at a nearby table suddenly collapsed. Describe the steps that you (or someone else) should take to help that person.
1. Determine if the victim is conscious by shaking the person's shoulder and shouting, "Are you all right?"
2. If there is no response, call for help and open the victim's airway.
3. Put your ear near the victim's mouth; look for chest and abdomen movement; listen for sounds of breathing; feel for breath on your cheek.
4. If none of these signs is present, the victim is not breathing; the next step is to follow the rescue steps outlined on p. 368 of the pupil's edition.

D   10. What civic groups or individuals in your community could organize CPR classes so that more people could become trained to perform this procedure?

Answers will vary.

Extend your knowledge

B   1. What person or group in your community would be responsible for carrying out an effective emergency medical services system? If a community did not have the 911 emergency telephone number, how might the residents obtain this valuable service?

Getting help in an emergency is usually accomplished by calling a telephone number to have a rescue unit dispatched to the scene. Ideally the telephone number is 911. Less than ideal is another specific emergency number. Least effective is "0" for operator. The 911 number is widely publicized and easy for people to remember. It is important for people not to have to learn a new emergency telephone number each time they move to a different community. How soon emergency care can be obtained can make the difference between life and death.

E   2. What steps would you take to motivate people to take the lifesaving CPR course?

Steps teenagers could take to help motivate people to take a CPR course include publicizing the value of taking a CPR course (posters, announcements, skits at PTA and other civic meetings to show the consequences of not knowing the lifesaving technique), door-to-door distribution of leaflets that promote the course, and conducting a survey to see how many people in the community know how to give CPR, and publicizing the outcome of the survey and the possible consequences based on its results.

C   3. In discussing the physiology of death, the terms clinical death and biological death are frequently used. Explain the relationship of each of these terms to the performance of CPR.

Clinical death refers to the absence of breathing and circulation. Biological death is the absence of breathing and circulation, and the absence of brain activity. CPR is recommended in the abrupt, unexpected cessation of breathing and circulation (clinical death). CPR is not indicated for situations such as a person being in the terminal stages of an incurable disease.

F   4. Good Samaritan laws protect lay people from liability suits resulting from an injury that a victim might sustain during a rescue effort. Does your community have these laws? Do you think these laws are adequate?

Answers will vary.

B   5. Often there are psychological problems related to performing CPR. Discuss one or more of the following concerns that a rescuer may have:
(a) fear of taking responsibility for someone else's life;
(b) mouth-to-mouth contact with a possibly dead or dying person;
(c) risk of "catching something";
(d) inability to perform when others are watching or when anxious and under pressure.

Answers will vary.

CHAPTER 32 Medical Care and Medicine Show

Apply your knowledge

A 1. List ten warning signals that mean you should call a doctor.
a. Pain is very bad and does not go away.
b. Blood is coughed up or appears in the stool or urine.
c. Diarrhea or vomiting does not stop.
d. Fever is high—38.5°C (102°F) or over.
e. Breathing is uneven, fast, or short.
f. Heartbeat is very fast or not regular.
g. Person is unconscious.
h. There are injuries such as broken bones, cuts, or wounds.
i. Person is confused or in a dazed state.
j. Person has been bitten by a strange animal.

A 2. Discuss what happens in the three stages of a medical checkup.
Medical history—The doctor or the assistant asks questions, such as what is the primary problem, how long have you had the problem, have you had the problem before, and do you have any other problems.
Physical examination—The doctor examines you using equipment such as tongue depressors, otoscope, ophthalmoscope, and sphygmomanometer.
Laboratory analysis—The third stage generally includes blood count and urinalysis, and possibly chest X rays and other laboratory tests if the doctor feels there is a need.

A 3. What are six ways of detecting a medical "quack"?
a. if people claim that they alone have a special formula or machine that cures a certain disease; b. if they guarantee that you will be cured very quickly; c. if they advertise and sell the product door-to-door, or use case histories and testimonials to promote their cure; d. if they tell you that they are being persecuted by the medical profession because of fear of competition; e. if they demand that their product be analyzed and recognized; f. if they say that surgery, X rays, or drugs are harmful and should not be used.

A 4. Give at least three reasons why people sometimes become victims of exaggerated or false medical claims.
1. "Quacks" use people's deepest fears of illness, pain, and death to sell their products.
2. When family doctors and specialists cannot supply treatment, cures, or ease pain because of worsening symptoms of disease, the patient becomes frightened and may become desperate to find a cure.
3. Desperate people may be easily swayed by overstated claims.

A 5. How do internists differ from family doctors?
Internists are physicians with advanced training who are skilled in diagnosing the illnesses people may have. Many family doctors are general practitioners. They provide general health care to all members of the family.

B 6. Describe the placebo effect.
A placebo has no medicine in it but it looks the same as the medicine being tested in an experiment. It is given to patients to see how they react to the suggestion that they are taking medicine. Researchers have found that one-third of the patients taking the placebo will show improvement.

A   7. Why are there many specialists in the medical field? What kinds of new specialists would you expect to see in the future?

There are many specialists today because medical science has grown so quickly that one person cannot learn everything there is to know about medicine. With more and more research in the areas of genetics and the central nervous system, perhaps new specialists will be called cerebrologist gene-recombinant specialists.

B   8. How are gynecologists and obstetricians related?

They are both concerned with the female reproductive system. The gynecologist diagnoses and treats physical problems of women, especially problems of the reproductive system. The obstetrician delivers babies and sees to the mother's health.

A   9. What is an otoscope?

An instrument used to examine the external canal and the eardrum.

A   10. What does the abbreviation *D.D.S.* mean?

Doctor of dental surgery.

Extend your knowledge

E   1. If you were a cardiologist, what would you want to know from your patient? Make a list of questions you would ask the patient.

a. What is your problem? b. How long have you had the problem? c. Have you ever had the problem before? d. Where does it hurt the most? e. Are you currently taking any medicine?

F   2. If you were a victim of medical quackery, what steps would you take to put the person or company out of business?

Contact the Better Business Bureau and warn others about the product and the people involved.

F   3. Make a list of 20 radio and television advertisements for medical or related products or services. Decide which are on the borderline of quackery. For each advertisement that you think is not true, explain your reasoning.

Answers will vary.

C   4. Write down, in detail, your medical history. Check with your parents about childhood diseases and immunizations.

Answers will vary.

B   5. Many medical terms come from Greek and Latin roots. For example, cardiology comes from *cardio*, meaning "heart" and *logy*, meaning "the study of." Using a dictionary that gives word histories, look up the following terms and list their literal meanings: dermatology, gynecology, neurology, ophthalmology, otology, pathology, urology.

dermatology: derma—*skin (the study of skin)*
gynecology: gyne—*woman (the study of woman)*
neurology: neuro—*nerve (the study of nerves)*
ophthalmology: opt—*eye (the study of the eye)*
otology: ot—*ear (the study of the ear)*
pathology: path—*suffering, disease (the study of disease)*
urology: ur—*urine (the study of urine)*

CHAPTER 33 Medical Consumer and Self-Care

Apply your knowledge

A   1. What is the difference between self-care and self-medication?

Self-care is a common-sense way to practice preventive medicine. Self-medication means that you buy and use medicine without consulting a physician.

A   2. Explain the total self-care concept.

Choosing the right medical facility, buying medicine, knowing the cost of health care, and investing in a medical insurance plan are self-care concepts.

A   3. Explain the difference between primary and secondary care.

In primary medical care, the treatment is given by a doctor at a clinic, emergency room, or doctor's office. In secondary care, the treatment is given by specialists at a private or community hospital.

A   4. List some of the ways you can practice self-care.

Self-care can be practiced by choosing the best doctor, going to the best medical facility, and having the most complete health insurance. Also, self-care includes using your common sense to avoid those things that can be harmful to your health.

A   5. Make a list of all the diseases to which you are immune.

Answers will vary.

A   6. List four types of disease-preventive measures.

Immunization; skin tests and chest X rays; breast self-examination; and learning how to take blood pressure and to avoid hypertension.

C   7. Name some OTC drugs that your family keeps in the medicine cabinet.

Answers will vary.

A   8. If you have to make an emergency visit to the hospital, why should you bring with you all the medications you are taking?

The doctor will know the type of illness you may have by examining the medicine. Also, your pills may act against any medication given to you at the hospital.

A   9. List all of the information that must appear on all medicines sold over the counter.

a. name of the product; b. name and address of the manufacturer, packager, and distributer; c. net contents of the package; d. active ingredients and the quantity of ingredients; e. name of any habit-forming drug contained in the medicine; f. cautions and warnings needed for the protection of the user; g. adequate directions for safe and effective use.

A   10. List all of the information that physicians must include on a prescription.

a. name of the medication; b. amount; c. dosage; d. date; e. expiration date; f. specific instructions, such as refrigerate, shake well; g. patient's name; h. how often medicine should be taken.

Extend your knowledge

C   1. Assume that your city has five hospitals and each one purchases an expensive Computerized Axial Tomograph. What effect will this have on health care costs? Do you think it is necessary for all hospitals to have the best equipment?

The cost of health care will greatly increase because of the expensive cost of equipment. There will be duplication of effort. Answers will vary.

2. Ask your pharmacist about "rebound effect" the next time you purchase any form of antihistamine.

"Rebound effect" means that if the antihistamine is used over a period of two days or more, the membrane of the nose will again produce more secretions.

E   3. Make a list of the medicines you think you should have in your medicine cabinet. Give a reason for each one.

Answers will vary.

D   4. Ask your parents if you can study the health insurance plan for your family. Check to see what medical expenses are covered by the insurance.

Answers will vary.

F   5. Examine several of the advertisements for medicine on television and in magazines. Check to see if there are any distortions or false claims.

Answers will vary.

CHAPTER 34 Health in the United States

Apply your knowledge

C
1. Why is it necessary for city health departments to pick up stray dogs?
Stray dogs can band together and attack people. They become hunters and tip over trash cans looking for food. Rodents and flies take advantage of the situation and eat the garbage. In this way, stray dogs add to the spread of diseases.

A
2. List five jobs your local health department does.
a. keeping stray animals off the street; b. inspecting kitchens in restaurants and hotels; c. removing wastes; d. examing water supplies; e. inspecting hotels, motels, and all public buildings; f. coordinating neighborhood health centers and clinics; g. collecting and analyzing vital statistics.

A
3. Why are vital data important to a city?
Information about marriages, births, deaths, and population are important in planning for the future of the city. Also, by having such statistics, public health officials can very quickly find out the possibility of potential epidemics in their state.

A
4. What are the jobs of the World Health Organization?
a. to act as a clearinghouse; b. to stop illegal traffic of narcotic drugs; c. to stop the spread of serious communicable diseases; d. to give emergency aid to countries dealing with epidemic diseases; e. to give financial and technical help to countries to control communicable diseases; f. to get all people to fight water and air pollution.

A
5. What are some of the services provided by the Public Health Service?
The Public Health Service conducts research programs in all areas of health and disease; investigates and controls serious outbreaks of communicable diseases anywhere in the country; prevents communicable diseases from being brought into the United States; certifies the safety, quality, and usefulness of vaccines and serums that prevent or treat diseases; gives information about the prevention and treatment of disease.

A
6. What are some of the services provided by the Food and Drug Administration?
The FDA certifies safety, quality, and proper dosage of drugs sold throughout the country. It checks on the safety of food and the honesty of statements on the labels of drugs, packaged foods, and cosmetics.

A
7. What are some ways to kill microorganisms?
Purify drinking water; dispose of sewage; pasteurize milk; inspect food supplies; and kill off insects that spread disease.

A
8. What is the role of the state health department?
The state health department takes on the task of problems too large for local or city departments. Special health services, such as running large facilities for mentally and physically handicapped people, are mostly funded by the state government.

A
9. How do voluntary health agencies work for public health?
Voluntary health agencies do important work in medical research and health education.

A   10. List five federal agencies that take care of public health.
Public Health Service, Food and Drug Administration, Occupational Safety and Health Administration, Welfare Administration, National Institute of Health. All of these organizations belong to the Department of Health, Education, and Welfare.

Extend your knowledge

C   1. Find out how common chickenpox and measles are at your school each year.
Answers will vary.

C   2. Make a survey of your class to find the number of students who have immunity to smallpox, tetanus, polio, diphtheria, and other diseases.
Answers will vary.

C   3. Visit your local Heart Association or the Red Cross and find out how you can be certified for cardiopulmonary resuscitation.
Request a certified CPR instructor to visit the class and provide instruction.

C   4. Ask your city or county health department about what kinds of health care are given to people who cannot pay for it. How does your community care for the handicapped?
Answers will vary.

D   5. Study the health program in your school. How are epidemics controlled? What responsibilities do the students have for the success of the health program?
Epidemics are generally controlled by the school health official, who can require that all students entering school be innoculated for a specific disease.

C   6. Using the address list in this chapter, write to five voluntary health agencies for free public health information. Share, with your class, the information you receive.
Answers will vary.

CHAPTER 35   Health Careers for You

Apply your knowledge

B   1. What are some of the reasons for the growing need for highly trained health personnel?
Changes in science and industry, for example, the use of computers, have affected the health field.

A   2. List five advantages of pursuing health careers.
Jobs almost everywhere; jobs for both men and women; on-the-job training; financial aid; job advancement.

B   3. Name five different health jobs that are entry-level careers. What are three jobs that would be considered intermediate-level careers? Name two jobs that would be considered higher-level careers.
Entry-level: laboratory assistant, dietetic assistant, central service technician, operating room technician, ward clerk. Intermediate-level: cytotechnologist, dental hygienist, pediatric assistant. High-level: medical technologist, physician.

B   4. How have science and industry affected health careers?
They have increased the need for specialists.

B   5. What is the advantage of getting a college degree for a health career?
The advantage is in the opportunity for advancement.

A   6. Name two kinds of jobs available today in the health field that were not available twenty years ago.
Diagnostic medical sonographic technician and noise technician.

B   7. How can an art major in college find a career in a health field?
The art major can work towards a career as a medical illustrator.

B   8. How are the two health careers in cytotechnology and certified laboratory assistance alike? How are they different?
Both use a microscope. Training is different.

A   9. In what ways do medical assistants help physicians as well as patients?
They prepare patients for examination, make appointments, help in emergency situations, type medical reports, and fill out insurance forms.

A   10. Besides immunizing pets, what are other jobs of the veterinarian?
Inspecting meat, poultry, dairies, plants and animals from abroad.

Extend your knowledge

C   1. Turn to the classified ads or "want ads," in your local newspaper, to see which health career has the most openings.
Answers will vary.

B   2. If methods to prevent and cure cancer are perfected, what new health careers would develop?
The areas of chemotherapy, immunogenetics, and virology might expand.

B   3. How would the cost of dental health care be affected if there were no careers such as dental hygienics or dental assistance?
The cost would probably increase.

E   4. What abilities or interests do you have that would be helpful to you in a health career. Name careers to which the abilities might apply.
Answers will vary.

B   5. Prepare a poster or exhibit based on what you have learned that will interest other students in a health career.
Results will vary.

110

CHAPTER TESTS

This section contains one test for each of the 35 text chapters:

TEST FOR CHAPTER ONE: HEALTH AND WELLNESS

I. On the line at the left of each of the following, write the letter of the choice that *best* completes the statement or answers the question.

_____ 1. Wellness is (A) physical health (B) mental health (C) emotional and social health (D) all of these.

_____ 2. Which of the following statements is *false*? (A) People have different attitudes about preventive health measures. (B) One of the latest health advances is a diagnosis to tell you exactly how long you will live. (C) People have different amounts of information about health care. (D) Some people ignore preventive health care recommendations.

_____ 3. Which of these is *not* a common excuse for not taking preventive health measures? (A) Thinking that concern about health is someone else's problem. (B) Believing good health is a matter of chance. (C) Not having a positive relationship with one's parents. (D) Finding preventive measures too difficult.

_____ 4. Which of the following questions is *not* a measure of mental and social well-being? (A) Have you fulfilled your need to create? (B) Do you have satisfying social relationships? (C) Have you had your blood pressure taken in the last year? (D) How do you relax when you are under stress?

_____ 5. Which of the following statements is *false*? (A) Mental illness can be successfully treated. (B) How you handle disappointments reflects your mental and social well-being. (C) It is almost impossible to separate mental and social health from physical health. (D) Events which cause emotional stress do not change your sense of physical well-being.

II. The following statements are true or false. Indicate True by placing (+) and False by placing (O) on the line at the left of the statement.

_____ 1. Physical fitness can be measured.

_____ 2. During the twentieth century, infectious diseases have been eliminated.

_____ 3. Health professionals have always relied on the behavioral sciences for information about well-being.

_____ 4. If you are not ill, then you are healthy.

_____ 5. Mental health and physical health are closely connected.

III. Match the term on the right with its description by placing the letter of the term in the blank to the left of the description.

_____ 1. offers tape recordings on health issues

_____ 2. person who can do the most to make you healthy

_____ 3. high blood pressure, strokes

_____ 4. state of physical, mental, and social well-being

_____ 5. help to avoid or postpone illness and injury

A. health
B. infectious diseases
C. preventive health habits
D. Tel-Med
E. noninfectious diseases
F. your doctor
G. you

IV. Answer the following questions at the bottom of your test paper.

1. What were the leading causes of death in 1900?
2. Why are diseases caused by bacteria and viruses called infectious diseases?
3. List four factors that cause people to take preventive action.
4. List the four food groups that together provide a balanced diet.
5. The health inventory in this chapter can help you take stock of your level of well-being in three areas. What are the three areas?

TEST FOR CHAPTER TWO: BASIS OF MOVEMENT

I. On the line at the left of each of the following, write the letter of the choice that *best* completes the statement or answers the question.

_____ 1. Which of the following statements is *false*?   (A) Bones protect the heart, lungs, and brain.   (B) All bones except those in the chest are connected by ligaments.   (C) Most cells of the blood are formed inside the bone.   (D) Bones differ greatly in size and shape.

_____ 2. Which of the following statements is *true*?   (A) Cartilage is not found in adult bodies.   (B) Most cartilage is replaced by bone cells and calcium salts as a child grows.   (C) Rickets results from decalcification.   (D) When bone tissues harden, the exchange of minerals between the bone and blood ceases to occur.

_____ 3. The human skull   (A) is fully grown at birth.   (B) is made up of the 206 flat bones of the cranium.   (C) holds the human brain.   (D) has fontanels throughout life.

_____ 4. Arthritis   (A) causes joints to swell and become painful.   (B) occurs only in young people.   (C) requires the care of a physician.   (D) (A) and (C).

_____ 5. Which of the following statements is *false*?   (A) Muscles are totally relaxed when a person is asleep.   (B) Each muscle is surrounded by blood vessels, nerves, and connective tissue.   (C) When a muscle contracts, it becomes shorter and thicker.   (D) Good muscle tone aids digestion.

II. The following statements are true or false. Indicate True by placing (+) and False by placing (O) on the line at the left of the statement.

_____ 1. Resting makes your bones stronger.

_____ 2. Muscles are made up of differently colored fibers with different functions.

_____ 3. If you are healthy you do not need to warm up before engaging in physical activity.

_____ 4. Energy is given off as work and heat during muscle contraction.

_____ 5. Broken bones do not bleed.

III. Match the term on the right with its description by placing the letter of the term in the blank to the left of the description.

_____ 1. condition that causes joints to swell

_____ 2. attaches muscle to bone

_____ 3. soft spaces between bones of the cranium in a baby

_____ 4. bone infection

_____ 5. many muscle fibers grouped together by connective tissue

A. fasciculus
B. hernia
C. tendon
D. osteomyelitis
E. voluntary muscles
F. arthritis
G. fontanels

IV. Answer the following questions at the bottom of your test paper.

1. List three types of muscles and where they may be found in the body.
2. Name the four kinds of joints found in the body.
3. List two functions calcium performs in the body.
4. What is the advantage to having arches in the foot?
5. What is the difference between tendons and ligaments?

TEST FOR CHAPTER THREE: KEEPING FIT THROUGH SPORTS AND RECREATION

I. On the line at the left of the following, write the letter of the choice that *best* completes the statement or answers the question.

_____ 1. Which condition can be prevented by drinking plenty of water before and during exercise?
(A) blisters   (B) pulled muscle   (C) heat cramps   (D) dislocations.

_____ 2. A charley horse   (A) damages the bones in the leg.   (B) comes from a hard blow to the front of the thigh.   (C) should be treated with a heating pad right away.   (D) is a rare occurence in contact sports.

_____ 3. Which of the following statements about muscles is *false*?   (A) Certain kinds of muscle pulls are common to certain sports.   (B) An injured muscle should be treated with cold packs.   (C) Muscle lameness is caused by a buildup of ascorbic acid.   (D) Muscle cramps usually happen in muscles that must carry weight.

_____ 4. Which of the following statements is *true*?   (A) Keeping physically fit can be accomplished by simply exercising your muscles.   (B) When your muscles remain bent for a long time they loosen up.   (C) Exercise relieves boredom.   (D) Coordination improves with practice.

_____ 5. Conditioning is a program of   (A) exercise   (B) rest   (C) eating   (D) all of these.

II. The following statements are true or false. Indicate True by placing (+) and False by placing (O) on the line at the left of the statement.

_____ 1. Eating before exercising increases energy.

_____ 2. As people get older, they no longer need to exercise.

_____ 3. Exercise strengthens the heart muscle.

_____ 4. A once-a-week exercise session improves your endurance.

_____ 5. Not warming up is a major cause of damaged muscles.

III. Match the term on the right with its description by placing the letter of the term in the blank to the left of the description.

_____ 1. ability to balance

_____ 2. ability of the body to withstand stress for long periods of time

_____ 3. ability to react quickly with sure movements

_____ 4. entire body is working smoothly

_____ 5. being able to stretch the body easily

A. flexibility
B. coordination
C. equilibrium
D. agility
E. speed
F. endurance
G. strength

IV. Answer the following questions at the bottom of your test paper.

    1. List five sports that increase your flexibility.
    2. What are two important benefits that come from exercise?
    3. How does exercise affect blood pressure and pulse rate?
    4. How can you prevent shinsplints?
    5. What happens when the body loses large amounts of water and salt through perspiration?

TEST FOR CHAPTER FOUR: EMOTIONAL NEEDS AND MATURE PERSONALITY

I. On the line at the left of each of the following, write the letter of the choice that *best* completes the statement or answers the question.

_____ 1. A philosophy of life may be affected by   (A) your experiences.   (B) family customs.   (C) personal beliefs.   (D) all of these.

_____ 2. Which of the following statements is *false*?   (A) Your level of self-confidence remains consistent throughout life.   (B) Self-confident people accept their shortcomings.   (C) Self-confidence is earned through experience.   (D) Your energy should be used to work on your strengths.

_____ 3. Mature behavior   (A) is a quality possessed by all adults.   (B) means accepting responsibility for your behavior.   (C) involves practicing self-control.   (D) (B) and (C).

_____ 4. Which of the following statements is *false*? The need to create can be fulfilled by (A) building a meaningful relationship.   (B) solving a problem.   (C) imitating the behavior of others.   (D) sewing.

_____ 5. Which of the following statements is *true*?   (A) Personal worth is based on the opinion of friends and acquaintances.   (B) Gaining self-respect is an important goal during adolescence.   (C) Conflicts with your parents have no value.   (D) Learning about who you are is not a difficult process.

II. The following statements are true or false. Indicate True by placing (+) and False by placing (O) on the line at the left of the statement.

_____ 1. Disturbed emotions unconsciously given to the body may lead to physical illness.

_____ 2. During adolescence, family relationships cease to influence the development of personality.

_____ 3. Hormones affect your feelings and attitudes.

_____ 4. Good friends do not argue and always share the same opinions.

_____ 5. A healthy personality includes the ability to be comfortable with oneself as well as others.

III. Match the term on the right with its description by placing the letter of the term in the blank to the left of the description.

_____ 1. full development

_____ 2. the thinking, acting, and feeling self as it reacts to the world

_____ 3. love, sense of personal worth, need to succeed

_____ 4. based upon personal standards

_____ 5. prejudging others based on body type, race, religion

A. emotional needs
B. personality
C. mood
D. maturity
E. responsible decisions
F. self-concept
G. stereotyping

IV. Answer the following questions at the bottom of your test paper.

1. List three traits or behaviors that show maturity.
2. What are two things you can do to discover areas in which you can feel a sense of achievement?
3. List three things that may contribute to the formation of your philosophy of life.
4. Give three guidelines for making responsible decisions.
5. What are four mistakes to avoid in rating others' personalities?

NAME: _____ DATE: _____

TEST FOR CHAPTER FIVE: EMOTIONS AND MENTAL HEALTH

I. On the line at the left of each of the following, write the letter of the choice that *best* completes the statement or answers the question.

_____ 1. A mentally healthy person   (A) depends on defense mechanisms to solve all his or her problems.   (B) avoids problems and conflicts.   (C) works cooperatively in give-and-take relationships.   (D) engages in behavior without thinking about it.

_____ 2. Which mental health specialist has a medical degree?   (A) a psychiatrist   (B) a psychologist   (C) a psychiatric nurse   (D) all of these

_____ 3. Which of the following is *not* a constructive way to get rid of hostile feelings?   (A) physical activity   (B) talking with someone who is objective   (C) making nasty remarks

_____ 4. Which method is used in treating emotional problems?   (A) individual therapy   (B) drug therapy   (C) group therapy   (D) all of these

_____ 5. Causes of mental illness may be   (A) physical.   (B) emotional.   (C) both.

II. The following statements are true or false. Indicate True by placing (+) and False by placing (O) on the line at the left of the statement.

_____ 1. One sign of mental illness is an ability to get along with others.

_____ 2. The role of a therapist is to force patients to change their behavior.

_____ 3. Fears of the unknown are always harmful.

_____ 4. Neurosis is a mental disorder in which a person is out of touch with reality.

_____ 5. Psychosomatic disorders are imaginary and do not damage the body.

III. Match the defense mechanism on the right with its description by placing the letter of the term in the blank to the left of the description.

_____ 1. thinking that you are much like another person

_____ 2. running away from problems

_____ 3. substituting a dream world for the real one

_____ 4. provides substitutes for real or imaginary shortcomings

_____ 5. always refusing the suggestions of others

A. compensation
B. negativism
C. daydreaming
D. escape
E. identification
F. rationalization

IV. Answer or complete the following at the bottom of your test paper.

    1. Depression and guilt feelings are major kinds of _____ .

    2. List the three major categories of mental illness.

    3. One constructive way to deal with anger is to attack the _____ , not the person.

    4. The treatment of mental and emotional disturbance is called _____ .

    5. A psychiatric social worker has a knowledge of ___ ___ available to patients and their families.

NAME: _____ DATE: _____

TEST FOR CHAPTER SIX: LIVING WITH STRESS

I. On the line at the left of each of the following, write the letter of the choice that *best* completes the statement or answers the question.

_____ 1. You can experience a stress reaction   (A) in a crisis.   (B) as a reaction to change.
(C) in everyday situations.   (D) all of these.

_____ 2. A stress reaction is characterized by   (A) lowered blood pressure.   (B) increased heart rate.   (C) slower breathing.   (D) a speedup in the digestive process.

_____ 3. Relaxation   (A) prevents physical symptoms from building up.   (B) is unnecessary when you have a busy schedule.   (C) speeds up the body's processes.   (D) increases body tension.

_____ 4. When coping with a stressful situation, it is helpful to   (A) prepare for it.   (B) allow yourself to acknowledge that you are experiencing stress.   (C) create positive images in your mind where you utilize energy from your stress reaction.   (D) all of these.

_____ 5. A healthy way to cope with the buildup of stress which comes after a disagreement with a friend is to   (A) sit and fume.   (B) yell at your friend.   (C) remove yourself from the situation until you can decide how to proceed.   (D) end the friendship.

II. The following statements are true or false. Indicate True by placing (+) and False by placing (O) on the line at the left of the statement.

_____ 1. The degree of stress needed in life is the same for everybody.

_____ 2. Happy events may cause stress.

_____ 3. A person experiencing a high level of stress will have fewer colds and minor illnesses.

_____ 4. People who most need to relax are those who find it most difficult to do.

_____ 5. When you relax the muscles in your body, you speed up the body's processes.

III. Match the major body system on the right with its possible problem by placing the letter of the term in the blank to the left of the description.

_____ 1. ulcers

_____ 2. prone to accidents

_____ 3. migraine headaches

_____ 4. colitis

_____ 5. high blood pressure

A. cardiovascular system
B. digestive system
C. skeletal-muscular system

IV. Answer the following questions at the bottom of your test paper.

    1. List three life changes that might involve stress.
    2. What are two common symptoms of stress?
    3. What are two ways to prepare your body to weather the stresses caused by life changes?
    4. List two of the ways in which your body prepares to cope with physical danger.
    5. Practicing relaxation has two important benefits. What are they?

TEST FOR CHAPTER SEVEN: HUMAN REPRODUCTION

I. On the line at the left of each of the following, write the letter of the choice that *best* completes the statement or answers the question.

_____ 1. During pregnancy, medicine or other drugs a woman takes   (A) may harm the unborn child.   (B) are O.K. except for hard drugs.   (C) are only a problem early in the pregnancy.   (D) are O.K. except for over-the-counter drugs.

_____ 2. Sperm are   (A) circular.   (B) found in seminiferous tubules.   (C) not mobile.   (D) mixed with urine and passed out of the body by the urethra.

_____ 3. Which of the following statements is *false*?   (A) The ovaries are formed during puberty.   (B) The ovum is moved by gravity and gentle suction.   (C) A Fallopian tube carries the ovum to the womb.   (D) The cervix is the neck of the uterus.

_____ 4. Which of the following statements is *true*?   (A) An ovum can be fertilized for up to two weeks after ovulation.   (B) Conception happens only when an ovum and sperm join.   (C) Cell division takes place in the fertilized ovum.   (D) (B) and (C).

_____ 5. Which of the following statements is *false*? During cell differentiation   (A) cells of many shapes are formed.   (B) spindle-shaped cells become muscle cells.   (C) flat cells form bone.   (D) the various cells join with others like it to form parts of the body.

II. The following statements are true or false. Indicate True by placing (+) and False by placing (O) on the line at the left of the statement.

_____ 1. All fraternal twins are of the same sex.

_____ 2. Children born to mothers who have been poorly nourished are more likely to have health problems.

_____ 3. Nicotine and alcohol pass through the placenta and may harm the tissues of an unborn baby.

_____ 4. Menstruation continues to occur during pregnancy.

_____ 5. All of the ova are present at birth.

III. Match the term on the right with its description by placing the letter of the term in the blank to the left of the description.

_____ 1. spongy lining of the uterus

_____ 2. the male sex hormone that controls the development of male sexual characteristics

_____ 3. the female sex hormone made by the ovaries

_____ 4. happens when an ovum and a sperm join

_____ 5. stage of life during which a person's reproductive system starts to work

A. estrogen
B. puberty
C. menopause
D. testosterone
E. fetus
F. endometrium
G. conception

IV. Answer or complete the following at the bottom of your test paper.

1. Name a disease which is not serious for a grown woman but may do great harm to a fetus in the first three months of pregnancy.
2. List two possible causes of congenital defects.
3. What joins the placenta to the fetus and passes oxygen and nutrients from the mother's blood to the blood of the fetus?
4. What is menstruation, and how often does it take place?
5. What are three male secondary sex characteristics that develop during puberty?

NAME: _____ DATE: _____

TEST FOR CHAPTER EIGHT: FAMILY LIFE

I. On the line at the left of each of the following, write the letter of the choice that *best* completes the statement or answers the question.

_____ 1. Members of a family affect one another in which area? (A) social (B) economic (C) emotional (D) all of these

_____ 2. Marriage (A) is a relationship which remains the same over the years. (B) takes no preparation. (C) is usually free from problems. (D) is a relationship which requires the willingness to work through life challenges.

_____ 3. Peer pressure is (A) direct influence from others. (B) pressure you put on yourself. (C) exerted by adults in your life. (D) a combination of (A) and (B).

_____ 4. Family planning (A) increases population growth. (B) has no impact on world resources. (C) does not deal with the process of adoption. (D) enables parents to provide their children with more emotional advantages.

_____ 5. An exclusive one-to-one dating arrangement (A) limits your chances to get to know many different people. (B) increases competition for dates. (C) makes it easy to re-enter the dating process if the steady relationship ends. (D) always widens one's circle of friends.

II. The following statements are true or false. Indicate True by placing (+) and False by placing (O) on the line at the left of the statement.

_____ 1. Making the decision of whether or not to get married involves self-examination.

_____ 2. Your ability to switch from one role to another remains the same throughout your life.

_____ 3. Emotions do not affect an individual's ability to communicate.

_____ 4. There are many reasons for deciding to date.

_____ 5. There are no disadvantages to "going steady."

III. Match the term on the right with its description by placing the letter of the term in the blank to the left of the description.

_____ 1. medications and devices that prevent conception

_____ 2. disagreements among people

_____ 3. person who is attracted only to members of the other sex

_____ 4. student, friend, team member

_____ 5. exchange of facts, ideas, and feelings

A. heterosexual
B. typical roles for a teenager
C. communication
D. homosexual
E. conflicts
F. peer pressure
G. contraceptives

IV. Answer the following questions at the bottom of your test paper.

1. What is the basic unit of society?
2. List two areas where family conflicts may arise.
3. What are three topics a couple should discuss before they decide to marry?
4. Give an example of a parent's responsibility to a child.
5. Give an example of a child's responsibility to a parent.

TEST FOR CHAPTER NINE: FROM GENERATION TO GENERATION

I. On the line at the left of each of the following, write the letter of the choice that *best* completes the statement or answers the question.

_____ 1. A symptom of Down's syndrome is   (A) mental retardation.   (B) a protruding tongue. (C) poor muscle tone.   (D) all of these.

_____ 2. Genes   (A) work in pairs.   (B) come from just one parent.   (C) carry environmental traits.   (D) are found in cells with no nuclei.

_____ 3. DNA   (A) is a protein.   (B) fights infection.   (C) causes production of new cells. (D) has an oval shape.

_____ 4. The nucleus of each cell contains   (A) two sex chromosomes.   (B) amniotic fluid. (C) 40 chromosomes.   (D) melanin.

_____ 5. Which of the following is a hereditary disorder?   (A) shinsplints   (B) Huntington's disease   (C) rubella   (D) systemic breathing

II. The following statements are true or false. Indicate True by placing (+) and False by placing (O) on the line at the left of the statement.

_____ 1. Only one defective gene is needed to cause a disease with dominant inheritance.

_____ 2. Mutations can sometimes be helpful.

_____ 3. All birth defects can be discovered through prenatal testing.

_____ 4. A person with blue eyes must have two genes for blue eyes.

_____ 5. Sickle-cell trait is a disease.

III. Match the term on the right with its description by placing the letter of the term in the blank to the left of the description.

_____ 1. passing of characteristics from parents to children

_____ 2. the study of heredity

_____ 3. substances which make up proteins

_____ 4. a prenatal test performed in order to find possible defects caused by chromosome error

_____ 5. a change in a gene

A. amino acids
B. recessive inheritance
C. mutation
D. amniocentesis
E. genetics
F. DNA
G. heredity

IV. Answer the following questions at the bottom of your test paper.

   1. List three characteristics of sickle-cell anemia.
   2. Which parent determines the sex of the child?
   3. Give two examples of inherited characteristics.
   4. Name the disease which is caused by the presence of an extra chromosome.
   5. Give an example of a disease with recessive inheritance.

TEST FOR CHAPTER TEN: ENVIRONMENTAL HAZARDS

I. On the line at the left of each of the following, write the letter of the choice that *best* completes the statement or answers the question.

_____ 1. You can prevent damage from noise pollution by (A) sitting far away from the sound system at a dance. (B) wearing ear plugs. (C) lowering the volume on the TV. (D) all of these.

_____ 2. Which of the following statements is *false*? (A) Water pollution was not a problem many years ago. (B) Use of public transportation by more people would not affect the amount of air pollution. (C) Long exposure to noise pollution may cause gradual hearing loss. (D) Noise may add to emotional problems.

_____ 3. Radioactive substances (A) can destroy bone marrow. (B) take a short time to disintegrate. (C) are not found naturally in the earth's surface. (D) are easily disposed of.

_____ 4. Carbon monoxide (A) is a nonpoisonous gas. (B) has a distinct odor. (C) comes from automobile exhaust. (D) has beneficial effects.

_____ 5. Which of the following statements is *false*? Sewage is (A) made up of food-processing wastes. (B) free from bacteria. (C) sometimes dumped into rivers. (D) a community problem.

II. The following statements are true or false. Indicate True by placing (+) and False by placing (O) on the line at the left of the statement.

_____ 1. Automobile accidents occur more frequently in places where the air is polluted.

_____ 2. It is not harmful to bathe in polluted water as long as you do not drink it.

_____ 3. Noise pollution can affect the entire body.

_____ 4. Scientists have calculated how much radiation a human body can stand.

_____ 5. Radioactive substances in tiny amounts are harmless.

III. Match the term on the right with its description by placing the letter of the term in the blank to the left of the description.

_____ 1. harmful particles of dust and ash

_____ 2. a measure of the loudness of sound

_____ 3. outbreak of infectious disease affecting a large number of people at the same time

_____ 4. capable of causing cancer

_____ 5. active form of oxygen produced by the action of sunlight on atmospheric impurities

A. epidemic
B. decibels
C. hepatitis
D. carcinogenic
E. noise pollution
F. ozone
G. particulates

IV. Answer or complete the following at the bottom of your test paper.

1. List three of the five basic air pollutants.
2. What three factors affect the amount of air pollution in a given area?
3. When cool, polluted air becomes trapped beneath the warmer, lighter air above, this is known as _____ _____ .
4. Epidemics of hepatitis, typhoid fever, and diarrhea have been traced to _____ _____ _____ .
5. What are the two largest pollutants?

TEST FOR CHAPTER ELEVEN: CANCER PREVENTION

I. On the line at the left of each of the following, write the letter of the choice that *best* completes the statement or answers the question.

_____ 1. Serious cancer problems can often be avoided by   (A) early detection.   (B) prevention.   (C) early treatment.   (D) all of these.

_____ 2. Which of the following statements is *false*?   (A) All cancers are the same.   (B) A benign tumor usually does not cause medical problems.   (C) There is no set rate of growth for cancer.   (C) Some families have a "familial tendency" toward certain types of cancer.

_____ 3. Which of the following is *not* an environmental factor that causes cancer?   (A) radiation   (B) decibels   (C) vinyl chloride   (D) asbestos

_____ 4. Which of the following is *not* a procedure used to detect cancer?   (A) PAP test   (B) physical checkup   (C) pelvic examination   (D) electroencephalography

_____ 5. You can take steps to prevent cancer by   (A) not smoking.   (B) eating more vegetables.   (C) avoiding exposure to radiation.   (D) all of these.

II. The following statements are true or false. Indicate True by placing (+) and False by placing (O) on the line at the left of the statement.

_____ 1. Responsibility for cancer prevention belongs to each person.

_____ 2. Different carcinogens cause different kinds of cancer.

_____ 3. Cancer cells are regular in size and shape.

_____ 4. Cancer cells are usually more sensitive to radiation than are normal cells.

_____ 5. Both biological and environmental factors combine to cause cancer.

III. Match the term on the right with its description by placing the letter of the term in the blank to the left of the description.

_____ 1. treatment of cancer with powerful chemicals

_____ 2. operation to remove tissue from the body so the doctor can check for abnormal cells

_____ 3. spreading of disease from place where it started to another part of the body

_____ 4. cancer of the blood cells

_____ 5. group of cells growing together in a mass

A. metastasis
B. leukemia
C. benign tumor
D. tumor
E. biopsy
F. chemotherapy

IV. Answer the following questions at the bottom of your test paper.

1. List three methods of treating cancer.
2. What is the most common type of cancer among women?
3. What are the Seven Warning Signals of cancer?
4. What is the difference between a benign tumor and a malignant tumor?
5. What is the main danger when people turn to cancer quacks for help?

TEST FOR CHAPTER TWELVE: COORDINATION AND CONTROL

I. On the line at the left of each of the following, write the letter of the choice that *best* completes the statement or answers the question.

_____ 1. Reflexes   (A) must be learned.   (B) are designed to protect you.   (C) are directed by the brain.   (D) require you to think.

_____ 2. Which of the following does *not* play a part in protecting the brain and spinal cord?
 (A) skull bones   (B) meninges   (C) anesthetics   (D) cerebrospinal fluid

_____ 3. Motor nerves   (A) carry impulses away from the brain to the muscles.   (B) carry impulses away from the spinal cord to the glands.   (C) cause glands to secrete juices.
 (D) all of these.

_____ 4. Which of the following is *not* a part of the brain?   (A) pons   (B) cerebellum
 (C) reflex   (D) medulla oblongata

_____ 5. Which of the following is *not* a disorder of the nervous system?   (A) multiple sclerosis
 (B) meningitis   (C) gonorrhea   (D) epilepsy

II. The following statements are true or false. Indicate True by placing (+) and False by placing (O) on the line at the left of the statement.

_____ 1. Anything that influences your nervous system affects the rest of your body.

_____ 2. Everyone needs the same amount of sleep.

_____ 3. Both rest and exercise can relieve feelings of tiredness.

_____ 4. It is possible to change habits of feeling.

_____ 5. The high development of the nervous system makes human beings different from other living species.

III. Match the term on the right with its description by placing the letter of the term in the blank to the left of the description.

_____ 1. inflammation of membranes that surround brain and spinal cord

_____ 2. pathway from senses to spinal cord and back to motor action

_____ 3. largest part of the brain

_____ 4. made up of brain and spinal cord

_____ 5. lowest portion of the brain

A. reflex arc
B. meninges
C. central nervous system
D. cerebellum
E. medulla oblongata
F. cerebrum
G. meningitis

IV. Answer the following questions at the bottom of your test paper.

    1. List the three smaller systems which make up the nervous sytem.

    2. What are the five sense organs of the body?

    3. Which part of the brain stores information, regulates memory, and controls the senses?

    4. Give two actions regulated by the medulla oblongata.

    5. List two things you can do to take care of your nervous system.

TEST FOR CHAPTER THIRTEEN: EYE AND EAR CARE

I. On the line at the left of each of the following, write the letter of the choice that *best* completes the statement or answers the question.

_____ 1. Contact lenses   (A) do not change the size of the object being looked at.   (B) do not fog up when the outside temperature changes.   (C) make it easier to see out of the sides of the eye.   (D) all of these.

_____ 2. Which of the following does not serve to protect the eyes?   (A) eyelids   (B) heavy padding of fat   (C) cochlea   (D) bones of the skull

_____ 3. Eye strain may be prevented by   (A) making sure you have plenty of light when doing close work.   (B) resting your eyes often when you study for a long time.   (C) not reading while riding in a car.   (D) all of these.

_____ 4. Which of the following statements is *false*?   (A) Half of all blindness that occurs is preventable.   (B) Damage to the retina is usually caused by changes inside the body. (C) visual problems may only be caused by injury to the eye muscles.   (D) Glaucoma can lead to total blindness.

_____ 5. Which of the following statements is *true*?   (A) The sclera gives the eyeball its shape. (B) In bright light, the pupil becomes larger.   (C) In dim light, the iris contracts. (D) Four parts of muscles make each eyeball move.

II. The following statements are true or false. Indicate True by placing (+) and False by placing (O) on the line at the left of the statement.

_____ 1. Tears contain a fluid that kills bacteria and protects the eye against infection.

_____ 2. There is nothing that can be done to correct deafness.

_____ 3. The major cause of defective hearing in young people is noise pollution.

_____ 4. One function of the inner ear is to control balance.

_____ 5. Most defective vision is caused by an eyeball that is not regular in shape.

III. Match the term on the right with its description by placing the letter of the term in the blank to the left of the description.

_____ 1. controls the amount of light that enters the eye

_____ 2. farsightedness

_____ 3. a condition where a clear image is not formed on the retina due to the fact that the curved surfaces of the cornea and lens are not regularly shaped

_____ 4. nearsightedness

_____ 5. fluid that feeds the lens and cornea

A. astigmatism
B. iris
C. aqueous humor
D. strabi
E. myopia
F. hyperopia
G. retina

IV. Answer or complete the following at the bottom of your test paper.

1. What are the three major types of hearing disorders?
2. Give two possible causes of conduction loss.
3. The ___ ___ connects the middle ear with the back of the nose and throat.
4. A doctor who specializes in the care and diseases of the eye is called an ___ .
5. List two chemicals that may injure your eyes.

TEST FOR CHAPTER FOURTEEN: TRANSPORT SYSTEM

I. On the line at the left of each of the following, write the letter of the choice that *best* completes the statement or answers the question.

_____ 1. Which of the following is *not* found in your blood?   (A) platelets   (B) diastole   (C) plasma   (D) red blood cells

_____ 2. Which of the following statements about blood is *false*?   (A) Blood is fluid tissue.   (B) Blood carries waste products to the kidneys.   (C) Blood carries digested food from the small intestine.   (D) None of these.

_____ 3. Which of the following is *true*? Hemoglobin   (A) is responsible for the blue color in the blood.   (B) is found only in the heart.   (C) picks up oxygen and carries it to all parts of the body.   (D) picks up carbon dioxide and carries it to all parts of the body.

_____ 4. Which of the following statements about leukemia is *false*?   (A) The cause of leukemia is not known.   (B) Leukemia can be slowed down.   (C) Scientists think leukemia is a cancer of the white blood cells.   (D) Leukemia drastically reduces the number of white blood cells.

_____ 5. Which of the following statements is *false*? Lymph nodes   (A) form all the red cells in the blood.   (B) are found along the lymph vessels.   (C) kill disease organisms that enter the lymph vessels.   (D) sometimes become swollen.

II. The following statements are true or false. Indicate True by placing (+) and False by placing (O) on the line at the left of the statement.

_____ 1. Blood that has a lot of oxygen is bluish in color.

_____ 2. Hemoglobin is found in red blood cells and carries oxygen to all parts of the body.

_____ 3. White blood cells fight infection.

_____ 4. In an emergency, a type AB person can receive blood from donors who have types A, B, or O.

_____ 5. Arteries carry blood back to the heart.

III. Match the term on the right with its description by placing the letter of the term in the blank to the left of the description.

_____ 1. heart disease that has been present since birth

_____ 2. hardening of the walls of the arteries

_____ 3. condition in which the arteries become narrower

_____ 4. carries blood out of the heart to the lungs

_____ 5. contraction of the heart

A. atherosclerosis
B. hypertension
C. congenital heart disease
D. arteriosclerosis
E. rheumatic heart disease
F. systole
G. pulmonary artery

IV. Answer or complete the following at the bottom of your test paper.

1. List four things you can do to take care of your circulatory system.
2. What is the main cause of anemia?
3. List the four types of human blood.
4. The upper part of each side of the heart is called the _____ , and the lower part of each side is called the _____ .
5. What are three factors related to high blood pressure?

TEST FOR CHAPTER FIFTEEN: RESPIRATION

I. On the line at the left of each of the following, write the letter of the choice that *best* completes the statement or answers the question.

_____ 1. Which of the following statements is *false*?   (A) Inspiration is the process of taking air into the lungs.   (B) Expiration is the process of forcing air out of the lungs. (C) Respiration and breathing are the same.   (D) The breathing habits of some people reduce the amount of oxygen they take in.

_____ 2. Your breathing pattern changes as a reaction to   (A) the way you feel.   (B) the amount of oxygen in your blood.   (C) the amount of dust in the air.   (D) all of these.

_____ 3. Which of the following pertain(s) to emphysema?   (A) alveoli become more elastic (B) coughing   (C) less oxygen available for the blood   (D) (B) and (C)

_____ 4. Which of the following statements is *false*?   (A) Influenza may be spread through talking. (B) Bronchitis is a shrinking of the bronchi.   (C) The air passages of the body are always exposed to bacteria.   (D) The upper respiratory tract can easily get many illnesses.

_____ 5. Asthma   (A) is not affected by one's emotional health.   (B) causes the mucous membranes of the bronchi to become irritated and swell.   (C) can be cured using over-the-counter medicine.   (D) is contagious.

II. The following statements are true or false. Indicate True by placing (+) and False by placing (O) on the line at the left of the statement.

_____ 1. When you are breathing normally, you use only one-eighth of your lung capacity.

_____ 2. The higher you go above sea level, the more oxygen there is in the air.

_____ 3. It is possible to live a long, useful life with only one lung.

_____ 4. Air pressure has no effect on breathing.

_____ 5. Oxidation is a process that takes place only when you are asleep.

III. Match the term on the right with its description by placing the letter of the term in the blank to the left of the description.

_____ 1. muscular floor of the chest cavity

_____ 2. air sacs which make up most of the lungs

_____ 3. causes mucous membranes of the bronchi to become swollen

_____ 4. hairline structures which filter harmful particles so that they will not get to the lungs

_____ 5. infection of lung tissue

A. alveoli
B. asthma
C. trachea
D. diaphragm
E. pneumonia
F. decompression
G. cilia

IV. Answer or complete the following at the bottom of your test paper.

1. The moist, smooth membranes that cover the outside of the lungs and inside of the chest cavity are called the _____ .
2. What are two things you can do to control hiccups?
3. When the air pressure is low, there is less _____ in the air.
4. Name two respiratory disorders that have been linked to cigarette smoking.
5. When you are in a stuffy room, you may not be taking in enough oxygen by breathing normally. When this happens, you may begin to _____ .

NAME: _____ DATE: _____

TEST FOR CHAPTER SIXTEEN: SKIN AND HAIR: YOUR PROTECTIVE COVERING

I. On the line at the left of each of the following, write the letter of the choice that *best* completes the statement or answers the question.

_____ 1. Which of the following is *false*? The dermis (A) is the outer portion of the skin. (B) contains blood vessels and nerves. (C) is a network of connective tissue and fatty tissue. (D) contains sweat glands, oil glands, and hair roots.

_____ 2. Hives (A) look like insect bites. (B) may be caused by an allergic reaction. (C) usually involve severe itching. (D) all of these.

_____ 3. Which of the following is *false*? Sunscreens (A) protect the skin from the sun's rays. (B) contain para-aminobenzoic acid. (C) remain effective after swimming. (D) should be applied 15 minutes before sunning.

_____ 4. Which of the following statements is *true*? Perspiration (A) comes from the oil glands in the skin. (B) is made up of water and sebum. (C) must be released through the pores to keep the body from overheating. (D) insulates the body when the environment is cold.

_____ 5. Which of the following statements is *false*? Skin (A) covers about 1.6 square meters of body surface in adults. (B) is a simple covering for the body. (C) prevents the air from drying up your body systems. (D) has two main layers.

II. The following statements are true or false. Indicate True by placing (+) and False by placing (O) on the line at the left of the statement.

_____ 1. The skin is your main defense against the entry of disease organisms.

_____ 2. Hair and nails contain no nerve endings.

_____ 3. Your skin constantly grows new cells and sheds the old.

_____ 4. It is possible to get poison ivy without ever touching the plant.

_____ 5. Ringworm and athlete's foot are common skin infections caused by melanin.

III. Match the term on the right with its description by placing the letter of the term in the blank to the left of the description.

_____ 1. an oily secretion of the skin

_____ 2. nonliving epidermis that surrounds the edges of nails

_____ 3. tiny openings that lead to sweat and oil glands

_____ 4. inflammation of the skin

_____ 5. outer portion of the skin

A. pores
B. dermatitis
C. melanin
D. epidermis
E. cuticle
F. sebum
G. dermis

IV. Answer the following questions at the bottom of your test paper.

1. What are the four skin-care rules for preventing acne?
2. What is the largest organ of the human body?
3. List three steps you can take to prevent athlete's foot.
4. List two types of dermatitis and an example of each.
5. How does the skin serve as an organ of expression?

TEST FOR CHAPTER SEVENTEEN: REGULATORS OF YOUR BODY

I. On the line at the left of each of the following, write the letter of the choice that *best* completes the statement or answers the question.

_____ 1. Which of the following statements is *false*?   (A) ACTH makes the adrenal glands produce their hormones.   (B) The pituitary gland produces hormones that control body growth. (C) The pituitary gland is located in the neck.   (D) The pituitary gland is thought to control the temperature of the human body.

_____ 2. The thyroid gland   (A) needs iodine to work properly.   (B) shrivels up if it does not get enough iodine.   (D) produces thyroxin.   (D) (A) and (C).

_____ 3. Adrenalin   (A) speeds up activity in the digestive tract.   (B) makes the body ready for action.   (C) is secreted by the kidneys.   (D) cannot be manufactured outside the body.

_____ 4. Which of the following statements is *false*?   (A) The most important female hormone is estrogen.   (B) The testes secrete a small amount of estrogen.   (C) The ovaries and testes develop during adolescence.   (D) The sex glands of the male are the testes.

_____ 5. Parathyroid glands   (A) are located in the neck.   (B) are located within the thyroid gland.   (C) aid in the metabolism of calcium and phosphorus.   (D) all of these.

II. The following statements are true or false. Indicate True by placing (+) and False by placing (O) on the line at the left of the statement.

_____ 1. People with diabetes can lead normal lives.

_____ 2. The thyroid gland needs calcium in order to work properly.

_____ 3. The thyroid gland is known as the master gland of the body.

_____ 4. Adrenalin makes the heart beat more strongly.

_____ 5. Hormones are chemicals.

III. Match the term on the right with its description by placing the letter of the term in the blank to the left of the description.

_____ 1. organs that produce reproductive cells

_____ 2. chemical change that goes on in cells to support life

_____ 3. low blood sugar

_____ 4. produce insulin

_____ 5. chemicals that act as the body's messengers

A. metabolism
B. adrenalin
C. islands of Langerhans
D. cortisone
E. gonads
F. hormones
G. hypoglycemia

IV. Answer the following questions at the bottom of your test paper.

1. How are endocrine glands different from other glands in the body?
2. What is the function of hormones?
3. List the eight glands that make up the endocrine system.
4. Why is insulin important?
5. What are two symptoms that indicate that the endocrine system is not working well?

TEST FOR CHAPTER EIGHTEEN: HEALTHY TEETH

I. On the line at the left of each of the following, write the letter of the choice that *best* completes the statement or answers the question.

_____ 1. Teeth are important to   (A) good nutrition.   (B) proper digestion.   (C) how you look.   (D) all of these.

_____ 2. Sugar   (A) contains nutrients necessary for healthy teeth.   (B) mixes with bacteria to cause damage to the teeth.   (C) takes two hours before it begins to do damage in the mouth.   (D) consumption does not increase tooth decay.

_____ 3. Which of the following statements is *false*?   (A) Chewing helps to keep gums healthy by improving the circulation of blood.   (B) Gingivitis is the swelling of unhealthy gums. (C) The chemical sodium fluoride has been found to increase the incidence of tooth decay. (D) Cell metabolism takes place in the teeth, gums, and jawbone.

_____ 4. Which of the following statements is *true*?   (A) The pulp cavity of the tooth holds nerves, blood vessels, and lymph vessels.   (B) Cuspids are the teeth used to grind food. (C) Wisdom teeth are also called incisors.   (D) It is not necessary to brush your inner teeth.

_____ 5. Which of the following is *false*?   (A) When a baby is born, all the primary teeth and some permanent teeth are already formed in the jawbones.   (B) Most people have 32 permanent teeth.   (C) If your water supply is not fluoridated, you cannot obtain fluoride protection in any other way.   (D) Your toothbrush should have soft bristles with rounded ends.

II. The following statements are true or false. Indicate True by placing (+) and False by placing (O) on the line at the left of the statement.

_____ 1. Prophylaxis is the only way to remove calculus.

_____ 2. Gingivitis is painful in its early stages.

_____ 3. A sinus infection can cause bad breath.

_____ 4. Periodontal disease is the chief cause of loss of teeth.

_____ 5. It is not necessary to take care of the primary teeth because they will be replaced by permanent teeth.

III. Match the term on the right with its description by placing the letter of the term in the blank to the left of the description.

_____ 1. swelling of the gums

_____ 2. improper bite

_____ 3. colorless, sticky layer of bacteria that forms in the mouth

_____ 4. tooth decay

_____ 5. infection at the root of a tooth

A. calculus
B. plaque
C. dental caries
D. abscess
E. halitosis
F. malocclusion
G. gingivitis

IV. Answer or complete the following at the bottom of your test paper.

1. Name the three parts which make up each tooth.
2. List three steps you can take to insure dental health.
3. What is thought to be the most common health problem in the United States?
4. What are two functions of teeth?
5. What do you call wisdom teeth that come in at the wrong angle and press against the second molars?

TEST FOR CHAPTER NINETEEN: USE OF TOBACCO

I. On the line at the left of each of the following, write the letter of the choice that *best* completes the statement or answers the question.

_____ 1. Smokeless tobacco   (A) is a very macho habit.   (B) is a safe use of tobacco.   (C) has no effect on your teeth.   (D) can lead to cancer.

_____ 2. Emphysema   (A) is not related to smoking.   (B) may begin with difficulty in breathing. (C) is a skin disorder.   (D) does not affect the performance of normal activities.

_____ 3. Cigarette smokers who are trying to quit smoking   (A) are concerned about gaining weight.   (B) can participate in programs designed to help them quit.   (C) are attempting to break a habit.   (D) all of these.

_____ 4. Which of the following statements about tars in tobacco is *false*?   (A) Tars are responsible for the respiratory diseases associated with smoking.   (B) Tars are safely eliminated by cigarette filters.   (C) Tars cause brown stains on the fingers of cigarette smokers. (D) Tobacco tars are not addictive.

_____ 5. Children   (A) are more likely to be sensitive to the effects of "secondhand" smoke. (B) whose parents smoke have more respiratory illnesses than children with nonsmoking parents.   (C) experience fewer respiratory infections than adults.   (D) (A) and (B).

II. The following statements are true or false. Indicate True by placing (+) and False by placing (O) on the line at the left of the statement.

_____ 1. Carbon monoxide reduces the oxygen-carrying capacity of the blood.

_____ 2. Smoking increases body temperature.

_____ 3. Smokers often have a cough caused by irritation of the lining of the throat.

_____ 4. Infants born to smoking mothers often weigh less than those born to nonsmoking mothers.

_____ 5. Sidestream smoke contains nicotine and carbon monoxide in greater concentrations than mainstream smoke.

III. Match the term on the right with its description by placing the letter of the term in the blank to the left of the description.

_____ 1. smoke inhaled and then exhaled by the smoker

_____ 2. contain a large number of chemicals

_____ 3. when a nonsmoker unwillingly inhales smoke from a burning cigarette

_____ 4. powerful, colorless poison found in tobacco smoke

_____ 5. smoke that goes directly into the air from the burning end of a cigarette

A. nicotine
B. involuntary smoking
C. sidestream smoke
D. carcinogens
E. mainstream smoke
F. tobacco tars
G. nonfilter

IV. Answer or complete the following at the bottom of your test paper.

    1. List three factors which influence an individual's chances of developing lung cancer.

    2. What are two benefits of breaking the smoking habit?

    3. According to the Surgeon General of the U.S. Public Health Service, of what three things is cigarette smoking the major preventable cause?

    4. What are three symptoms of mild nicotine poisoning?

    5. List two diseases which smokers are more likely to contract than nonsmokers.

NAME: _____ DATE: _____

TEST FOR CHAPTER TWENTY: USE OF ALCOHOL

I. On the line at the left of each of the following, write the letter of the choice that *best* completes the statement or answers the question.

_____ 1. Which of the following statements is *false*?   (A) Alcohol is high in calories.   (B) Alcohol has important nutrients.   (C) Alcohol is fattening.   (D) Alcoholics frequently suffer from malnutrition.

_____ 2. Drinking a large amount of alcohol may make a person   (A) loud.   (B) talkative.   (C) quarrelsome.   (D) all of these.

_____ 3. Which of the following statements is *true*?   (A) Regular intake of large amounts of alcohol does not damage body organs.   (B) Alcohol does not affect a person's ability to drive.   (C) Drinking large amounts of alcohol may paralyze the nerve centers that control the lungs.   (D) Alcohol is a stimulant.

_____ 4. Which of the following statements is *false*?   (A) Alcoholism does not affect an individual's personality.   (B) Alcohol can be addictive.   (C) Teenage drinkers risk slowing down their mental growth.   (D) Some people become heavy drinkers to escape from emotional problems.

_____ 5. When someone loses consciousness from drinking too much alcohol,   (A) call an ambulance immediately.   (B) make sure the person can breathe freely.   (C) remove any food from the mouth.   (D) all of these.

II. The following statements are true or false. Indicate True by placing (+) and False by placing (○) on the line at the left of the statement.

_____ 1. Alcohol has its greatest effect on the brain.

_____ 2. Drinking too much alcohol in too short a time may cause alcohol poisoning.

_____ 3. It is possible to predict accurately who will become an alcoholic.

_____ 4. A person who loses consciousness from drinking too much alcohol needs immediate medical attention.

_____ 5. There are about 300 calories in a 12-ounce glass of beer.

III. Match the term on the right with its description by placing the letter of the term in the blank to the left of the description.

_____ 1. process of purifying liquids by heating them until they become gas

_____ 2. caused by the action of certain yeasts on sugars found in fruit and grains

_____ 3. organization for children of alcoholics

_____ 4. withdrawal from a drug

_____ 5. amount of alcohol in a person's blood

A. Alateen
B. Alcoholics Anonymous
C. detoxification
D. 10%
E. blood alcohol level
F. fermentation
G. distillation

IV. Answer or complete the following at the bottom of your test paper.

1. List four signs that a person has an alcohol problem.
2. Name the organization made up of former alcoholics who try to help each other to stop drinking.
3. Alcohol dulls the nerve centers of the brain that control ____ , ____ , and ____ .
4. What are three signs that a person is intoxicated?
5. Give two reasons why people drink alcoholic beverages.

TEST FOR CHAPTER TWENTY-ONE: DRUGS: USE AND ABUSE

I. On the line at the left of each of the following, write the letter of the choice that *best* completes the statement or answers the question.

_____ 1. Stimulants   (A) slow down the body's processes.   (B) cause the heart to beat slower. (C) increase circulation and respiration.   (D) lower blood pressure.

_____ 2. Barbiturates   (A) slow down a person's reaction time.   (B) produce drowsiness. (C) decrease mental functioning.   (D) all of these.

_____ 3. Which of the following statements is *false*? Narcotics   (A) are derived from the opium poppy flower.   (B) are highly addictive.   (C) do not result in physical addiction. (D) have varying capacities to relieve pain.

_____ 4. Which of the following statements is *true*? Hallucinogens   (A) are usually taken by injection.   (B) are psychologically addictive.   (C) can only be made in chemical laboratories.   (D) cause extreme physical dependence.

_____ 5. Which of the following statements is *false*?   (A) Aspirin is a commonly used analgesic. (B) Anesthetics cause numbness.   (C) Penicillin is a powerful vaccine.   (D) Epilepsy can be controlled with medication.

II. The following statements are true or false. Indicate True by placing (+) and False by placing (O) on the line at the left of the statement.

_____ 1. Most drugs are used to restore or maintain health.

_____ 2. Methadone is a nonaddictive, legal substitute for heroin.

_____ 3. Caffeine is the most widely used psychoactive drug in America.

_____ 4. Marijuana produces distortions in a person's ability to judge time and space.

_____ 5. Regular users of marijuana may require more of the drug to get "high" than first-time users would need.

III. Match the term on the right with its description by placing the letter of the term in the blank to the left of the description.

_____ 1. help the body to fight germs that cause disease

_____ 2. strong feeling of well-being

_____ 3. drugs sold over the counter

_____ 4. change a person's mood or behavior

_____ 5. drug extracted from opium

A. OTC drugs
B. depressant
C. psychoactive drugs
D. morphine
E. hallucinations
F. euphoria
G. vaccines

IV. Answer the following questions at the bottom of your test paper.

1. Why should leftover prescription drugs be thrown out?
2. List the four categories of commonly abused drugs.
3. What are two symptoms of drug withdrawal?
4. Why does a given amount of alcohol drunk over several hours have less effect on a person than the same amount taken over a shorter period of time?
5. Which drug group has the immediate effects of a quick elevation of mood and a sudden feeling of power?

TEST FOR CHAPTER TWENTY-TWO: SEXUALLY TRANSMITTED DISEASES

I. On the line at the left of each of the following, write the letter of the choice that *best* completes the statement or answers the question.

_____ 1. Which of the following statements about syphilis is *false*? Syphilis (A) has more than one stage. (B) is important to treat at an early stage. (C) is incurable. (D) can be discovered through a blood test.

_____ 2. Which of the following statements is *false*? People with sexually transmitted diseases (A) should tell their sexual partners. (B) need not worry because the disease will go away on its own. (C) should not engage in sexual activity. (D) should consult a doctor or health clinic.

_____ 3. Which of the following statements about gonorrhea is *false*? (A) Symptoms of gonorrhea take two months to appear. (B) A male with gonorrhea usually has pain when he urinates. (C) A female always shows symptoms when she has gonorrhea. (D) Gonococci can live in the inner mucous membranes.

_____ 4. Which of the following statements about genital herpes is *false*? (A) The first symptom of genital herpes virus is usually pain in the genital area. (B) Herpes can be cured with penicillin. (C) Herpes infections are triggered by emotional stress. (D) A person with herpes should avoid sexual contact during the time of active infection.

_____ 5. Sexually transmitted diseases (A) are not cured by self-medication. (B) can be contracted more than once. (C) are prevented by avoiding sexual contact with infected people. (D) all of these.

II. The following statements are true or false. Indicate True by placing (+) and False by placing (O) on the line at the left of the statement.

_____ 1. Gonorrhea and syphilis are two forms of the same disease.

_____ 2. Gonorrhea infections can usually be treated with antibiotics.

_____ 3. Spirochetes can live outside the body.

_____ 4. During the latent stage of syphilis, an infected person may evidence no symptoms.

_____ 5. Pregnant women may pass the syphilis infection to their newborn babies.

III. Match the term on the right with its description by placing the letter of the term in the blank to the left of the description.

_____ 1. an open sore

_____ 2. bacteria which can enter the eye of a newborn

_____ 3. spiral-shaped bacteria

_____ 4. a small skin lesion associated with herpes

_____ 5. the most common sexually transmitted disease

A. vesicle
B. spirochetes
C. vaginitis
D. chancre
E. antibiotics
F. gonococci
G. gonorrhea

IV. Answer or complete the following at the bottom of your test paper.

1. Which two sexually transmitted diseases are causing epidemics all over the United States?
2. Genital herpes is caused by a ＿＿ that is introduced into the body through sexual contact.
3. Gonorrhea infection which goes untreated may develop into ＿＿ or ＿＿ .
4. What are the four stages of syphilis?
5. How can a physician find out if a gonococcal infection is present?

TEST FOR CHAPTER TWENTY-THREE: THE COMMON COLD AND OTHER MISERIES

I. On the line at the left of each of the following, write the letter of the choice that *best* completes the statement or answers the question.

_____ 1. Infectious diseases   (A) may be given to others by carriers.   (B) are due to an imbalance of blood and other body fluids.   (C) help people live long and healthier lives. (D) always cause death.

_____ 2. Which of the following statements is *false*? Your body   (A) can do nothing to defend itself against infection.   (B) uses protein to make antibodies.   (C) produces antitoxins to neutralize harmful toxins produced by pathogens.   (D) possesses leukocytes which digest invading organisms.

_____ 3. Which of the following statements is *false*?   (A) Colds and flu are passed from one person to another through mucus released in sneezing.   (B) Flu epidemics frequently occur in the spring.   (C) No new influenza has appeared since the late 1960s.   (D) Viruses mutate rapidly.

_____ 4. When you have a cold, you should   (A) rest.   (B) breathe humidified air.   (C) drink a lot of liquids.   (D) all of these.

_____ 5. Which of the following statements is *false*? Mononucleosis   (A) is a viral infection. (B) is contracted only by kissing a person who has the disease.   (C) causes sore throats and chills.   (D) can be diagnosed with a blood test.

II. The following statements are true or false. Indicate True by placing (+) and False by placing (O) on the line at the left of the statement.

_____ 1. There is no medication that will cure the common cold.

_____ 2. Hepatitis is a contagious disease.

_____ 3. Most viruses can be killed with antibiotics.

_____ 4. A cold is most contagious in the first few days of symptoms.

_____ 5. Antitoxins are prescription drugs that have been developed to cure influenza.

III. Match the term on the right with its description by placing the letter of the term in the blank to the left of the description.

_____ 1. a swelling of the liver

_____ 2. time during which pathogens multiply

_____ 3. disease-causing microorganisms

_____ 4. can be passed from one person to another

_____ 5. protein substances made by white blood cells

A. pathogens
B. mononucleosis
C. communicable diseases
D. antitoxins
E. hepatitis
F. antibodies
G. incubation period

IV. Answer or complete the following at the bottom of your test paper.

1. What are the two most common pathogens?
2. What are three of the most common symptoms of the common cold?
3. The greatest number of cases of mononucleosis is found among young people ＿＿ to ＿＿ years old.
4. A yellow discoloration of the skin is called ＿＿ and may occur in people who have ＿＿.
5. Name two factors which lower an individual's resistance to infection.

TEST FOR CHAPTER TWENTY-FOUR: IMMUNIZATIONS

I. On the line at the left of each of the following, write the letter of the choice that *best* completes the statement or answers the question.

_____ 1. Which of the following statements is *false*?   (A) Boosters are doses of vaccine. (B) Different types of vaccines last for different periods of time.   (C) In order for antibodies to be produced, symptoms of a disease must be present.   (D) Many school systems refuse to admit children who have not been immunized.

_____ 2. Rubella is   (A) dangerous to pregnant women.   (B) called German measles. (C) a disease that causes lockjaw.   (D) (A) and (B).

_____ 3. Which of the following statements is *false*?   (A) Measles can cause blindness.   (B) One symptom of mumps is swollen glands.   (C) Severe cases of measles may cause sterility. (D) Measles is a serious childhood disease.

_____ 4. Which of the following statements is *true*? Tetanus   (A) bacteria make a poison that attacks the nervous system.   (B) affects all but the facial muscles.   (C) is a childhood disease.   (D) has no known cause.

_____ 5. Which of the following statements is *false*? Vaccines   (A) cause side effects. (B) should be given under the direction of trained health professionals.   (C) eliminate disease-causing pathogens.   (D) cause the body to make antibodies.

II. The following statements are true or false. Indicate True by placing (+) and False by placing (O) on the line at the left of the statement.

_____ 1. Vaccines can cause side effects.

_____ 2. Tetanus has never been known to cause death.

_____ 3. Vaccine boosters are not needed after the age of 5.

_____ 4. All people are born with some natural immunity.

_____ 5. Polio sometimes causes the paralysis of breathing muscles.

III. Match the term on the right with its description by placing the letter of the term in the blank to the left of the description.

_____ 1. vaccines

_____ 2. lasts only a short time

_____ 3. whooping cough

_____ 4. a type of vaccine

_____ 5. builds up after having a disease

A. toxoids
B. pertussis
C. diphtheria
D. acquired immunity
E. immunizations
F. active immunity
G. passive immunity

IV. Answer or complete the following at the bottom of your test paper.

    1. Poliomyelitis is a disease that can cause lifelong _____ .

    2. List two childhood diseases.

    3. What three diseases does a combination DPT vaccine protect against?

    4. What do you call the ability to form antibodies against pathogens before they can cause disease?

    5. Name three diseases that a person can have only once.

TEST FOR CHAPTER TWENTY-FIVE: NUTRITIONAL NEEDS

I. On the line at the left of each of the following, write the letter of the choice that *best* completes the statement or answers the question.

_____ 1. Which of the following statements about fiber is *false*? Fiber   (A) is the indigestible part of plants.   (B) helps the passage of food through the digestive system.   (C) increases the production of bacteria in the large intestine.   (D) is found in fruits, seeds, and whole-grain cereals.

_____ 2. Water   (A) is found in every body cell.   (B) dissolves nutrients.   (C) is essential to life.   (D) all of these.

_____ 3. Carbohydrates   (A) cause all weight problems.   (B) include starches and sugars.   (C) are stored in the lungs.   (D) meet all the body's nutritional needs.

_____ 4. Which of the following statements about nutrients is *false*?   (A) Eating a lot of food insures that a person is properly nourished.   (B) Carbohydrates can be found in ice cream.   (C) Fats add flavor to foods.   (D) Iron attracts oxygen.

_____ 5. Calories   (A) are nutrients.   (B) are substances found in foods.   (C) are measures of energy.   (D) are needed in equal amounts by men and women.

II. The following statements are true or false. Indicate True by placing (+) and False by placing (O) on the line at the left of the statement.

_____ 1. Taking large amounts of vitamins guarantees a healthy body.

_____ 2. Water is the most important element needed for life.

_____ 3. Vitamin C is found in tomatoes.

_____ 4. Fat helps the body to absorb certain vitamins.

_____ 5. Your body can make all the amino acids necessary for protein building.

III. Match the term on the right with its description by placing the letter of the term in the blank to the left of the description.

_____ 1. insures proper working of thyroid gland

_____ 2. disease caused by lack of thiamine

_____ 3. speed up chemical processes

_____ 4. how fast your body uses energy

_____ 5. disease caused by lack of niacin

A. beriberi
B. pellagra
C. basal metabolic rate
D. iodine
E. carbohydrates
F. vitamins
G. nutrients

IV. Answer or complete the following at the bottom of your test paper.

1. List five nutrients found in food.
2. Name the vitamin connected with each of the following: (1) energy and growth, (2) healthy eyes, (3) blood clotting, (4) strong bones and teeth, (5) preventing the destruction of vitamin A.
3. _____ prevents pernicious anemia.
4. Another name for vitamin C is _____ _____ .
5. How do you get the nine essential amino acids that your body cannot manufacture?

NAME: _____ DATE: _____

TEST FOR CHAPTER TWENTY-SIX: SNACKS AND SPECIAL DIETS

I. On the line at the left of each of the following, write the letter of the choice that *best* completes the statement or answers the question.

_____ 1. Which of the following statements about dieting is *false*? (A) Diet pills interfere with healthy body functions. (B) Members of weight-reducing clinics support each other. (C) Your body can easily go without nutrients for long stretches of time. (D) It is best to check with your doctor before dieting.

_____ 2. Which of the following statements about fad diets is *true*? (A) They can harm the body's metabolism. (B) They may make you feel tired. (C) They are a healthy way to lose weight. (D) (A) and (B).

_____ 3. Underweight people (A) don't need to worry about nutrients. (B) just need to eat more food. (C) need to develop new eating habits. (D) look forward to trying new dishes.

_____ 4. Vegetarians (A) should plan their meals carefully. (B) do not eat meat. (C) may find it hard to get needed amino acids. (D) all of these.

_____ 5. Athletes (A) should eat at least three hours before a game. (B) should eat fatty foods before a sports event. (C) have no need for fluids. (D) have nutritional needs which are very different from those of nonathletes.

II. The following statements are true or false. Indicate True by placing (+) and False by placing (O) on the line at the left of the statement.

_____ 1. Snacking is always bad for you.

_____ 2. Protein cannot be stored in the body the same way as fat.

_____ 3. Pure vegetarians eat nuts and cheese.

_____ 4. An athlete should eat a candy bar ten minutes before a game to give him or her extra energy.

_____ 5. Large amounts of vitamin E will not improve an athlete's ability.

III. Match the term on the right with its description by placing the letter of the term in the blank to the left of the description.

_____ 1. lack of appetite for food

_____ 2. examples of fad diets

_____ 3. those who do not eat meat

_____ 4. found in snack foods that have no nutrients

_____ 5. use only dairy products such as milk, cheese, and butter

A. vegetarians
B. anorexia
C. lacto-vegetarians
D. bulimia
E. liquid-protein, grapefruit, high-fat
F. empty calories
G. lacto-ovo-vegetarians

IV. Answer the following questions at the bottom of your test paper.

1. List three strategies that may help a person to lose weight.
2. As the morning wears on, what happens to a person who has not eaten a good breakfast?
3. Which vitamins are harmful if taken in massive doses?
4. An overweight person is at risk for several diseases. List two of them.
5. One pound of body weight equals how many calories?

TEST FOR CHAPTER TWENTY-SEVEN: NUTRITION, LABELS, AND THE CONSUMER

I. On the line at the left of each of the following, write the letter of the choice that *best* completes the statement or answers the question.

_____ 1. Sugar   (A) contains calories and other nutrients.   (B) adds to overweight and tooth decay.   (C) can only be obtained from cakes and other desserts.   (D) is an essential part of one's diet.

_____ 2. Food-product labels   (A) list the ingredients that make up the food.   (B) place the largest ingredient by weight first.   (C) list food ingredients by weight in decreasing order.   (D) all of these.

_____ 3. Which of the following statements is *false*?   (A) Sugar is used as a preservative.   (B) Acids and bases keep jelly from hardening.   (C) Manufacturers guarantee the freshness of food after the date stamped on the package.   (D) Some foods lose their flavor in a short time.

_____ 4. Which of the following statements is *true*?   (A) People who have high blood pressure should use less salt.   (B) It is not possible to fertilize without using chemicals.   (C) Flavoring agents are made of all-natural ingredients.   (D) Coloring agents have nutritional value.

_____ 5. Additives   (A) may be harmful.   (B) are needed to keep food fresh.   (C) restore lost nutrients.   (D) all of these.

II. The following statements are true or false. Indicate True by placing (+) and False by placing (O) on the line at the left of the statement.

_____ 1. Foods lose nutritional value when they are processed.

_____ 2. Nitrites prevent the growth of botulinum.

_____ 3. Sulfur dioxide is a preservative.

_____ 4. Open dating assures consumers that the food is nutritious.

_____ 5. Foods sold in health food stores are more nutritious than those sold in supermarkets.

III. Match the term on the right with its description by placing the letter of the term in the blank to the left of the description.

_____ 1. added to hot dogs, bacon, sausage to prevent botulinum from growing

_____ 2. keep oil and water mixed

_____ 3. severe form of food poisoning

_____ 4. additives that keep food from spoiling

_____ 5. grown without use of synthetic fertilizers or insect or weed killers

A. toxins
B. preservatives
C. botulism
D. organic food
E. nitrites
F. emulsifiers
G. enriched

IV. Answer the following questions at the bottom of your test paper.

1. List three factors which determine a person's daily needs for various nutrients.
2. Name the function of each of the following additives: (1) acids and bases, (2) improving agents, (3) taste enhancers, (4) antioxidants.
3. What do the terms *made from, prepared from, contains,* and *contents* all refer to?
4. How can you lower your intake of food additives?
5. Why are preservatives, antioxidants, and enriched additives needed in packaged foods?

TEST FOR CHAPTER TWENTY-EIGHT: DIGESTION AND ELIMINATION

I. On the line at the left of each of the following, write the letter of the choice that *best* completes the statement or answers the question.

_____   1. Insulin   (A) is secreted by the liver.   (B) helps the body use sugar.   (C) is an enzyme.
             (D) plays an important role in elimination.

_____   2. Ulcers   (A) are usually found in the stomach or the duodenum.   (B) are often caused
             by an increase in acid in the digestive tract.   (C) are more frequent in cigarette smokers.
             (D) all of these.

_____   3. Which of the following promote good digestion?   (A) a stimulating debate about impor-
             tant issues   (B) drinking ice water with the meal   (C) eating slowly   (D) using water
             to ease large bites of food down the throat

_____   4. Which of the following statements is *false*?   (A) The villus in the small intestine has a
             lymph vessel.   (B) Many bacteria live in the large intestine.   (C) Enuresis does not
             occur in school-aged children.   (D) Urine is constantly being formed in the body.

_____   5. The kidneys   (A) are connected to the bladder by the urethra.   (B) may be damaged
             by infection in the blood.   (C) filter roughage from the blood.   (D) are responsible
             when the stomach "rumbles."

II. The following statements are true or false. Indicate True by placing (+) and False by placing (O) on the line at the left of the statement.

_____   1. Peristaltic waves are controlled by the brain.

_____   2. Bile is stored in the gall bladder.

_____   3. The stomach is the most important organ of the digestive system.

_____   4. The kidneys can be harmed by large amounts of alcohol.

_____   5. The major part of digestion takes place in the large intestine.

III. Match the term on the right with its description by placing the letter of the term in the blank to the left of the description.

_____   1. projections on inner lining of small intestine   A. alimentary canal
                                                                     B. esophagus
_____   2. digestive tract   C. papillae
                                                                     D. duodenum
_____   3. enzyme found in saliva   E. enzymes
                                                                     F. villi
_____   4. projections on the surface of the tongue   G. amylase

_____   5. first section of small intestine

IV. Answer or complete the following at the bottom of your test paper.

1. List the four different kinds of taste buds.
2. The pancreas produces two kinds of secretions. What are they?
3. After digestion, what do carbohydrates, fats, and proteins change to?
4. What are two causes of diarrhea?
5. Give two examples of how strong emotions can affect the digestive system.

TEST FOR CHAPTER TWENTY-NINE: PERSONAL SAFETY

I. On the line at the left of each of the following, write the letter of the choice that *best* completes the statement or answers the question.

_____ 1. Which of the following statements is *false*?   (A) Most work-related accidents take place around machines.   (B) Accidents in industry occur evenly throughout the day. (C) Lack of safety-guards causes a large number of accidents with saws.   (D) Eye protection is an important safety measure in the use of grinding-wheels.

_____ 2. Accidents   (A) are not a problem among older people because they are more careful. (B) do not occur in the home.   (C) frequently result from carelessness.   (D) are not a significant factor in causing death.

_____ 3. Bicycle accidents may result from   (A) riding a bike that is too large.   (B) chain slippage.   (C) collision with another vehicle.   (D) all of these.

_____ 4. Motorcycle accidents are frequently caused by   (A) pedals falling off.   (B) keeping a considerable distance when following cars.   (C) pulling out from parked cars without looking.   (D) attending to traffic rules.

_____ 5. Which of the following statements is *false*?   (A) Riding a bicycle can be dangerous. (B) Bike riding is a healthful way to get exercise.   (C) Hitting a bump can cause a bicycle to go out of control.   (D) Careless bike riders harm only themselves.

II. The following statements are true or false. Indicate True by placing (+) and False by placing (O) on the line at the left of the statement.

_____ 1. Careless driving of tractors is the major cause of farm accidents.

_____ 2. Rest periods for workers cut down on the number of accidents.

_____ 3. It is safe to skate on ice that is 5 centimeters thick.

_____ 4. Bicycle riders should obey traffic signs and lights.

_____ 5. People pay more attention to the possible dangers in surroundings they see every day.

III. Match the term on the right with its description by placing the letter of the term in the blank to the left of the description.

_____ 1. crash helmets, goggles, heavy gloves

_____ 2. involved in more accidents than any other vehicle

_____ 3. caused by unsafe buildings, tools, and equipment

_____ 4. fire drills at home

_____ 5. following the car ahead too closely

A. EDITH
B. work-related accidents
C. tailgating
D. safety equipment
E. motorcycles
F. home accidents
G. bicycles

IV. Answer the following questions at the bottom of your test paper.

1. What are two dangerous driving conditions which lead to automobile accidents?
2. List three rules for safety in the home.
3. List three rules for safe swimming.
4. What are three unsafe driving practices?
5. Why do insurance companies charge higher rates for teenage drivers?

TEST FOR CHAPTER THIRTY: BASIC FIRST AID

I. On the line at the left of each of the following, write the letter of the choice that *best* completes the statement or answers the question.

_____ 1. Which of the following statements is *false*?   (A) Swelling and pain occur very quickly with dislocations.   (B) Apply heat to a sprain as quickly as possible.   (C) It is important to keep a patient with a sprain warm.   (D) Sometimes an x-ray must be taken to determine whether an injury is a sprain, dislocation, or fracture.

_____ 2. Which of the following conditions require immediate first aid?   (A) poisoning   (B) hemorrhaging   (C) extensive burns   (D) all of these

_____ 3. Which of the following is *true*? Most burns are caused by   (A) matches.   (B) electricity.   (C) chemicals.   (D) heat.

_____ 4. Heatstroke   (A) results from overexposure to the sun.   (B) makes the skin hot and dry.   (C) victims should never be moved.   (D) (B) and (C).

_____ 5. Which of the following statements is *false*? An emergency situation   (A) needs fast action.   (B) can only be dealt with by trained medical personnel.   (C) should be dealt with in a calm manner.   (D) calls for the use of first aid.

II. The following statements are true or false. Indicate True by placing (+) and False by placing (O) on the line at the left of the statement.

_____ 1. When the skin is broken only slightly, there is no danger of infection.

_____ 2. You should keep the victim of a snakebite moving around as much as possible.

_____ 3. It is more dangerous to move a person with a fracture than to wait for medical help.

_____ 4. The most important factor in treating shock is keeping the victim from losing body heat.

_____ 5. A person who has been bitten by an animal must always have antirabies vaccination.

III. Match the term on the right with its description by placing the letter of the term in the blank to the left of the description.

_____ 1. substance that works against a poison

_____ 2. band of cloth tied near a wound to stop bleeding

_____ 3. painful injury to tendons around a joint

_____ 4. strong attack of involuntary muscle contractions

_____ 5. loss of large amounts of water and salt in perspiration

A. antidote
B. sprain
C. sunstroke
D. convulsion
E. heat exhaustion
F. fracture
G. tourniquet

IV. Answer the following questions at the bottom of your test paper.

1. If someone is bleeding heavily, what should you do until medical help arrives?
2. What are three general rules governing first-aid treatment of burns?
3. Describe the condition of the skin in first-degree burns, second-degree burns, and third-degree burns.
4. Give three first-aid rules that should be followed in emergency situations.
5. What should you be sure *not* to do if you know that a person has swallowed lye or acid?

NAME: _____ DATE: _____

TEST FOR CHAPTER THIRTY-ONE: CARDIOPULMONARY RESUSCITATION (CPR)

I. On the line at the left of each of the following, write the letter of the choice that *best* completes the statement or answers the question.

_____ 1. Which of the following statements is *false*? Common causes of sudden death are (A) heart attacks.   (B) choking.   (C) frostbite.   (D) suffocation.

_____ 2. A rescuer who provides basic life support has been trained to recognize   (A) respiratory arrest.   (B) absence of a pulse.   (C) blocked airways.   (D) all of these.

_____ 3. The distress signal for choking is   (A) raising the right hand.   (B) grabbing the back of the neck.   (C) clutching the neck between the thumb and index finger.   (D) bending over from the waist.

_____ 4. Which of the following statements is *false*? CPR   (A) can be administered only by a paramedic, nurse, or doctor.   (B) stands for cardiopulmonary resuscitation.   (C) combines artificial respiration with artificial circulation.   (D) courses are offered by the American Heart Association and the American National Red Cross.

_____ 5. How can you determine if someone is breathing?   (A) Try to spot movement of the chest.   (B) Listen for breathing sounds.   (C) Feel for breath on your cheek. (D) Do all of these.

II. The following statements are true or false. Indicate True by placing (+) and False by placing (O) on the line at the left of the statement.

_____ 1. Café coronaries are heart attacks that take place in restaurants.

_____ 2. A person who is choking should receive the same treatment whether conscious or unconscious.

_____ 3. Alcoholic beverages reduce sensation in the mouth.

_____ 4. Pressure applied to a victim can sometimes cause rib fractures.

_____ 5. The rescuer can find out if the victim's heart is beating by feeling the pulmonary artery.

III. Match the term on the right with its description by placing the letter of the term in the blank to the left of the description.

_____ 1. artificial circulation provided by external pressure on the breastbone

_____ 2. absence of heartbeat

_____ 3. procedure to save choking victim

_____ 4. absence of breathing

_____ 5. emergency care to restore breathing

A. Heimlich maneuver
B. rescue breathing
C. respiratory arrest
D. external cardiac compression
E. basic life support
F. cardiac arrest
G. cardiopulmonary resuscitation

IV. Answer the following questions at the bottom of your test paper.

1. What are four warning signals of a heart attack?
2. List three ways to prevent choking in children.
3. What is the best way to provide rescue breathing?
4. What should you do to dislodge an object in the airway of a child?
5. What are the A-B-C steps of cardiopulmonary resuscitation?

TEST FOR CHAPTER THIRTY-TWO: SELECTING HEALTH CARE

I. On the line at the left of each of the following, write the letter of the choice that *best* completes the statement or answers the question.

_____   1. Placebos   (A) are sometimes effective.   (B) contain no medicine.   (C) look just like medicine.   (D) all of these.

_____   2. Which of the following statements is *false*?   (A) Many diseases are self-limited. (B) "Quacks" use people's fears to sell their products.   (C) There is no such thing as a disease "running its course."   (D) The human body has many defense systems that fight illness.

_____   3. Which of the following statements is *true*?   (A) Otolaryngologists treat ear disorders. (B) Radiologists use x-rays to treat patients.   (C) Thoracic surgeons perform surgery on the heart.   (D) Orthopedic surgeons perform surgery on the chest.

_____   4. Which of the following statements is *false*?   (A) The doctor may use a stethoscope during an examination.   (B) There are many kinds of blood tests.   (C) A PAP test examines the fluid in the spinal cord.   (D) Use of a tongue depressor gives a better view of the tonsils.

_____   5. Which of the following is a dental specialist?   (A) periodontist   (B) endodontist (C) otologist   (D) (A) and (B)

II. The following statements are true or false. Indicate True by placing (+) and False by placing (O) on the line at the left of the statement.

_____   1. Illness is sometimes caused by emotional problems.

_____   2. An obstetrician treats gastrointestinal disorders.

_____   3. Anesthetics are used to test reflexes.

_____   4. All doctors must pass a state board examination before receiving a license to practice medicine.

_____   5. Information about your social setting may be used in treating illness.

III. Match the term on the right with its description by placing the letter of the term in the blank to the left of the description.

_____   1. shines light into the ear   A. otoscope
                                                                    B. sphygmomanometer
_____   2. treats disorders of the urinary tract   C. internist
_____   3. measures blood pressure   D. stethoscope
_____   4. has special training in diagnosing illness   E. dermatologist
                                                                    F. otologist
_____   5. treats skin diseases   G. urologist

IV. Answer the following questions at the bottom of your test paper.

1. Give two examples of chronic illnesses.
2. List five signs that indicate that it is necessary to call a doctor.
3. Give two examples of crises that can cause people to turn to psychologists for help.
4. A visit to a doctor may involve a three-stage process. What are the three parts?
5. Why are more doctors becoming specialists?

TEST FOR CHAPTER THIRTY-THREE: SELF-CARE AND THE HEALTH CONSUMER

I. On the line at the left of each of the following, write the letter of the choice that *best* completes the statement or answers the question.

_____ 1. An HMO   (A) gives prepaid health care.   (B) regulates new drugs at the state level. (C) is an aspirin substitute.   (D) is required on drug labels.

_____ 2. Which of the following statements is *false*? Medications   (A) need not remain sterile. (B) may decompose.   (C) may lose their strength.   (D) may become poisonous.

_____ 3. Which of the following statements is *true*?   (A) Only new drugs are tested for harmful effects.   (B) The FDA can only suggest that a product be removed from the market. (C) The New Drug Section of the FDA gives drug manufacturers permission to sell their products.   (D) The manufacturers of new drugs need only submit a list of the ingredients in their products.

_____ 4. Decongestants   (A) cause drowsiness.   (B) encourage the membranes in the nose to produce more secretions.   (C) work effectively for two weeks.   (D) are expectorants.

_____ 5. Immunization   (A) is a way of using medicine that can keep you from getting certain diseases.   (B) is given primarily to adults.   (C) is usually given by injection. (D) (A) and (C).

II. The following statements are true or false. Indicate True by placing (+) and False by placing (O) on the line at the left of the statement.

_____ 1. Many drugs advertised on television may be harmful to you.

_____ 2. Aspirin is used to cure arthritis.

_____ 3. Drugs bought for self-treatment may be harmful.

_____ 4. If the United States implements a national health insurance plan, it will be the first country to do so.

_____ 5. Taking antibiotics without a doctor's advice can make you resistant to their effects.

III. Match the term on the right with its description by placing the letter of the term in the blank to the left of the description.

_____ 1. being absorbed into the bloodstream

_____ 2. health insurance for persons over 65 years of age

_____ 3. make you cough more

_____ 4. quiets cough center

_____ 5. prevents growth of bacteria

A. Medicaid
B. expectorants
C. antiseptic
D. antacids
E. systemic
F. Medicare
G. antitussive

IV. Answer the following questions at the bottom of your test paper.

1. Briefly describe primary medical care, secondary medical care, and tertiary care.
2. What is the function of the FDA?
3. List four of the seven pieces of information that are found on the labels of OTC drugs.
4. What are two preventive measures you can take to protect your health?
5. Name the function of each of the following OTC medications: (1) antiseptics, (2) antacids, (3) decongestants.

TEST FOR CHAPTER THIRTY-FOUR: HEALTH IN THE UNITED STATES

I. On the line at the left of each of the following, write the letter of the choice that *best* completes the statement or answers the question.

_____   1. One communicable disease is   (A) tuberculosis   (B) ulcers   (C) epilepsy
(D) arthritis

_____   2. Government is concerned with public health and demonstrates this by   (A) disposing of wastes.   (B) inspecting water supplies.   (C) providing fire protection.   (D) all of these.

_____   3. Which of the following statements is *false?* The CDC   (A) is concerned with the safety of workers on their jobs.   (B) limits its services to people who live in the United States.   (C) tracks down the source of epidemics.   (D) is located in Atlanta, Georgia.

_____   4. Vital data do *not* include records of   (A) marriages.   (B) weight and height of each schoolchild in the district.   (C) numbers of deaths.   (D) causes of death.

_____   5. Which of the following is *not* a voluntary health agency?   (A) National Association for Mental Health   (B) Arthritis Foundation   (C) Administration of the Aging
(D) National Foundation—March of Dimes.

II. The following statements are true or false. Indicate True by placing (+) and False by placing (O) on the line at the left of the statement.

_____   1. The federal government is responsible for public health services that cross state boundaries.

_____   2. The American National Red Cross is a division of the Department of Health and Human Services.

_____   3. Epidemiologists search for the source of infection when an outbreak of infectious disease occurs.

_____   4. WHO plays a role in preventing illegal drug traffic.

_____   5. The most important federal agency in the area of public health is the National Institutes of Health.

III. Match the term on the right with its description by placing the letter of the term in the blank to the left of the description.

_____   1. record of deaths and the causes of deaths

_____   2. supports research programs in the areas of health and disease

_____   3. agency of the United Nations

_____   4. voluntary agency that provides health education

_____   5. concerned with the control of communicable diseases

A. vital data
B. American Medical Association
C. World Health Organization
D. Public Health Service
E. federal health services
F. Centers for Disease Control
G. American Heart Association

IV. Answer the following questions at the bottom of your test paper.

1. List three functions performed by your local health department.
2. What are two methods for killing microorganisms?
3. What are three functions of the Public Health Service?
4. The average life span depends on three major factors. What are they?
5. List three activities of the World Health Organization.

TEST FOR CHAPTER THIRTY-FIVE: HEALTH CAREERS FOR YOU

I. On the line at the left of each of the following, write the letter of the choice that *best* completes the statement or answers the question.

_____ 1. Health-care jobs   (A) require many years of special training.   (B) let you learn while you work.   (C) require little special training.   (D) all of these.

_____ 2. Which of the following statements is *false*? Speech pathologists   (A) work to prevent hearing disorders.   (B) evaluate the language of adults.   (C) must have graduated from a two-year training program.   (D) work in community organizations.

_____ 3. Which of the following statements is *false*? Certified laboratory assistants work in the areas of   (A) bacteriology.   (B) morphology.   (C) hematology.   (D) urinalysis.

_____ 4. Which of the following organizations support(s) job training in the area of health?   (A) New Drugs Section of FDA   (B) labor unions   (C) federal government   (D) (B) and (C)

_____ 5. Which of the following statements is *false*?   (A) An inhalation therapy technician helps supply oxygen to patients.   (B) Prosthetists treat foot disorders.   (C) Food technologists design new packing techniques.   (D) Histologic technicians prepare body tissues for microscopic examination.

II. The following statements are true or false. Indicate True by placing (+) and False by placing (O) on the line at the left of the statement.

_____ 1. All health jobs require some technical expertise.

_____ 2. Ward clerks do routine tasks necessary to make hospital patients comfortable.

_____ 3. Health careers is one of the fastest-growing fields of employment.

_____ 4. Veterinarians inspect water plants and dairies.

_____ 5. Central service technicians prepare patients to receive EKGs.

III. Match the term on the right with its description by placing the letter of the term in the blank to the left of the description.

_____ 1. works with pathologists

_____ 2. jobs in which a person can work and learn at the same time

_____ 3. require least amount of formal education

_____ 4. treats foot disorders

_____ 5. x-ray machines

A. entry-level careers
B. podiatrist
C. pediatric assistant
D. cytotechnologist
E. tomographic scanners
F. on-the-job training
G. medical technologist

IV. Answer the following questions at the bottom of your test paper.

1. What are three entry-level health careers?
2. List two responsibilities of radiation therapy technologists.
3. What are examples of three high-level health careers?
4. What is the job title for the person who conducts chemical, serologic, and bacteriologic tests to help diagnose diseases?
5. What two tasks might be performed by a pediatric assistant?

Answers to Chapter Tests

CHAPTER 1

MULTIPLE CHOICE	TRUE/FALSE	MATCHING
1. D 2. B 3. C 4. C 5. D	1. + 2. ○ 3. ○ 4. ○ 5. +	1. D 2. G 3. E 4. A 5. C

QUESTIONS

1. pneumonia, influenza, tuberculosis
2. They spread when conditions are favorable for their growth.
3. They see a health problem as one which has a good chance of affecting them.
   They think that there would be serious consequences if the problem did affect them.
   They believe there is a course of action that can reduce the threat.
   They believe this course of action is reasonable.
4. milk; fruits and vegetables; meats, fish, or chicken; bread and cereal products
5. physical, mental, social

CHAPTER 2

MULTIPLE CHOICE	TRUE/FALSE	MATCHING
1. B 2. B 3. C 4. D 5. A	1. ○ 2. + 3. ○ 4. + 5. ○	1. F 2. C 3. G 4. D 5. A

QUESTIONS

1. voluntary: skeleton
   involuntary: walls of stomach
   cardiac: heart
2. hinge, ball-and-socket, gliding, pivot
3. makes bones hard and strong; helps muscles to contract, blood to clot, and nerves to carry impulses
4. spread body weight evenly over foot, provide necessary support to let foot be used as a lever when you stand on your toes
5. Tendons attach muscle to bone; ligaments connect bones.

CHAPTER 3

MULTIPLE CHOICE	TRUE/FALSE	MATCHING
1. C 2. B 3. C 4. D 5. D	1. ○ 2. ○ 3. + 4. ○ 5. +	1. C 2. F 3. D 4. B 5. A

QUESTIONS

1. badminton, ballet, calisthenics, diving, figure skating, frisbee, gymnastics, judo, karate, mountain climbing, racquetball, skateboarding, skiing, soccer, volleyball, wrestling, yoga
2. tones the muscles, strengthens the heart
3. It raises them.
4. by wearing shoes that fit properly, learning how to run correctly, warming up before you jog
5. cramps, nausea

CHAPTER 4

MULTIPLE CHOICE	TRUE/FALSE	MATCHING
1. D 2. A 3. D 4. C 5. B	1. + 2. ○ 3. + 4. ○ 5. +	1. D 2. B 3. A 4. E 5. G

QUESTIONS

1. setting realistic goals, making wise decisions, practicing self-control, accepting responsibility for one's behavior
2. take aptitude tests, talk with counselors, try new activities
3. family customs or standards, religion, ideas you have read, personal experience, personal beliefs
4. use available resources, explore the choices, think about the results
5. drawing conclusions from one event, placing too much value on surface traits, using a "personality test" from a magazine, stereotyping

CHAPTER 5

MULTIPLE CHOICE   TRUE/FALSE   MATCHING

1. C 2. A 3. C 4. D 5. C   1. ○ 2. ○ 3. ○ 4. ○ 5. ○   1. E 2. D 3. C 4. A 5. B

QUESTIONS

1. anxieties
2. neurosis, psychosis, psychosomatic disorder
3. issue
4. psychotherapy
5. community resources

CHAPTER 6

MULTIPLE CHOICE   TRUE/FALSE   MATCHING

1. D 2. B 3. A 4. D 5. C   1. ○ 2. + 3. ○ 4. + 5. ○   1. B 2. C 3. A 4. B 5. A

QUESTIONS

1. (any listed on page 70, Life Change Scale)
2. dry mouth, depression, irritability, loss of appetite, eating uncontrollably
3. eat a well-balanced diet, get enough sleep, exercise regularly
4. Pulse, heartbeat, and breathing rates all increase.
   Hormones rush into the bloodstream.
   Temperature rises and you begin to perspire.
5. improvement in day-to-day performance
   increase in ability to adapt to sudden stress reactions

CHAPTER 7

MULTIPLE CHOICE   TRUE/FALSE   MATCHING

1. A 2. B 3. A 4. D 5. C   1. ○ 2. + 3. + 4. ○ 5. +   1. F 2. D 3. A 4. G 5. B

QUESTIONS

1. German measles, or rubella
2. disease, drugs, damage during pregnancy
3. umbilical cord
4. loss of endometrium (spongy lining of the uterus); usually once a month
5. deeper voice; hair growth on face, under arms, in genital area; stronger and harder arm, leg, and chest muscles; thicker and tougher skin; wider shoulders

CHAPTER 8

MULTIPLE CHOICE   TRUE/FALSE   MATCHING

1. D 2. D 3. D 4. D 5. A   1. + 2. ○ 3. ○ 4. + 5. ○   1. G 2. E 3. A 4. B 5. C

Answers to Chapter Tests

QUESTIONS

1. the family
2. money, religion, choice of friends, drinking, drugs, what television program to watch, length of time on the phone
3. meeting physical and emotional needs, education necessary to realize individual potentials, costs of maintaining a home, affordability of important things and agreement of what these things are, children, goals in life
4. giving the kind of care that will help the child grow into a physically, emotionally, and socially healthy person; care and protection
5. showing respect, following the standards that have been set up for behavior, doing a share of the work in maintaining the home

CHAPTER 9

MULTIPLE CHOICE   TRUE/FALSE   MATCHING

1. D 2. A 3. C 4. A 5. B   1. + 2. + 3. ○ 4. + 5. ○   1. G 2. E 3. A 4. D 5. C

QUESTIONS

1. serious infections, tires easily, slowed growth, slow-to-heal leg ulcers, poor vision or blindness, strokes, need blood transfusions, have pain in any body part caused by sickle cells blocking small capillaries
2. father
3. hair color, eye color, height, facial appearance
4. Down's syndrome
5. Tay-Sachs, cystic fibrosis, sickle-cell anemia

CHAPTER 10

MULTIPLE CHOICE   TRUE/FALSE   MATCHING

1. D 2. B 3. A 4. C 5. B   1. + 2. ○ 3. + 4. ○ 5. +   1. G 2. B 3. A 4. D 5. F

QUESTIONS

1. carbon monoxide, sulfur oxide, nitrogen oxide, hydrocarbons, small particles that float in the air
2. weather conditions, geographic location, type of industry
3. temperature inversion
4. polluted water supplies
5. human waste, industrial waste

CHAPTER 11

MULTIPLE CHOICE   TRUE/FALSE   MATCHING

1. D 2. A 3. B 4. D 5. D   1. + 2. + 3. ○ 4. + 5. +   1. F 2. E 3. A 4. B 5. D

QUESTIONS

1. surgery, chemotherapy, radiation therapy
2. breast cancer

3. a change in bowel or bladder habits
   a sore that does not heal
   any unusual bleeding or discharge
   a thickening or lump in the breast or elsewhere
   indigestion or difficulty in swallowing
   an obvious change in a wart or mole
   a nagging cough or hoarseness
4. benign tumors: cells are normal and in orderly pattern, do not spread to other parts of the body or attack organs needed for life
   malignant tumors: cells are not normal and grow in irregular pattern, spread to other parts of the body or attack organs needed for life
5. losing valuable time

CHAPTER 12

MULTIPLE CHOICE	TRUE/FALSE	MATCHING
1. B 2. C 3. D 4. C 5. C	1. + 2. ○ 3. + 4. + 5. +	1. G 2. A 3. F 4. C 5. E

QUESTIONS

1. central nervous system, peripheral nervous system, autonomic nervous system
2. eyes, ears, nose, tongue, skin
3. cerebrum
4. breathing, heart action, circulation
5. wear seat belts, eat a well-balanced diet, get enough rest, avoid poisons and unnecessary drugs

CHAPTER 13

MULTIPLE CHOICE	TRUE/FALSE	MATCHING
1. D 2. C 3. D 4. C 5. A	1. + 2. ○ 3. ○ 4. + 5. +	1. B 2. F 3. A 4. E 5. C

QUESTIONS

1. conduction deafness
   nerve deafness
   central deafness
2. too much wax or infection in the auditory canal
   an eardrum that is torn or inflamed
   broken or joined malleus, incus, or stapes
   thick fluid in the middle ear
3. eustachian tube
4. ophthalmologist
5. ammonia, liquid bleach, alkali, strong acid, cleaning agents

CHAPTER 14

MULTIPLE CHOICE	TRUE/FALSE	MATCHING
1. B 2. D 3. C 4. D 5. A	1. ○ 2. + 3. + 4. + 5. ○	1. C 2. D 3. A 4. G 5. F

QUESTIONS

1. get enough exercise, choose a proper diet, maintain normal blood pressure, avoid cigarette smoking
2. not enough hemoglobin
3. A, B, AB, O

Answers to Chapter Tests

4. atrium, ventricle.
5. heredity, overweight, emotional tension

CHAPTER 15

MULTIPLE CHOICE	TRUE/FALSE	MATCHING
1. C 2. D 3. D 4. B 5. B	1. + 2. ○ 3. + 4. ○ 5. ○	1. D 2. A 3. B 4. G 5. E

QUESTIONS

1. pleura
2. hold your breath, sip water, try to breathe slowly and regularly
3. oxygen
4. cancer of the lungs and larynx, chronic bronchitis, emphysema
5. yawn

CHAPTER 16

MULTIPLE CHOICE	TRUE/FALSE	MATCHING
1. A 2. D 3. C 4. C 5. B	1. + 2. + 3. + 4. + 5. ○	1. F 2. E 3. A 4. B 5. D

QUESTIONS

1. Wash with soap and water at least twice a day.
   Avoid greasy creams and oily preparations.
   Eat a well-balanced diet.
   Get enough rest and exercise.
2. skin
3. Wash feet carefully with soap.
   Dry feet thoroughly.
   Use your own towel.
   Avoid footwear that causes your feet to perspire.
4. contact dermatitis: poison ivy, poison oak, poison sumac
   allergic dermatitis: hives
5. the look on your face, sweating on palms and forehead, blushing, impression made by personal appearance

CHAPTER 17

MULTIPLE CHOICE	TRUE/FALSE	MATCHING
1. C 2. D 3. B 4. C 5. D	1. + 2. ○ 3. ○ 4. + 5. +	1. E 2. A 3. G 4. C 5. F

QUESTIONS

1. They do not have ducts or tubes that lead to other parts of the body.
2. Hormones regulate many systems of the body so they will work together.
3. pituitary gland, thyroid gland, parathyroid glands, islands of Langerhans, adrenal glands, gonads, pineal gland, thymus gland
4. It is needed for breaking down sugar so that it can be used by body cells.
5. unusual thirst, unexplained weight change, extreme tiredness or nervousness, signs of abnormal growth and development

CHAPTER 18

MULTIPLE CHOICE	TRUE/FALSE	MATCHING
1. D 2. B 3. C 4. A 5. C	1. + 2. ○ 3. + 4. + 5. ○	1. G 2. F 3. B 4. C 5. D

QUESTIONS

1. crown, neck, roots
2. Brush teeth twice a day.
   Use dental floss.
   Visit the dentist for checkups.
3. dental disease
4. cutting, tearing, crushing, and grinding food; preparing food for digestion
5. impacted wisdom teeth

CHAPTER 19

MULTIPLE CHOICE	TRUE/FALSE	MATCHING
1. D 2. B 3. D 4. B 5. D	1. + 2. ○ 3. + 4. + 5. +	1. E 2. F 3. B 4. A 5. C

QUESTIONS

1. age at which smoking began, number of cigarettes smoked per day, how deeply smoke is inhaled, total number of years smoking, total number of cigarettes smoked over the years
2. live longer, healthier, cough less, breathe more easily, feel better
3. illness, disability, premature death
4. dizziness, faintness, rapid pulse, clammy skin, nausea, vomiting, diarrhea
5. heart disease, chronic bronchitis, emphysema, lung cancer

CHAPTER 20

MULTIPLE CHOICE	TRUE/FALSE	MATCHING
1. B 2. D 3. C 4. A 5. D	1. + 2. + 3. ○ 4. + 5. ○	1. G 2. F 3. A 4. C 5. E

QUESTIONS

1. drinks in order to perform a job
   drives while intoxicated
   does something under the influence of alcohol that he or she would not have done without alcohol
   becomes seriously injured as a result of using alcohol
   has come into conflict with the law as a result of being intoxicated
   has been intoxicated four times in a year
2. Alcoholics Anonymous
3. judgment, attention, memory, self-control
4. slow movements, slurred speech, unsteady walk, dizziness, loud, talkative, affectionate, quarrelsome
5. like the taste
   think it is sophisticated
   seems to relax them and ease their worries for a time
   to escape feelings of immaturity and inferiority
   to forget disappointments and failures

Answers to Chapter Tests

CHAPTER 21

MULTIPLE CHOICE	TRUE/FALSE	MATCHING
1. C 2. D 3. C 4. B 5. C	1. + 2. ○ 3. + 4. + 5. ○	1. G 2. F 3. A 4. C 5. D

QUESTIONS

1. The chemicals may change over time.
2. depressants, narcotics, stimulants, hallucinogens
3. trembling, hallucinations, vomiting, nausea
4. Alcohol is metabolized quickly in the body.
5. amphetamines

CHAPTER 22

MULTIPLE CHOICE	TRUE/FALSE	MATCHING
1. C 2. B 3. C 4. B 5. D	1. ○ 2. + 3. ○ 4. + 5. +	1. D 2. F 3. B 4. A 5. G

QUESTIONS

1. gonorrhea, syphilis
2. virus
3. arthritis, sterility
4. primary stage
   secondary stage
   latent stage
   late syphilis
5. by taking samples of fluids from the cervix, vagina, and urethra

CHAPTER 23

MULTIPLE CHOICE	TRUE/FALSE	MATCHING
1. A 2. A 3. C 4. D 5. B	1. + 2. + 3. ○ 4. + 5. ○	1. E 2. G 3. A 4. C 5. F

QUESTIONS

1. bacteria, viruses
2. fever, cough, weakness, muscle aches
3. 15, 19
4. jaundice, hepatitis
5. poor nutrition, illness, smoking, emotional stress, age, too much alcohol

CHAPTER 24

MULTIPLE CHOICE	TRUE/FALSE	MATCHING
1. C 2. D 3. C 4. A 5. C	1. + 2. ○ 3. ○ 4. + 5. +	1. E 2. G 3. B 4. A 5. D

QUESTIONS

1. paralysis
2. Answers will vary somewhat: examples include measles, mumps, and rubella.
3. diphtheria, pertussis, tetanus
4. active immunity
5. diphtheria, scarlet fever, measles, mumps, chicken pox

CHAPTER 25

MULTIPLE CHOICE   TRUE/FALSE   MATCHING

1. C 2. D 3. B 4. A 5. C   1. ○ 2. ○ 3. + 4. + 5. ○   1. D 2. A 3. F 4. C 5. B

QUESTIONS

1. fats, carbohydrates, proteins, vitamins, minerals
2. (1) vitamin B, (2) vitamin A, (3) vitamin K, (4) vitamin D, (5) vitamin E
3. vitamin B_{12}
4. ascorbic acid
5. must be in the proteins you eat

CHAPTER 26

MULTIPLE CHOICE   TRUE/FALSE   MATCHING

1. C 2. D 3. C 4. D 5. A   1. ○ 2. + 3. ○ 4. ○ 5. +   1. B 2. E 3. A 4. F 5. C

QUESTIONS

1. eat only at meals, snack only on fruits and vegetables, refuse second helpings, eat slowly, compare size of serving with amount of exercise needed to burn calories
2. energy level drops
3. vitamin A and vitamin D
4. hypertension, diabetes, coronary heart disease, diseases of circulatory system
5. 3,500

CHAPTER 27

MULTIPLE CHOICE   TRUE/FALSE   MATCHING

1. B 2. D 3. C 4. A 5. D   1. + 2. + 3. + 4. ○ 5. ○   1. E 2. F 3. C 4. B 5. D

QUESTIONS

1. sex, age, body size, level of activity
2. (1) put "fizz" into soft drinks, (2) glaze on baked goods, (3) bring out flavors, (4) prevent foods from changing in taste, color, and smell
3. what makes up food
4. by eating as many fresh foods as possible
5. to prolong freshness, keep bacteria from multiplying, stop formation of toxins

CHAPTER 28

MULTIPLE CHOICE   TRUE/FALSE   MATCHING

1. B 2. D 3. C 4. C 5. B   1. ○ 2. + 3. ○ 4. + 5. ○   1. F 2. A 3. G 4. C 5. D

Answers to Chapter Tests

QUESTIONS

1. sweet, salty, sour, bitter
2. insulin, pancreatic juice
3. simple sugar, glycerol and fatty acids, amino acids
4. nervous upsets, eating food to which you are allergic, presence of microorganisms in food or drink
5. can cause problems with peristaltic waves and gland secretions, dry mouth, "dry" stomach and intestines

CHAPTER 29

MULTIPLE CHOICE	TRUE/FALSE	MATCHING
1. B 2. C 3. D 4. C 5. D	1. + 2. + 3. ○ 4. + 5. ○	1. D 2. G 3. B 4. A 5. C

QUESTIONS

1. stormy weather, narrow roads, slippery road surfaces, darkness, fog, headlight glare
2. light stairways well; do not leave toys or other objects on stairs; keep ice and snow off porches, steps, and sidewalks; use a stepladder to reach high places; be sure that the ladder is steady; be careful when walking on waxed floors or loose rugs; keep electric cords in good condition; do not use electrical appliances in places where they may be dangerous (for example, don't use a hair dryer next to the bathtub); keep knives, garden tools, broken glass, boiling water, matches, household chemicals, and medicines out of the reach of children; keep poisons in plainly marked containers and out of the reach of children; be careful of swinging doors; be alert for gas leaks around gas appliances; put out burning matches or cigarettes carefully; do not use gasoline or flammable cleaning fluids indoors; do not start an automobile in a closed garage; be sure that guns are unloaded and out of reach; arrange bedclothes so that babies cannot get blankets and pillows over their noses and mouths; keep plastic bags out of the reach of children; do not use plastic bags as slipcovers for pillows or mattresses; keep small objects that might be swallowed or that might stick in windpipes away from babies; place window guards on upper-story windows in homes where there are small children; securely lock or remove any large container, such as an empty refrigerator, in which a child could suffocate; use caution when working with power tools; power lawn mowers are very dangerous; do not leave small children alone even for a few minutes; know what to do if fire strikes; practice Exit Drills In The Home (EDITH)
3. learn to swim well; swim out of doors only when the water temperature will not chill your body; pick a place to swim where you know the depth and current of the water, a place free from weeds that may trap you; swim where a lifeguard is present; never swim alone; know how well you can swim, and do not take chances; know how long you are able to swim; stop before you get chilled or overtired; do not swim long distances unless someone in a boat accompanies you; do not swim out to a drowning person unless you have had special training in lifesaving, but throw the person something that will float, such as an oar or a life belt; learn how to handle a boat or a canoe correctly; wear a life jacket; use boats that are in good condition and do not overload them; do not skate on ice that is less than 10 centimeters (4 inches) thick; be careful when wading in streams, since slippery rocks and a fast current can cause anyone to slip and fall; do not attempt to swim long distances underwater without coming up for air (otherwise, you may lose consciousness and drown)

4. driving over the speed limit, passing on a hill or curve, cutting in ahead of other cars, tailgating, turning without signaling
5. They have more accidents.

CHAPTER 30

MULTIPLE CHOICE	TRUE/FALSE	MATCHING
1. B 2. D 3. A 4. B 5. B	1. ○ 2. ○ 3. + 4. + 5. ○	1. A 2. G 3. B 4. D 5. E

QUESTIONS

1. Place a clean cloth over wound and press down firmly; if no bones are broken, raise injured part of body; apply pressure to artery leading to wound; use a tourniquet as a last resort.
2. Cut clothing from around burned area.
   Blisters should not be opened.
   Do not use any substance on burned area.
3. skin not broken, may be reddened
   skin blistered
   burn deep and skin destroyed
4. If there is more than one injured person, care for the most seriously injured first; keep calm and act quickly and quietly, speak in a normal tone of voice, try not to worry the victim; find out if the injured person is bleeding (serious bleeding must be stopped as quickly as possible); check for breathing, make sure that the victim has an open air passage, if the victim is not breathing, start artificial respiration at once; check for the victim's pulse, if there is no pulse, cardiopulmonary resuscitation (CPR) must be started; if there are signs of poisoning or drug use, begin the right treatment at once; do not move an injured person unless you must for the person's safety; do not let the person sit up or stand until you know how bad the injury is; get trained medical help fast; however, do not leave the victim in order to get help unless you have no other choice.
5. induce vomiting

CHAPTER 31

MULTIPLE CHOICE	TRUE/FALSE	MATCHING
1. C 2. D 3. C 4. A 5. D	1. ○ 2. ○ 3. + 4. + 5. ○	1. D 2. F 3. A 4. C 5. B

QUESTIONS

1. pressure or pain in center of chest, sweating, nausea, shortness of breath, feeling of weakness
2. Keep small articles out of their reach.
   Encourage children to stay seated and calm while eating.
   Remove all bones and shells from foods before giving them to a small child. Don't give nuts, candy containing nuts, or unchopped pieces of meat to small children.
   Be certain that toys do not contain small parts that could be chewed or pulled off.
3. Use mouth-to-mouth technique.
4. Turn child upside down and deliver blows on the back between shoulder blades.
5. Airway = Breathing = Circulation

CHAPTER 32

MULTIPLE CHOICE	TRUE/FALSE	MATCHING
1. D 2. C 3. B 4. C 5. D	1. + 2. ○ 3. ○ 4. + 5. +	1. A 2. G 3. B 4. C 5. E

Answers to Chapter Tests

QUESTIONS

1. arthritis, stomach ulcers, epilepsy, some types of cancer
2. pain is very bad and does not go away; blood is coughed up or appears in the stool or urine; diarrhea or vomiting does not stop; fever is high—38.5°C (102°F) or over; breathing is uneven, fast, or short; heartbeat is very fast or not regular; the person is unconscious; there are injuries, such as broken bones, cuts, or wounds; the person is confused or in a dazed state; the person has been bitten by a strange animal
3. breakup of relationship, death, personal failure, overwork
4. medical history, physical examination, laboratory analysis
5. Medical science is growing so quickly that it is impossible for one person to learn to treat all illnesses.

CHAPTER 33

MULTIPLE CHOICE   TRUE/FALSE   MATCHING

1. A   2. A   3. C   4. A   5. D   1. +   2. ○   3. +   4. ○   5. +   1. E   2. F   3. B   4. G   5. C

QUESTIONS

1. primary: treatment by a doctor in a clinic, emergency room, or doctor's office
   secondary: treatment given by a specialist at a private or community hospital
   tertiary: treatment given by specialists at a university hospital
2. to make sure all products meet government safety and health standards
3. name of product; name and address of manufacturer, packer, or distributor; net content of the package; active ingredients and the amount of certain ingredients; warnings and cautions needed for the protection of the user; proper directions for safe and effective use; expiration date
4. get skin tests and chest x-rays, remember the early warning signs of cancer and avoid environmental dangers that can cause cancer, learn how to take your own blood pressure and how to avoid hypertension, conduct breast self-examination
5. (1) cleaning wounds, killing bacteria; (2) decreasing acid in the stomach; (3) easing congestion

CHAPTER 34

MULTIPLE CHOICE   TRUE/FALSE   MATCHING

1. A   2. D   3. B   4. B   5. C   1. +   2. ○   3. +   4. +   5. ○   1. A   2. D   3. C   4. G   5. F

QUESTIONS

1. keeping stray animals off the street; inspecting kitchens in restaurants and hotels; removing wastes; examining the water supply; inspecting hotels, motels, and all public buildings; coordinating neighborhood health centers and clinics; collecting and analyzing vital data (needed information)
2. purifying drinking water, pasteurizing milk, disposing of sewage, inspecting food supplies, killing off insects that spread disease

3. supporting research programs in all areas of health and disease; investigating and controlling serious outbreaks of communicable diseases; preventing communicable diseases from entering the United States from other countries; certifying the safety, quality, and usefulness of vaccines; giving information about the prevention and treatment of disease
4. preventive medicine, health care methods, state of our environment
5. giving new information about medical and health matters; stopping the illegal traffic of narcotic drugs; stopping serious communicable diseases from spreading from country to country; giving financial and technical help to countries that need help in controlling communicable diseases; giving emergency aid to countries which must deal with epidemic diseases; getting all people to use good methods of fighting water, soil, food, and air pollution

CHAPTER 35

MULTIPLE CHOICE

1. D 2. C 3. B 4. D 5. B

TRUE/FALSE

1. ○ 2. + 3. + 4. + 5. ○

MATCHING

1. D 2. F 3. A 4. B 5. E

QUESTIONS

1. certified laboratory assistant, electrocardiograph technician, central service technician, dietetic assistant, operating room technician, ward clerk
2. to know rules for radiation safety, to provide care and comfort to patient and apply surgical dressings, to check physician's prescription
3. medical technologist, therapeutic recreation specialist, speech pathologist, physician, veterinarian
4. medical technologist
5. secretarial tasks, taking temperatures, measuring height and weight, sterilizing instruments, preparing young patients for examination or treatment

UNIT TESTS

This section contains one test for each of nine units and two tests for the longest unit, Unit Five. Each test is divided into three parts: 5 matching questions, 20 multiple-choice questions, and 1 essay question. The matching questions are basic competency questions. They test only the students' understanding of the main concepts of the unit. The multiple-choice questions range from average to challenging in difficulty. They demand a more comprehensive understanding of the main concepts of the unit and of specific details. The essay question has purposely been included in order to encourage students to assimilate the facts they learn and to practice and extend their writing skills. The ability to write clearly and coherently is a skill that should be developed whenever possible.

Each test may be administered in two ways to allow for convenient scoring.

(1) A complete test, including all three parts, may be given with the following scoring system:

5 matching questions at 2 points each	10 points
20 multiple-choice questions at 4 points each	80 points
1 essay question at 10 points	10 points
	Total: 100 points

(2) A partial test, consisting of the first two parts, may be given with the following scoring system:

5 matching questions at 4 points each	20 points
20 multiple choice questions at 4 points each	80 points
	Total: 100 points

NAME: _____ DATE: _____

TEST FOR UNIT ONE: ACTIVE BODY

I. Match each term on the left with the *best* description on the right. Place the letter of the description on the line provided.

_____ 1. Health   A. their movements can be controlled

_____ 2. Muscle cramp   B. physical, mental, and social well-being

_____ 3. Cartilage   C. happens to tired, strained muscles

_____ 4. Voluntary muscles   D. replaced by bone as children grow

_____ 5. Tendon   E. tissue that connects muscle to bone

II. On the line at the left of each of the following, write the letter of the choice that *best* completes the statement or answers the question.

_____ 1. Good health depends on   (A) adequate rest.   (B) balanced diet. (C) physical exercise.   (D) all of the above.

_____ 2. Heart attack, cancer, high blood pressure, and stroke are examples of (A) diseases spread by bacteria and viruses.   (B) noninfectious diseases.   (C) diseases that take place early in life.   (D) diseases that are not influenced by health habits.

_____ 3. What would happen to your leg if it were in a cast and you were not able to move it for months?   (A) The bone would become dry and brittle.   (B) Blood vessels in the bone would die.   (C) The bone would become weak due to a loss of calcium.   (D) Nothing would happen.

_____ 4. A physically healthy person   (A) keeps track of past illness. (B) is aware of how the body is presently performing and changing. (C) knows what to expect of the body at certain times in the future. (D) does all of these.

_____ 5. The hip joint is a   (A) gliding joint   (B) pivot joint   (C) hinge joint   (D) ball-and-socket joint.

_____ 6. Lactic acid   (A) helps muscles to contract.   (B) helps blood to clot.   (C) is the hollow portion inside bone.   (D) is the waste product of muscle contraction.

_____ 7. The fluid that helps to protect the brain and spinal cord by acting as a cushion is called   (A) synovial   (B) cerebrospinal   (C) fontanels (D) lymphatic.

_____ 8. Which statement about muscles is false?   (A) Muscles relax completely when a person is asleep.   (B) Healthy muscle has good tone. (C) Muscles help in circulating blood and in digesting food.   (D) When a muscle contracts, heat is released.

9. Which statement about bone is false? (A) There are many blood vessels going into and out of bone. (B) Blood cells are made inside the bone marrow. (C) Calcium and phosphorus are stored in the bone. (D) Bone is hard, dry, and is the only nonliving structure of the body.

10. The tissue which connects bone to bone is called (A) tendon (B) marrow (C) ligament (D) synovial.

11. The type of muscle which makes up the stomach and helps to mix the food is (A) smooth (B) striated (C) cardiac (D) voluntary.

12. Sore muscles (A) are caused by excessive stretching of muscles that have not been used regularly. (B) are related to the amount of lactic acid which builds up in the muscle tissue. (C) can be prevented by proper warm-up and conditioning. (D) All of these answers are correct.

13. When bone is infected and becomes inflamed, the condition is called (A) osteomyelitis (B) arthritis (C) epiphysis (D) hernia.

14. The most important organ in your body that determines endurance is the (A) heart (B) stomach (C) liver (D) kidneys.

15. In order for an exercise to be helpful to the heart muscle, it must cause the heart to beat (A) at least 70 times per minute. (B) at least 30 times per minute. (C) at least 500 times per minute. (D) at least 150 times per minute.

16. When tiny muscle fibers are torn due to contraction under a heavy load or force, the injury is called (A) muscle lameness (B) pulled muscle (C) charley horse (D) dislocation.

17. When blood vessels, nerves, soft tissue, and muscles on the front part of the thigh (quadriceps femoris) are damaged, the condition is called (A) sprain (B) charley horse (C) muscle cramps (D) muscle lameness.

18. The best way to avoid muscle cramps is to (A) warm up properly. (B) wear proper protective clothing. (C) drink an adequate amount of fluids. (D) do all of the above.

19. When the ligament between joints is torn, the condition is called a (A) sprain (B) lame muscle (C) muscle cramp (D) charley horse.

20. The proper procedure for treatment of a sprain is to (A) continue walking on it to prevent stiffening. (B) apply a cold pack for twenty minutes, every half hour. (C) apply heat immediately to reduce swelling. (D) apply a cold pack continuously for thirty-six hours.

III. Essay

Why do people avoid preventive health measures even though they know these measures can reduce the risk of noninfectious disease?

TEST FOR UNIT TWO: UNDERSTANDING YOURSELF

I. Match each term on the left with the *best* description on the right. Place the letter of the description on the line provided.

_____ 1. Security

_____ 2. Self-confidence

_____ 3. Defense mechanism

_____ 4. Mental illness

_____ 5. Mental health

A. a feeling experienced when physical and emotional needs are satisfied

B. gained by strengthening your abilities

C. ability to adapt yourself, to make good use of your skills, and to receive satisfaction out of life

D. caused by physical or emotional disorders

E. often gives a false sense of security

II. On the line at the left of each of the following, write the letter of the choice that *best* completes the statement or answers the question.

_____ 1. The need to create   (A) is felt only during adolescence and adult-hood.   (B) requires training for expression.   (C) is believed to be one of the strongest emotional needs.   (D) is felt only by children.

_____ 2. In building strengths and overcoming weaknesses, you   (A) always need the help of others.   (B) must first know the difference between characteristics you can do something about and those you cannot control. (C) need only to base your behavior on the importance of getting along with others.   (D) must take stock of yourself once or twice a year.

_____ 3. Surface causes for human behavior   (A) are usually different from the underlying causes, which are related to basic emotional needs. (B) are the only causes we need to consider.   (C) are usually emo-tional causes.   (D) sometimes do not exist.

_____ 4. In understanding human behavior, it is necessary to   (A) relate an act to basic emotional needs.   (B) know all the causes of a single act. (C) know all about the person involved.   (D) do all of these.

_____ 5. Which of these is *not* an escape mechanism?   (A) repression (B) conversion   (C) rationalization   (D) regression.

_____ 6. Direct ways of satisfying basic emotional needs include   (A) building strengths.   (B) working toward overcoming weaknesses.   (C) under-standing yourself and others.   (D) all of these.

_____ 7. A good way to get rid of anger is   (A) to be disagreeable to your friends.   (B) to hold the anger inside so that it does not show. (C) to perform a demanding physical activity.   (D) none of these.

_____ 8. Most antisocial or criminal acts are   (A) hostile behavior directed against an individual or a group.   (B) intelligent rebellion. (C) caused by poverty.   (D) necessary ways of showing hostility.

9. Which of the following is a true statement?   (A) Fear is a feeling that can never be a help to you.   (B) Fear is caused by adrenaline in the blood stream.   (C) Fear sometimes causes you to be stronger than normal.   (D) Fear of the unknown cannot be overcome.

10. Fear, anxieties, and worries are   (A) often useful in preparing us for action.   (B) seldom of any value.   (C) characteristics we could get along without.   (D) not felt by mentally healthy people.

11. Which of the following is *not* a defense mechanism?   (A) rationalization   (B) guilt feelings   (C) compensation   (D) regression.

12. In the United States, patients with mental illness use   (A) only a small percentage of the hospital beds.   (B) all of the hospital beds. (C) almost half of the hospital beds.   (D) none of the hospital beds.

13. Stress is   (A) always harmful.   (B) not experienced by mentally healthy people.   (C) a response only to physical danger.   (D) sometimes necessary.

14. By five years of age, a child has   (A) developed behavior patterns which cannot be changed.   (B) set up patterns of behavior and ways of reacting to different situations.   (C) learned most of the personal feelings and the feelings about others that will ever be learned. (D) not developed any important attitudes or feelings yet.

15. In evaluating one's own personality, it is important to consider (A) how comfortable one feels about oneself.   (B) how comfortable one feels with others.   (C) how successfully one meets the demands of life.   (D) all of these.

16. Which of the following statements is *false*?   (A) Some adults act immature at times.   (B) High school students seldom show maturity in their behavior.   (C) Most people act mature at some times and immature at other times.   (D) A person is considered to be mature if that person acts mature most of the time.

17. Finding your "identity" means   (A) that you have a sense of purpose in life.   (B) that you have a set of values and goals.   (C) that you feel comfortable about yourself and about being with other people. (D) all of these.

18. A demand made on the body is known as   (A) distress   (B) stress (C) stressor   (D) none of these.

19. When making an important decision, it is a good idea to   (A) think about all the choices that you have.   (B) seek help.   (C) think about what might happen as a result of your decision.   (D) do all of these.

20. Which of the following statements is *false*?   (A) Parental acceptance of a child helps to develop a mature personality in the child. (B) Parental rejection may do lasting damage to a child.   (C) Family relationships are not important during adolescence.   (D) The family is one of the biggest influences on personality.

III. Essay

Describe a mentally healthy person.

NAME: _____ DATE: _____

TEST FOR UNIT THREE: HUMAN SEXUALITY

I. Match each term on the left with the *best* description on the right. Place the letter of the description on the line provided.

_____ 1. Ovum

_____ 2. Sperm

_____ 3. Testes

_____ 4. Ovaries

_____ 5. Placenta

A. female reproductive cell

B. two organs in the female which produce eggs and hormones

C. the organ by which the fetus is attached to the uterus

D. two organs in the male which produce sperm and hormones

E. male reproductive cell

II. On the line at the left of each of the following, write the letter of the choice that *best* completes the statement or answers the question.

_____ 1. In boys, puberty usually occurs between the age of (A) 10 and 12. (B) 12 and 15. (C) 9 and 14. (D) 15 and 18.

_____ 2. Usually, girls mature (A) at the exact age that boys mature. (B) earlier than boys mature. (C) later than boys mature. (D) more slowly than boys mature.

_____ 3. The testes are formed in the (A) scrotum before birth. (B) scrotum after birth. (C) abdomen before birth. (D) abdomen after birth.

_____ 4. A sperm cell (A) can move by itself. (B) can be moved only by liquids. (C) matures and is released about once a month. (D) is not a living cell until fertilization takes place.

_____ 5. An ovum (A) can move by itself. (B) is moved by gravity and by suction. (C) does not move until fertilized. (D) never moves until it disintegrates.

_____ 6. Menopause (A) usually happens between the ages of 30 and 40. (B) is the period when production of ova stops. (C) happens once each month. (D) is normally completed in three to seven days.

_____ 7. Ovulation is (A) the name given to the fertilized ovum. (B) the process of fertilization. (C) the release and descent of a mature ovum from an ovary. (D) all of these.

_____ 8. Conception can happen (A) only when a sperm and an ovum unite. (B) only during menstruation. (C) three weeks out of every month. (D) only when the ovum has been discharged into the vagina.

_____ 9. A sign that a woman may be pregnant is (A) a missed menstrual period. (B) enlargement of the breasts. (C) a feeling of tiredness. (D) all of these.

10. The endometrium   (A) is the lining of the uterus.   (B) is the name for the fertilized ovum.   (C) separates from the walls of the uterus and is discharged through the vagina after conception takes place. (D) is none of these.

11. In the growing embryo,   (A) flat cells become skin cells. (B) spindle-shaped cells become muscle cells.   (C) six-sided cells become liver cells.   (D) all of these developments take place.

12. The umbilicus is   (A) another word for navel.   (B) the cord which attaches the placenta to the baby.   (C) the lining of the uterus. (D) none of these.

13. Which of these statements is *false*?   (A) Nicotine and alcohol are absorbed into the blood and can pass through the placenta into the baby's body.   (B) The exact amount of nicotine and alcohol that may be harmful to a fetus is not known.   (C) German measles in a pregnant woman may do great damage to an unborn baby.   (D) An expectant mother does not need medical care until about the fourth month of pregnancy.

14. Identical twins   (A) are called Siamese twins.   (B) begin as one fertilized ovum.   (C) are attached to separate placentas.   (D) are not necessarily the same sex.

15. Fraternal twins   (A) are always the same sex.   (B) are attached to a single placenta.   (C) begin life as two fertilized ova.   (D) begin as two ova fertilized by one sperm cell.

16. Which of these statements is *false*?   (A) Semen is a mixture of sperm and fluids from glands.   (B) Millions of sperm are carried in semen. (C) Semen can pass out of the body during sleep.   (D) Semen is emitted through the urethra and the penis at the same time as urine.

17. Fertilization of the egg usually takes place   (A) in the vagina. (B) in the uterus.   (C) in the Fallopian tube.   (D) in the ovaries.

18. Relationships within the family can greatly influence   (A) your decisions.   (B) your ability to get along with people outside of the family.   (C) your happiness.   (D) all of these.

19. Separation rates and divorce rates are highest for those who marry (A) late in life.   (B) between the ages of 30 and 34.   (C) between the ages of 24 and 28.   (D) between the ages of 15 and 19.

20. Correct information about contraception can be obtained: (A) from a physician, a hospital clinic, or a Planned Parenthood Association. (B) only from a physician.   (C) from any adult.   (D) only if you can afford it.

III. Essay

Knowing whether or not to get married, and when to get married, are important decisions. What do you think a couple should consider before getting married?

TEST FOR UNIT FOUR: ENVIRONMENT AND HEREDITY

I. Match each term on the left with the *best* description on the right. Place the letter of the description on the line provided.

_____ 1. Tumor

_____ 2. Amniocentesis

_____ 3. Carcinogen

_____ 4. Chromosomes

_____ 5. Genetics

A. a group of cells that grow together in a mass or a lump

B. paired structures on which genes are arranged

C. the study of heredity

D. a substance that causes cancer

E. the process of removing fluid from the uterus to examine the cells of the fetus

II. On the line at the left of each of the following, write the letter of the choice that *best* completes the statement or answers the question.

_____ 1. Which of the following statements is *false*? (A) There are many types of cancer. (B) Cancer can occur in any tissue or organ of the body. (C) The rate of growth of cancer cells is always the same. (D) Cancer cells do not form useful tissues and organs.

_____ 2. Cancer (A) can be prevented. (B) is one of the major causes of death in the United States today. (C) has no single cause. (D) all of these.

_____ 3. Metastasis is (A) a substance that causes cancer. (B) the process of a cancer spreading to another part of the body. (C) a cancer treatment. (D) none of these.

_____ 4. Which of the following is a *true* statement? (A) All tumors are fatal. (B) Benign tumors grow to a certain size and then stop growing. (C) Cancers are benign tumors. (D) Cancers do not occur among infants.

_____ 5. Which of the following statements is *false*? (A) Exposure to asbestos for many years may cause a type of lung cancer. (B) Workers who come in contact with vinyl chloride may get a type of liver cancer. (C) Heavy smokers have a much higher rate of lung, larynx, and esophageal cancer than nonsmokers. (D) Sailors, farmers, and others who spend many hours in the sun are immune to skin cancer.

_____ 6. A biopsy is (A) a type of tumor. (B) a form of radiation. (C) the removal of a small amount of tissue to look for abnormal cells under a microscope. (D) a form of chemotherapy.

_____ 7. Which of the following is *not* a pollutant? (A) sulfuric acid piped from factories into streams. (B) oxygen in the atmosphere. (C) untreated sewage that has been run directly into streams. (D) carbon monoxide from automobile exhausts.

_____ 8. Carbon monoxide is (A) colorless and odorless. (B) poisonous. (C) in the air from automobile exhausts. (D) all of these.

_____ 9. Substances harmful to fish in the water include (A) human waste and other garbage. (B) pesticides and detergents. (C) oils and fertilizers. (D) all of these.

_____ 10. Lifelong hearing loss may be caused by being exposed for too long a time to noise levels above (A) 10 decibels (B) 20 decibels (C) 60 decibels (D) 85 decibels.

_____ 11. A radioactive substance (A) is a material that gives off radiation. (B) can cause leukemia. (C) can cause a genetic disorder. (D) is all of these.

_____ 12. The way amino acids are to be arranged in order to make up the proteins is determined by (A) DNA (B) the genetic code (C) genes (D) all of these.

_____ 13. Enzymes, hormones, and hemoglobin are essentially (A) antibiotics (B) genes (C) proteins (D) all of these.

_____ 14. A person with blue eyes must have two genes for blue eyes. This is because the gene for blue eyes is (A) dominant (B) on the X chromosome (C) recessive (D) none of these.

_____ 15. When both parents appear normal, and yet have a child with an inherited birth defect, the type of inheritance is called (A) recessive (B) dominant (C) sex-linked (D) cloning.

_____ 16. Which one of the following genetic defects does not appear at birth? (A) cleft lip or palate (B) Huntington's disease (C) polydactylism (D) Down's syndrome.

_____ 17. How many chromosomes do sperm and egg cells have? (A) 46 (B) 45 (C) 23 (D) 22.

_____ 18. If the mother has brown eyes because she has inherited the genes for brown eyes from both of her parents, and if the father has blue eyes because both his parents have blue eyes, what are the chances of any of their children being brown-eyed? (A) 50 percent chance (B) 100 percent chance (C) 25 percent chance (D) no chance.

_____ 19. One of the factors which can increase the risk of Down's syndrome is (A) age of the mother. (B) deformed sperm. (C) age of the father. (D) environment.

_____ 20. A genetic disorder affecting the shape and the oxygen-carrying ability of red blood cells is called (A) galactocemia (B) Tay-Sachs disease (C) sickle-cell anemia (D) sickle-cell trait.

III. Essay

What are the seven warning signals of cancer?

NAME: _____ DATE: _____

TEST FOR UNIT FIVE: FUNCTIONING BODY (Part One)

I. Match each term on the left with the *best* description on the right. Place the letter of the description on the line provided.

_____ 1. Inspiration

_____ 2. Neurons

_____ 3. Reflex

_____ 4. Myopia

_____ 5. Hypertension

A. cells in the nervous system that carry messages or impulses

B. nearsightedness

C. a condition in which a person's blood pressure is continually high

D. the process of taking air into the lungs

E. an automatic reaction directed by the spinal cord

II. On the line at the left of each of the following, write the letter of the choice that *best* completes the statement or answers the question.

_____

1. What distinguishes humans from all other living species?   (A) the endocrine system   (B) the nervous system   (C) the circulatory system   (D) the respiratory system.

_____

2. Which one of the following is a function of the autonomic system? (A) playing the piano   (B) scratching an itch   (C) combing hair (D) blushing.

_____

3. Which nerves carry impulses to muscles to bring about contractions? (A) sensory   (B) motor   (C) dendrite   (D) involuntary.

_____

4. The part of the brain which is responsible for coordinating muscle movement so that posture and balance can be maintained is the (A) cerebellum   (B) pons   (C) midbrain   (D) cerebrum.

_____

5. A disease of the nervous system that affects the membrane surrounding the brain and the spinal cord is called   (A) stroke   (B) poliomyelitis   (C) meningitis   (D) epilepsy.

_____

6. The brain can become permanently damaged if it is deprived of oxygen for   (A) 10 seconds   (B) 4 to 5 minutes   (C) 30 seconds (D) even 2 seconds.

_____

7. The electroencephalograph records   (A) shock waves.   (B) brain waves.   (C) sound waves through the ear.   (D) heat waves throughout the body.

_____

8. The pathway of light from the front part of the eye to the retina is (A) sclera, pupil, lens, aqueous humor.   (B) cornea, lens, pupil, iris. (C) conjunctiva, lens, iris, aqueous humor.   (D) conjunctiva, cornea, aqueous humor, lens.

_____

9. The muscle which helps to change the shape of the lenses for near vision is   (A) ciliary   (B) hamstring   (C) triceps   (D) sclera.

_____ 10. The person who is qualified to care for diseased eyes and to prescribe medication is an (A) optometrist (B) optician (C) ophthalmologist (D) otologist.

_____ 11. The pathway of sound from the outer ear to the inner ear is (A) external auditory canal, malleus, oval window, incus, stapes. (B) external auditory canal, malleus, incus, stapes. (C) external auditory canal, incus, malleus, stapes. (D) inner ear, stapes, malleus, incus.

_____ 12. The eustachian tube is important because (A) it keeps bacteria out of the middle ear. (B) it balances the air pressure in the middle ear. (C) it has liquid in it to keep the air moist. (D) it transports sound waves from the outer ear to the inner ear.

_____ 13. The part of the inner ear responsible for receiving sound waves is the (A) cochlea (B) semicircular canal (C) vestibule (D) pinna.

_____ 14. Which one of the following is not a function of the circulatory system? (A) to carry digested food from the small intestine. (B) to carry hormones from the endocrine glands. (C) to help fight infection and to help blood in clotting. (D) to produce white and red blood cells.

_____ 15. A condition in which the leukocyte number increase to ten or more times the usual number is called (A) anemia (B) hemophilia (C) leukemia (D) hemorrhage.

_____ 16. Blood pressure (A) is the amount of pressure within the heart. (B) is the amount of pressure in the veins. (C) is the amount of pressure in the capillaries. (D) is the pressure of blood against the walls of the arteries.

_____ 17. The most common form of heart disease in the United States (A) is called rheumatic heart disease. (B) involves the coronary arteries. (C) is due to enlargement of the aorta. (D) is heart murmur.

_____ 18. Which one of the following is the correct order of air passage? (A) nose, larynx, trachea, bronchi, alveoli (B) nose, larynx, bronchi, trachea, alveoli (C) alveoli, trachea, larynx, nose, bronchi (D) nose, bronchi, alveoli, trachea, larynx.

_____ 19. A respiratory disorder in which the alveoli sacs lose their elasticity is called (A) bronchitis (B) emphysema (C) asthma (D) pneumonia.

_____ 20. With asthma, (A) home remedies are the best cure. (B) not enough mucus is secreted, and the bronchi are dry. (C) dust is the only cause. (D) a less than normal amount of air gets through to the lungs because of the excess mucus in the bronchi tubes.

III. Essay

Discuss four ways by which a young person can reduce the risk of acquiring cardiovascular diseases later in life.

204

TEST FOR UNIT FIVE: FUNCTIONING BODY (Part Two)

I. Match each term on the left with the *best* description on the right. Place the letter of the description on the line provided.

_____ 1. Metabolism

_____ 2. Iodine

_____ 3. Islands of Langerhans

_____ 4. Hypoglycemia

_____ 5. ACTH

A. gland tissue that produces insulin

B. low blood sugar

C. chemical change that goes on in cells to support life

D. hormone produced by the pituitary

E. substance that the thyroid gland needs in order to work properly

II. On the line at the left of each of the following, write the letter of the choice that *best* completes the statement or answers the question.

_____ 1. The layer of skin that contains blood vessels, nerves, and glands is the (A) dermis   (B) subdermis   (C) epidermis   (D) layer just beneath the fatty tissue and the muscles.

_____ 2. Contact dermatitis is caused by   (A) eating vegetables that are not cooked properly.   (B) oils on plants that irritate the skin. (C) allergy to seafood.   (D) all of these.

_____ 3. The best way to get a suntan is to   (A) limit exposure to the sun at first and then slowly increase the time.   (B) use a sunlamp for at least one hour.   (C) expose the skin to the ultraviolet light of the sun for several days.   (D) use suntan lotions.

_____ 4. The skin helps to lower body temperature by   (A) opening its pores to allow cool air to rush in.   (B) evaporating the perspiration released through its pores.   (C) closing its pores to prevent warm air from entering.   (D) shivering until all the pores are wide open.

_____ 5. A skin infection that causes itching and sores on the scalp is called (A) hives   (B) boils   (C) acne   (D) ringworm.

_____ 6. Acne can be best prevented by   (A) washing the infected area with soap and warm water as often as possible.   (B) avoiding greasy creams and oily preparations.   (C) eating well-balanced meals. (D) doing all of the above.

_____ 7. Hair and nails have one thing in common, that is,   (A) they both are outgrowths of the epidermis.   (B) they both contain nerve endings. (C) they both grow at the same rate.   (D) they both are pigmented.

_____ 8. Endocrine glands   (A) do not have ducts leading to organs. (B) secrete directly into the circulatory system.   (C) secrete hormones.   (D) do all of the above.

_____ 9. An endocrine gland that controls body growth is the   (A) pituitary (B) thymus   (C) adrenal   (D) none of the above.

10. The gland that influences the rate of metabolism of the cell is the
(A) thymus   (B) thyroid   (C) pineal   (D) parathyroid.
11. The parathyroid glands   (A) regulate the level of calcium and
phosphorus in the blood.   (B) control the thyroid gland.   (C) are
found directly on top of the adrenal glands.   (D) all of the above.
12. Which hormone is responsible for an increase in muscle tone and for
preparation for an emergency?   (A) insulin   (B) testosterone
(C) adrenaline   (D) thyroxine.
13. Which one of the following endocrine glands is not found in the neck or
the head region?   (A) pituitary   (B) parathyroid   (C) thyroid
(D) adrenal.
14. Which one of the following is not a function of the pituitary gland?
(A) control of body temperature.   (B) control of the secretions of
the thyroid, gonads, and adrenal glands.   (C) secretion of adrenaline
during an emergency.   (D) secretion of ACTH to make the adrenal
gland produce cortisone.
15. Which one of the following statements is true?   (A) Only the enamel
of the tooth is alive.   (B) The entire tooth is hard and nonliving.
(C) Teeth contain many nerves but lack blood vessels.   (D) The tooth,
with the exception of the enamel, is alive.
16. Dental caries can be prevented if   (A) a proper diet is eaten.
(B) fluoride is used.   (C) flossing and brushing are performed
regularly.   (D) all of these preventive measures are taken.
17. An orthodontist is a specialist in   (A) correcting malocclusion.
(B) cleaning teeth.   (C) filling cavities.   (D) doing none of the
above.
18. The three major parts of the tooth are the   (A) enamel, dentine, and
root canal   (B) crown, neck, and root   (C) gum, root, and jawbone   (D) pupl cavity, nerves, and blood vessels.
19. Gums can be injured by   (A) improper use of dental floss.
(B) aggressive use of a toothbrush.   (C) accumulation of tartar between teeth.   (D) all of these.
20. Halitosis   (A) can be caused by infection of the nose, the sinus, and
the tonsils.   (B) can be eliminated permanently by using mouthwash.
(C) is not related to the teeth.   (D) always occurs after a meal.

III.

Explain how the adrenal gland can help prepare an athlete for an important game.

206

TEST FOR UNIT SIX: SOCIAL DRUGS: YOUR DECISION

I. Match each term on the left with the *best* description on the right. Place the letter of the description on the line provided.

_____ 1. Nicotine

_____ 2. Involuntary smoking

_____ 3. Alcohol

_____ 4. OTC drugs

_____ 5. caffeine

A. a drug that causes insomnia and nervousness

B. a depressant drug

C. a poisonous drug in tobacco that causes the heart rate and the blood pressure to increase

D. unwillingly inhaling smoke from a burning tobacco product

E. drugs that can be bought without prescription

II. On the line at the left of each of the following, write the letter of the choice that *best* completes the statement or answers the question.

_____ 1. Tobacco smoke contains   (A) nicotine, which seems to be the addictive element in tobacco.   (B) tars which destroy the cilia in the lungs of smokers.   (C) carbon monoxide and hydrogen cyanide gases. (D) all of these.

_____ 2. Which of the following statements is *false*?   (A) Excessive use of tobacco can damage vision or hearing.   (B) The brown stains from cigarette smoke on teeth and hands are caused by tar. (C) Smoking puts additional strain on the heart and on circulation. (D) Cigarette smoking causes many premature deaths.

_____ 3. Smoking causes   (A) lowering of the temperature of the skin. (B) a lessened ability to taste and smell.   (C) the small arteries to become smaller.   (D) all of these.

_____ 4. Coronary heart disease   (A) is caused only by smoking.   (B) causes more than twice as many deaths among cigarette smokers as among nonsmokers.   (C) is seldom serious today.   (D) affects only males.

_____ 5. The risk of lung cancer   (A) is greater for smokers than for nonsmokers.   (B) is about the same for pipe smokers and for cigarette smokers.   (C) has increased in recent years for women who smoke. (D) A and C.

_____ 6. Sidestream smoke   (A) is the smoke inhaled and then exhaled by the smoker.   (B) is the smoke that goes directly into the air from the burning end of a tobacco product.   (C) is not as harmful to the nonsmoker as mainstream smoke.   (D) B and C.

_____ 7. When a person quits the smoking habit, the individual   (A) increases the likelihood of living longer.   (B) begins to breathe easier and to cough less.   (C) gives the body a chance to repair the damage caused by smoking.   (D) does all of these.

8. Alcohol is   (A) low in calories.   (B) usually used in moderate amounts by alcoholics.   (C) not habit-forming.   (D) absorbed directly from the stomach and the small intestine into the bloodstream.

9. Alcoholism   (A) can result in severe damage to the heart, the liver, and the kidneys.   (B) cannot be defined as a serious illness.   (C) is a rare disease today.   (D) affects a person's physical health but not a person's mental health.

10. While alcohol probably has some effect on all the organs, its greatest effect is on the   (A) muscles   (B) digestive tract   (C) brain (D) heart.

11. Which of these statements is *false*?   (A) Alcohol is a drug. (B) Alcoholic beverages, if used in moderation, act as a sedative. (C) An ounce or more of alcohol is likely to cause a person to become dizzy and lightheaded.   (D) Drinking alcoholic beverages helps a person to keep warm on a cold day.

12. Which of these statement is *true*?   (A) Alcohol dulls the nerve centers of the brain.   (B) The blood vessels of the skin contract after the use of alcohol.   (C) Alcohol always causes some degree of indigestion. (D) Alcohol is a stimulant.

13. Drinking a large quantity of alcohol   (A) can result in unconsciousness but not in death.   (B) has no effect on an alcoholic.   (C) may paralyze the nerve centers in the brain that control the action of the heart and the lungs, thereby causing death.   (D) cannot be dangerous if the alcohol is consumed over a period of several hours.

14. Which one of the following is not a depressant?   (A) alcohol (B) tranquilizer   (C) cocaine   (D) barbiturate.

15. Amphetamines   (A) are powerful depressants.   (B) stimulate the central nervous system.   (C) have no medical use.   (D) slow the heartbeat and breathing.

16. Heroin is   (A) a weak pain reliever   (B) a barbiturate (C) made from codeine   (D) an opiate.

17. A narcotic that can be found in OTC decongestants and in OTC pain killers is   (A) cocaine   (B) codeine   (C) heroin   (D) valium.

18. Which one of the following drugs is not a narcotic?   (A) codeine (B) morphine   (C) marijuana   (D) heroin.

19. Women who are pregnant should be careful when taking drugs because (A) the drugs can pass through the placenta to the fetus.   (B) the drugs will have a greater effect on the fetus.   (C) birth defects can occur.   (D) all of these can happen.

20. A drug found in tea, coffee, chocolate, and colas is   (A) cocaine (B) caffeine   (C) codeine   (D) phencyclidine.

III. Essay

What are some signs that a person has an alcohol problem?

TEST FOR UNIT SEVEN: PREVENTING COMMUNICABLE DISEASES

I. Match each term on the left with the *best* description on the right. Place the letter of the description on the line provided.

_____ 1. Antibody

_____ 2. Communicable disease

_____ 3. Sexually transmitted disease

_____ 4. Active immunity

_____ 5. Passive immunity

A. a disease that may be passed from one person to another

B. a disease spread from one person to another through sexual contact

C. a person is given antibodies produced by another person or animal

D. a person's body produces its own antibodies

E. a substance made in the blood that acts against disease organisms

II. On the line at the left of each of the following, write the letter of the choice that *best* completes the statement or answers the question.

_____ 1. Two serious infectious diseases that changed history by causing death to certain armies were   (A) chickenpox and measles   (B) smallpox and typhoid fever   (C) influenza and cancer   (D) tuberculosis and heart disease.

_____ 2. A carrier is a person who   (A) carries disease organisms.   (B) spreads disease organisms to other persons.   (C) is not sick with the disease that is being carried.   (D) is all of these.

_____ 3. The incubation period is   (A) the same for all diseases.   (B) the time between the appearance of symptoms and the end of the disease in the body.   (C) the time between the entrance of disease organisms into the body and the appearance of symptoms.   (D) the time period that a disease organism is studied in the laboratory.

_____ 4. The body's first line of defense against disease organisms is provided by the   (A) endocrine system   (B) skin, mucous membranes, and bodily secretions   (C) digestive system   (D) circulatory system.

_____ 5. Which of the following statements is *false*?   (A) Influenza is an infectious disease.   (B) Symptoms of influenza are fever, cough, and muscle aches.   (C) Epidemics of influenza do not occur today.   (D) Influenza is often called the "flu."

_____ 6. Hepatitis   (A) means inflammation of the lungs.   (B) is caused by a virus.   (C) is a swelling of the liver.   (D) B and C

_____ 7. Mononucleosis   (A) is a rare disease.   (B) happens most often in young children.   (C) is caused by a virus that may be spread through the saliva.   (D) cannot be prevented.

_____ 8. Tetanus   (A) is also called lockjaw.   (B) is caused by a bacterium. (C) involves muscle spasms.   (D) all of these are true.

_____ 9. DPT vaccine gives protection against   (A) rubella, polio, and tetanus (B) measles, polio, and pertussis   (C) diphtheria, pertussis, and tetanus   (D) diphtheria, polio, and tetanus.

_____ 10. Which of the following statements is *false*?   (A) Mumps may occur in children, teenagers, or adults.   (B) Patients with mumps get swollen hands and feet.   (C) Mumps may cause sterility or brain damage. (D) In some cases, vaccination can produce immunity to mumps.

_____ 11. Rubella   (A) is called German measles.   (B) is called three-day measles.   (C) can cause a fetus to become deformed if a pregnant woman contracts the disease.   (D) is all of these.

_____ 12. Tetanus organisms enter the body   (A) in food.   (B) through wounds.   (C) in air that is breathed.   (D) in water.

_____ 13. Which of the following statements is *false*?   (A) It is important to keep a record of your immunizations.   (B) Tetanus immunizations should be kept up-to-date with booster shots about every ten years. (C) We now have a vaccine available for every communicable disease. (D) The good effects of immunization outweigh the risks.

_____ 14. Which of the following statements is *false*?   (A) The most common pathogens are bacteria and viruses.   (B) Infectious diseases are caused by pathogens.   (C) No infectious disease can be prevented by vaccine.   (D) Viruses are smaller than bacteria.

_____ 15. Gonorrhea   (A) is caused by bacteria called gonococci.   (B) can usually be treated successfully with antibiotics.   (C) can be diagnosed by checking a sample of secretion from the cervix, vagina, or urethra. (D) all of these are true.

_____ 16. Complications of gonorrhea are   (A) sterility or crippling arthritis (B) cancer   (C) vision loss or hearing loss   (D) heart diseases.

_____ 17. During childbirth, gonorrhea usually attacks the newborn's   (A) eyes (B) ears   (C) brain   (D) heart.

_____ 18. Which of the following statements is *false*?   (A) The bacterium that causes syphilis enters the body through a break in the skin or through mucous membranes.   (B) A pregnant woman may pass the syphilis infection to her unborn baby.   (C) Even without treatment, the symptoms of syphilis will disappear.   (D) During the latent stage of syphilis, the person usually has a rash and sores.

_____ 19. A chancre   (A) is a painless open sore.   (B) usually appears 2 to 6 weeks after contact with an infected person.   (C) is very infectious. (D) is all of these.

_____ 20. A person with a sexually transmitted disease   (A) can treat the disease successfully with self-medication.   (B) should tell his or her partner so that the partner can also be examined.   (C) cannot catch the same disease again.   (D) B and C.

III. Essay

If there is a chance that a person has a sexually transmitted disease, what steps should this person take?

210

TEST FOR UNIT EIGHT: FOOD, DIET, DIGESTION

I. Match each term on the left with the *best* description on the right. Place the letter of the description on the line provided.

_____ 1. Amino acids   A. stored sugar

_____ 2. Glycogen   B. Recommended Daily Allowance

_____ 3. Empty-calorie foods C. a severe form of food poisoning

_____ 4. RDA   D. the body's building blocks that form specific proteins

_____ 5. Botulism   E. foods that are high in calories and low in nutrients

II. On the line at the left of each of the following, write the letter of the choice that *best* completes the statement or answers the question.

_____ 1. Fats are (A) very bad for you because they can cause hardening of the arteries. (B) important to your diet because they help absorb certain vitamins and add flavor to foods. (C) a very poor source of energy. (D) only found in meat.

_____ 2. Iron is important in your diet because (A) hemoglobin in red blood cells is made from it. (B) without it muscles cannot efficiently contract. (C) a lack of it can cause a form of anemia. (D) all of these facts are true.

_____ 3. An overweight person can safely lose weight by (A) following the quick weight-loss diet. (B) reducing the calories taken in and by exercising. (C) fasting for fifteen days. (D) taking diet pills.

_____ 4. Athletes (A) do not need a special diet. (B) need more vitamins A, C, and E. (C) should eat a nice, juicy steak before a competition. (D) should eat honey, yogurt, and high proteins before a competition.

_____ 5. Heat cramps can be prevented during a sports event (A) by eating sugar cubes or hard candy during the game. (B) by avoiding any form of liquid. (C) by drinking fruit juice or water in small amounts. (D) if large amounts of salt tablets are taken.

_____ 6. A person who eats no meat or eggs, but drinks milk, is called a (A) lacto-vegetarian (B) lacto-ovo-vegetarian (C) ovo-vegetarian (D) pure vegetarian.

_____ 7. In order to lose one pound of fat, how many calories must be used? (A) 500 (B) 1000 (C) 3500 (D) 10 000.

_____ 8. The level of cholesterol in the body can increase by (A) stress. (B) lack of exercise. (C) eating too many saturated fats. (D) all of the above.

_____ 9. The U.S. RDA   (A) differs according to age, body size, sex, and how active a person is.   (B) gives the exact amounts of nutrients needed by everyone in the world.   (C) is ten times what the average person needs to avoid diseases.   (D) is established by the food manufacturers.

_____ 10. What is the purpose of drying and smoking foods, and of using salt, sugar, and nitrites on foods?   (A) to enrich them.   (B) to flavor them.   (C) to gel them.   (D) to preserve them.

_____ 11. The advantage of using additives is to   (A) make certain food available all year round.   (B) restore nutrients that were lost during processing.   (C) improve color and taste.   (D) do all of the above.

_____ 12. Sugar   (A) has nutritive value in addition to calories.   (B) can be found in many foods as an additve.   (C) is found only in sweet foods, such as cake, candy, and cookies.   (D) must be added to foods because most starches do not contain sugar.

_____ 13. Open dating   (A) assures consumers that foods on grocery shelves are fresh.   (B) allows consumers to compare the prices of two packages of similar foods.   (C) tells how many additives are included in the food.   (D) tells who packaged the food and the location of the manufacturer.

_____ 14. Organic foods   (A) are grown without the use of synthetic fertilizers, pesticides, or herbicides.   (B) are grown with many organic chemicals, such as DDT and hormones.   (C) are inexpensive to grow because no chemicals are used.   (D) can be grown in today's environment due to lack of harmful contaminants.

_____ 15. The stomach   (A) completely digests all the foods that enter it.   (B) is the most important organ of the digestive system.   (C) mixes the food with gastric juices, which results in a soupy liquid called chyme.   (D) does all of the above.

_____ 16. The liver   (A) is responsible for producing red blood cells.   (B) secretes bile, which aids in breaking down fats.   (C) is responsible for digesting starch.   (D) does all of the above.

_____ 17. Insulin   (A) is secreted by the pancreas.   (B) is a hormone which helps glucose to enter the cells.   (C) deficiency leads to diabetes.   (D) does all of the above.

_____ 18. Ulcers are usually caused by   (A) nervous tension, which causes acid to be secreted in large amounts.   (B) overeating.   (C) too much mucus.   (D) an insufficient amount of insulin.

_____ 19. Which one of the following is the correct order for the passage of food?   (A) esophagus, duodenum, colon, stomach.   (B) duodenum, stomach, small intestine, colon.   (C) esophagus, stomach, small intestine, colon.   (D) esophagus, colon, duodenum, stomach.

_____ 20. Constipation can generally be caused by   (A) lack of exercise.   (B) a diet that lacks fibers.   (C) weak muscle tone in the colon.   (D) all of the above.

III. Essay

Explain the statement, "You are what you eat."

TEST FOR UNIT NINE: SAFETY AND EMERGENCY CARE

I. Match each term on the left with the *best* description on the right. Place the letter of the description on the line provided.

_____ 1. Accidents

A. artificial circulation and artificial respiration

_____ 2. Antidote

B. main cause of death among young people

_____ 3. Artificial respiration

C. works against a poison

_____ 4. Cardiopulmonary resuscitation

D. forcing air into and out of the lungs of a person who has stopped breathing

_____ 5. Cardiac arrest

E. absence of a heartbeat or pulse

II. On the line at the left of each of the following, write the letter of the choice that *best* completes the statement or answers the question.

_____ 1. Accidents may be caused by which of the following driving practices? (A) driving over the speed limit. (B) passing on a hill or curve. (C) following the car ahead too closely. (D) all of these.

_____ 2. Which of the following products is most often involved in a serious accident? (A) a ladder (B) a football (C) a boat (D) a bicycle.

_____ 3. Which of the following is *not* a water safety rule? (A) Learn to swim well enough so that you can swim alone. (B) Swim out of doors only when the water will not chill your body. (C) Do not swim long distances unless someone in a boat accompanies you. (D) Do not skate on ice that is less than 10 centimeters (4 inches) thick.

_____ 4. In automobile driving safety, drivers below the age of 25 have (A) the poorest record. (B) the second to the best record. (C) an average record. (D) the best record.

_____ 5. In giving first aid, it is important first to (A) stop any serious bleeding. (B) give artificial respiration. (C) treat for shock. (D) clean any wound.

_____ 6. If a person has taken poison by mouth and is still conscious, you should (A) immediately give large amounts of liquid. (B) give artificial respiration at once. (C) put the victim to bed and keep the victim warm. (D) all of these.

_____ 7. Treatment for shock includes (A) keeping the victim warm and on his or her back. (B) forcing the victim to stand and walk. (C) giving large amounts of liquid. (D) none of these.

_____ 8. Bleeding (A) is always serious and must be stopped at once. (B) is called a hemorrhage if it is serious or an abnormal amount. (C) can usually be stopped by applying firm pressure directly onto the wound. (D) B and C.

_____ 9. If a sick or injured child is not breathing, you should start artificial respiration   (A) as soon as you have a physician's permission. (B) as soon as you have a parent's permission.   (C) immediately. (D) A and B.

_____ 10. You should avoid moving a person who   (A) has a fracture of the hip. (B) has a fracture of the neck or back.   (C) is in shock.   (D) is in any of these conditions.

_____ 11. When a bone is out of place at a joint, the condition is   (A) a dislocation   (B) a sprain   (C) a fracture   (D) a strain.

_____ 12. A first-degree burn   (A) is the most serious kind of burn.   (B) is a burn in which the skin is reddened.   (C) is a burn in which the skin is destroyed.   (D) A and C.

_____ 13. Which of the following statements is _true_?   (A) A person whose clothes are burning should run, or be rushed, toward water.   (B) A person whose clothes are on fire should be rolled on the ground or wrapped in heavy material.   (C) Heat exhaustion is caused by too much salt in the blood.   (D) Rub frostbitten toes with snow.

_____ 14. In giving first aid for sunstroke, you should   (A) use ice bags or wet cloths.   (B) give the victim a stimulant.   (C) keep the victim warm. (D) keep the person standing and active.

_____ 15. Early warning signs of a heart attack may include   (A) pain in the chest.   (B) sweating, nausea, and shortness of breath.   (C) the symptoms becoming less severe and then returning.   (D) all of these.

_____ 16. To find out if an unconscious victim is breathing,   (A) check the victim's eyes.   (B) check for cyanosis.   (C) check the victim's pulse.   (D) look, listen, and feel for signs of air and chest movement.

_____ 17. In most cases the easiest way to open a victim's airway is to   (A) wipe out the mouth and throat.   (B) strike the victim on the back. (C) turn the victim's head to one side.   (D) tilt the victim's head back.

_____ 18. When only one rescuer performs CPR, the ratio of chest presses to breaths for any adult victim is   (A) 12 chest presses to 2 breaths. (B) 5 chest presses to 1 breath.   (C) 7 chest presses to 1 breath. (D) 15 chest presses to 2 breaths.

_____ 19. The distress signal for choking is   (A) rapid, heavy breathing. (B) violent thrashing of the victim's arms.   (C) clutching the neck between the thumb and the index finger.   (D) A and B.

_____ 20. The Heimlich maneuver is   (A) used only on young children. (B) a way of avoiding a car accident.   (C) a simple procedure used to save a choking victim.   (D) none of these.

III. Essay

Most home accidents can be prevented. List as many safety measures (or safety rules) as you can think of that would help prevent an accident in the home.

214

TEST FOR UNIT TEN: HEALTH CAREERS AND SERVICES

I. Match each term on the left with the *best* description on the right. Place the letter of the description on the line provided.

_____ 1. Internist

A. regulates safety of drugs

_____ 2. Placebo effect

B. treatment by a doctor at a clinic or office

_____ 3. FDA

C. improvement in a patient's health even though the medication used was not real

_____ 4. Dietician

D. supervises food preparation

_____ 5. Primary care

E. specialist in diagnosing illness

II. On the line at the left of each of the following, write the letter of the choice that *best* completes the statement or answers the question.

_____ 1. For which symptom should you see a doctor immediately? (A) runny nose (B) sunburn (C) high fever (D) headache.

_____ 2. Approximately what percent of patients taking a placebo will show improvement? (A) 33 percent (B) 50 percent (C) 10 percent (D) 90 percent.

_____ 3. A medical specialist who is concerned with all forms of skin disease is a (A) cardiologist (B) dermatologist (C) allergist (D) pathologist.

_____ 4. A gastroenterologist is a specialist in the area of which system? (A) nervous (B) circulatory (C) digestive (D) skeletal.

_____ 5. To which specialist would you go if you had a broken bone? (A) ophthalmologist (B) orthopedic surgeon (C) pathologist (D) anesthesiologist.

_____ 6. Which one of the following statements is generally used by a quack? (A) "The *Cat Scan* shows a tumor that we can treat with radiation." (B) "I have a special treatment that has cured hundreds of sick people." (C) "I'm going to recommend a specialist to you." (D) "I can't guarantee a cure, but the therapy may control some of the pain."

_____ 7. Which one of the following groups of diseases is not on the immunization schedule of pediatricians? (A) mumps and rubella (B) tetanus and polio (C) cold and flu (D) diphtheria and rubeola.

_____ 8. Which one of the following abbreviations on a prescription means "twice a day"? (A) ad lib. (B) b.i.d. (C) stat (D) o.d.

_____ 9. Which one of the following is not required on labels of OTC drugs? (A) net contents of package. (B) name of any habit-forming drug contained within it. (C) proper directions for safe and effective use. (D) all of the above information must be included on the label.

10. The Computerized Tomographic Scanner (CTS)   (A) is used to destroy cancerous tumors.   (B) can diagnose diseases and recommend treatment.   (C) is an X-ray machine that can take many cross-sectional views of the body.   (D) does all of these.

11. Preventive medicines does not mean   (A) relying on medicine for the prevention of diseases.   (B) working to keep yourself healthy and finding ways to keep from getting disease.   (C) being immunized against diseases.   (D) having a breast self-examination.

12. Information about the causes of death in a city or a state is important because   (A) population growth statistics must be kept up-to-date.   (B) funeral parlors must keep up with the needs of the population.   (C) health officials can quickly find out the possible potential for epidemics in their state.   (D) of all of these reasons.

13. Which of the following is not a function of the World Health Organization?   (A) to stop illegal traffic of narcotic drugs.   (B) to stop the spread of communicable diseases.   (C) to stop aggression by military support.   (D) to spread information about family planning.

14. Communicable diseases can be prevented by   (A) vaccination.   (B) pasteurization of milk.   (C) sanitary disposal of sewage.   (D) all of these methods.

15. Which of the four organizations includes the other three?   (A) The Food and Drug Administration   (B) The National Institutes of Health   (C) The Public Health Service   (D) The Department of Health and Human Services

16. Health careers that require the least amount of formal education are called   (A) entry-level   (B) intermediate-level   (C) advanced-level   (D) higher-level

17. Which one of the following is an entry-level career?   (A) dietetic assistant   (B) dental hygienist   (C) veterinarian   (D) speech pathologist.

18. Which one of the following careers requires four years of college and also a master's degree?   (A) pediatric assistant   (B) dental hygienist   (C) ward clerk   (D) speech pathologist.

19. Which one of the following health careers would you select if you did not like the sight of blood?   (A) histologic technician   (B) dental hygienist   (C) food technologist   (D) veterinarian.

20. Radiation therapy technologist   (A) is a higher-level career.   (B) applies simple surgical dressings and checks the doctor's prescription for mathematical errors.   (C) studies the growth and development of infants and children.   (D) carries out serologic tests.

III. Essay

Write a statement indicating how you will continue to maintain your wellness after completing the health class.

Answers To Unit Tests

UNIT 1

MATCHING

1. B
2. C
3. D
4. A
5. E

MULTIPLE CHOICE

1. D	6. D	11. A	16. A
2. B	7. B	12. D	17. B
3. C	8. A	13. A	18. D
4. D	9. D	14. A	19. A
5. D	10. C	15. D	20. B

UNIT 2

MATCHING

1. A
2. B
3. E
4. D
5. C

MULTIPLE CHOICE

1. C	6. D	11. B	16. B
2. B	7. C	12. C	17. D
3. A	8. A	13. D	18. C
4. A	9. C	14. B	19. D
5. C	10. A	15. D	20. C

UNIT 3

MATCHING

1. A
2. E
3. D
4. B
5. C

MULTIPLE CHOICE

1. B	6. B	11. D	16. D
2. B	7. C	12. A	17. C
3. C	8. A	13. D	18. D
4. A	9. D	14. B	19. D
5. B	10. A	15. C	20. A

UNIT 4

MATCHING

1. A
2. E
3. D
4. B
5. C

MULTIPLE CHOICE

1. C	6. C	11. D	16. B
2. D	7. B	12. A	17. C
3. B	8. D	13. C	18. B
4. B	9. D	14. C	19. A
5. D	10. D	15. A	20. C

UNIT 5 (Part 1)

MATCHING

1. D
2. A
3. E
4. B
5. C

MULTIPLE CHOICE

1. B	6. B	11. B	16. D
2. D	7. B	12. B	17. B
3. B	8. B	13. A	18. A
4. A	9. A	14. D	19. B
5. C	10. C	15. C	20. D

UNIT 5 (Part 2)

MATCHING

1. C
2. E
3. A
4. B
5. D

MULTIPLE CHOICE

1. A	6. D	11. A	16. D
2. B	7. A	12. C	17. A
3. A	8. D	13. D	18. B
4. B	9. A	14. C	19. D
5. D	10. B	15. D	20. A

UNIT 6

MATCHING

1. C
2. D
3. B
4. E
5. A

MULTIPLE CHOICE

1. D	6. B	11. D	16. D
2. A	7. D	12. A	17. B
3. D	8. D	13. C	18. C
4. B	9. A	14. C	19. D
5. D	10. C	15. B	20. B

UNIT 7

MATCHING

1. E
2. A
3. B
4. D
5. C

MULTIPLE CHOICE

1. B	6. D	11. D	16. A
2. D	7. C	12. B	17. A
3. C	8. D	13. C	18. D
4. B	9. C	14. C	19. D
5. C	10. B	15. D	20. B

UNIT 8

MATCHING

1. D
2. A
3. E
4. B
5. C

MULTIPLE CHOICE

1. B	6. A	11. D	16. B
2. D	7. C	12. B	17. D
3. B	8. D	13. A	18. A
4. A	9. A	14. A	19. C
5. C	10. D	15. C	20. D

UNIT 9

MATCHING

1. B
2. C
3. D
4. A
5. E

MULTIPLE CHOICE

1. D	6. A	11. A	16. D
2. D	7. A	12. B	17. D
3. A	8. D	13. B	18. D
4. A	9. C	14. A	19. C
5. A	10. D	15. D	20. C

UNIT 10

MATCHING

1. E
2. C
3. A
4. D
5. B

MULTIPLE CHOICE

1. C	6. B	11. A	16. A
2. A	7. C	12. C	17. A
3. B	8. B	13. C	18. D
4. C	9. D	14. D	19. C
5. B	10. C	15. D	20. B

STUDENT ACTIVITIES

In this section, one or more reproducible student activity sheets for each of the ten units have been provided. The following list keys each activity title to the appropriate unit.

UNIT	ACTIVITY TITLE
Unit One: Active Body	Wellness Inventory
	Daily Health Inventory
	Self-Inventory
	Which Activity Is Best for You?
	Who Is Better?
	What Do You Know About Exercising?
Unit Two: Understanding Yourself	Life Goals
	Stress Evaluation for High School Students
Unit Three: Human Sexuality	The Year You Were Born
	Family Services
Unit Four: Environment and Heredity	I Am Different. I Am Unique.
	Work Sheet for Inheritance of Dominant Trait
	Work Sheet for Inheritance of Recessive Trait
	Work Sheet for Inheritance of Sex-linked Trait
	Environmental Risks Inventory
	The Effects of Noise
Unit Five: Functioning Body	Eye Activities
	Vision Test
	Cardiovascular Risk Factors
	How Large and Strong Are Your Lungs?
	What Do You Know About Skin Problems?
Unit Six: Social Drugs	What Do You Know About Smoking?
	What Do You Know About Alcohol?
	An Inventory On Drugs
	Classifying Drugs
	The Cigarette Habit
Unit Seven: Preventing Communicable Diseases	Control of Communicable Diseases
	Personal Health Record
	What Do You Know About Sexually Transmitted Diseases?
Unit Eight: Foods, Diet, and Digestion	Nutrition Inventory
	Looking at What You Eat
	How Do Dry Cereals Differ?
	How Many Calories Do You Burn in One Day?
	How Many Calories Do You Consume in One Day?

Unit Nine: Safety and Emergency Care   Check up on the Safety in Your Home

Unit Ten: Health Careers and Services   How Does Your Restaurant Rate?

Preceding the activities themselves is a section of teaching suggestions for activities where it was thought recommendation might be useful. These teaching suggestions explain the purpose of an activity and describe how it might be effectively used. Where appropriate, answers are furnished or additional information is provided.

TEACHING SUGGESTIONS FOR UNIT ONE ACTIVITY: WELLNESS INVENTORY

This activity can be used at the beginning of the semester as a preinventory and again as a postinventory to determine if any behavior changes have been made. The activity can be used at the beginning of Chapter 1 to emphasize the wellness concept. In the preinventory, the scores will average in the 30s and 40s. Encourage students to be very honest about themselves.

TEACHING SUGGESTIONS FOR UNIT ONE ACTIVITY: WHICH ACTIVITY IS BEST FOR YOU?

After the students make their selections and have the total for at least three activities, use the following questions to initiate discussion:

1. Are the three activities you selected similar in skill requirements? Explain.
2. Determine the necessary skills for ballet dance and for bowling. How does the score for ballet dance compare with the three activities you selected? How does the score for bowling compare with the three activities?
3. Compare the scores from everyone in the class to see if there is an agreement about the score for each activity.
4. Decide as a class which activity requires the most skills.
5. Decide as a class which activity requires the least skills.
6. Do you think you have adequate skills to participate in the activities you selected? Explain.

Ballet dance is an example of an activity that requires the most skills and will probably be rated high by the students. Bowling is generally rated low on skill requirements.

TEACHING SUGGESTIONS FOR UNIT ONE ACTIVITY: WHO IS BETTER?

This activity allows male and female students to compete against each other. The purpose of the competition is to debunk some of the myths and stereotypes regarding dexterity, strength, and endurance. After the students complete all three exercises and discuss their results, they should understand that not all girls can pass a thread through a tiny opening faster than the boys, and that not all boys are stronger than girls. The purpose is to show that everyone is unique and should not be stereotyped by sex.

Materials needed for Part I: petri dish or flat container, approximately 30 centimeters (12 inches) of sewing thread, 25 tiny beads, 50 centimeters (20 inches) of durable string; for Part II: masking-tape strips on the floor. See page 28 of the text.

TEACHING SUGGESTIONS FOR UNIT ONE ACTIVITY: WHAT DO YOU KNOW ABOUT EXERCISING?

This activity can be used as a pretest to find out what students know and what needs to be explained in more detail. The activity can be used to introduce the chapter on sports and recreation. After students have responded to the questions individually, the class may be divided into teams of three. They can discuss the questions and decide as a team whether to accept the statement as true or to discuss the reason why the statement is false. The questions can also be rearranged and used as a posttest.

ANSWERS:

O	1.	O	6.	O	11.	O	16.	+	21.
+	2.	+	7.	O	12.	O	17.	O	22.
O	3.	O	8.	+	13.	O	18.	+	23.
O	4.	O	9.	O	14.	O	19.	O	24.
O	5.	+	10.	O	15.	O	20.	O	25.

TEACHING SUGGESTIONS FOR UNIT TWO ACTIVITY: STRESS EVALUATION FOR HIGH SCHOOL STUDENTS

Some sources of stress are different for high school students than for adults. Some come from the students themselves. The pressures and stresses will differ from one school to another and from one student to another. This activity is to be done individually. No student should be required to share his or her results. The major emphasis, regardless of results, is students understanding that change, good or bad, can have an effect on them. The more changes a body goes through, the more stressful it is to the organs and systems. The discussion may bring out many other stresses experienced by students. Your may want to ask students to suggest stresses not included, then revise the evaluation sheet or have students make up their own for extra credit.

TEACHING SUGGESTIONS FOR UNIT THREE ACTIVITY: FAMILY SERVICES

Suggest to the students that they use only one or two words to describe a service whenever possible. Examples of words that could be used are "counseling," "housing," "financial assistance," "legal services," and "medical treatment." This will help the students to get more information on the chart. Precede the activity with a class discussion on what kind of family services are usually needed and list these on the chalkboard as a reference for the students to use.

TEACHING SUGGESTIONS FOR UNIT FOUR ACTIVITY: I AM DIFFERENT. I AM UNIQUE

This activity allows the students to see that skin color, clothing, hair style, and body size are very superficial ways of grouping people. The activity recognizes the individuality of everyone in the room. If the students segregate themselves according to sex, race, or familiarity, the exercise forces them to see everyone as an individual rather than as a member of a group. It is important that students see *themselves* as individuals before any attempt is made to help them improve their health status. No discussion on dominance, recessiveness, or other genetic terms is necessary.

TEACHING SUGGESTIONS FOR UNIT FOUR ACTIVITY: WORK SHEETS FOR DOMINANT TRAIT, RECESSIVE TRAIT, AND SEX-LINKED INHERITANCE

The three work sheets can be used to introduce the students to the concepts of dominant, recessive, and sex-linked inheritance. The work sheets may be given as a homework assignment, as a chapter evaluation, or as a discussion outline.

222

ANSWERS TO THE WORK SHEET

Dominant inheritance

	h	h
H	Hh	Hh
H	Hh	Hh

Each child born to the couple has a 100 percent chance of inheriting the disease, and no chance of inheriting all normal genes.

Polydactylism (poly=many/dactyl=digit) means many digits, or extra fingers or toes. It is present at birth. The extra digit can be surgically removed without any trace of polydactylism. Only the genes will be carried to the next generation. Father is *dd*. Mother is *Dd*.

	D	d
d	Dd	dd
d	Dd	dd

Each child born to the couple has a 50 percent chance of inheriting the trait, and a 50 percent chance of inheriting all normal genes.

Recessive inheritance

	P	p
p	Pp	pp
p	Pp	pp

Each child born to the couple has a 50 percent chance of inheriting the PKU problem.

Cystic Fibrosis is caused by the absence of some essential hormone or enzyme. The victim secretes abnormal amounts of mucus, saliva, and sweat. Father is *Cc*. Mother is *Cc*.

	C	c
C	CC	Cc
c	Cc	cc

Each child born to the couple has a 25 percent chance of inheriting the disease.

	X^N	X^c
X^c	$X^N X^c$	$X^c X^c$
Y	$X^N Y$	$X^c Y$

Each son or daughter born to the couple will have a 50 percent chance of being color-blind.

Hemophilia is a failure of blood to clot. The person lacks the factors necessary for normal clotting. Father is $X^h Y$. Mother is $X^N X^N$.

	X^N	X^N
X^h	$X^N X^h$	$X^N X^h$
Y	$X^N Y$	$X^N Y$

In this generation, the children will now show the trait for hemophilia. However, in the next generation, each daughter may contribute the trait to her sons.

TEACHING SUGGESTIONS FOR UNIT FOUR ACTIVITY: ENVIRONMENTAL RISKS INVENTORY

The inventory is a good way to introduce the chapter on environmental hazards. Although not all topics on the inventory will be covered in this chapter, students should be made aware of the hazards. To see if any behavioral change has taken place, the inventory can be given again after the chapter has been completed.

TEACHING SUGGESTIONS FOR UNIT FIVE ACTIVITY: HOW FLEXIBLE ARE YOUR LENSES?

The lenses of the eye are elastic and flexible. They are able to change in shape to accommodate for objects at different distances. The lenses are somewhat flat for distant vision, but they take on a spherical shape for close vision.

The distance recorded in centimeters to the exact point where reading material brought close to the eye becomes blurred is the "near point" of vision for that eye. As a person becomes older, the lenses lose their elasticity and cannot become spherical for close vision. The near point increases in distance as the person ages. Thus, many elderly people require reading glasses, or must hold the reading material almost at arm's length, in order to see clearly.

As an extra assignment, instruct students to find the near points of their parents, grandparents, teachers, and of other people of varying ages to see how they compare with the chart.

TEACHING SUGGESTIONS FOR UNIT FIVE ACTIVITY: VISION TEST

Does having 20/20 vision mean that the eyes are necessarily in good working condition? Many eye doctors think not and are critical of the way people neglect the health of their eyes. During an eye examination in school, the student is asked to cover one eye and to look at the letters on the chart. Unfortunately, even if the test results show 20/20 vision, the student may not be able to recognize certain shapes, coordinate eye movement, or stare at a given point. It is recommended that any discomfort of the eye be examined by a professional eye doctor.

224

Instruct the students that the vision test they are using does not test for hyperopia, glaucoma, astigmatism, and other eye problems.

TEACHING SUGGESTIONS FOR UNIT FIVE ACTIVITY: HOW LARGE AND STRONG ARE YOUR LUNGS?

This activity can be done in one class period. You will need extra-large balloons. Stretch the balloons as much as possible before collecting the data. The students will learn that vital capacity is greater in the larger and taller person. On the average, the males will have a greater vital capacity. Caution students not to hyperventilate as they try to blow out the candle.

TEACHING SUGGESTIONS FOR UNIT FIVE ACTIVITY: WHAT DO YOU KNOW ABOUT SKIN PROBLEMS?

This activity can be used as a pretest to find out what students know about acne and other skin problems. There are many misconceptions about acne. The students can be divided into teams of three. They should decide which statements are false and why they are false. The questions can be used as an introduction to the chapter. The questions can be used as a posttest also.

ANSWERS:

O 1.	+ 6.	O 11.	+ 16.	+ 21.
O 2.	+ 7.	O 12.	O 17.	O 22.
O 3.	O 8.	+ 13.	O 18.	+ 23.
+ 4.	O 9.	+ 14.	+ 19.	O 24.
O 5.	+ 10.	+ 15.	+ 20.	+ 25.

TEACHING SUGGESTIONS FOR UNIT SIX ACTIVITY: WHAT DO YOU KNOW ABOUT SMOKING?

This activity can be used as a pretest to find out what students know about smoking and what areas you will have to expand on. There are many misconceptions about smoking. The questions can be used as an introduction to the chapter.

ANSWERS:

O 1.	+ 6.	+ 11.	+ 16.	O 21.
O 2.	+ 7.	O 12.	+ 17.	O 22.
O 3.	+ 8.	O 13.	+ 18.	+ 23.
O 4.	O 9.	+ 14.	+ 19.	+ 24.
+ 5.	+ 10.	O 15.	+ 20.	+ 25.

TEACHING SUGGESTIONS FOR UNIT SIX ACTIVITY: WHAT DO YOU KNOW ABOUT ALCOHOL?

This activity can be used as a pretest to find out how much each student knows about alcohol. Students can do the activity individually, or it can be used with groups. Divide the students into teams of three. Each team will work together to decide which statement is true and what makes the false statements incorrect. This method allows the students to interact with other members of the class.

ANSWERS:

+ 1.	O 6.	+ 11.	+ 16.	O 21.
+ 2.	O 7.	O 12.	+ 17.	O 22.
O 3.	O 8.	O 13.	+ 18.	O 23.
+ 4.	+ 9.	O 14	O 19.	O 24.
O 5.	O 10.	O 15.	+ 20.	O 25.

TEACHING SUGGESTIONS FOR UNIT SIX ACTIVITY: AN INVENTORY ON DRUGS

This activity allows students to evaluate the amounts of chemical substances they consume each day. Students who abuse drugs may or may not record their daily consumption accurately. In order to help these students, a positive approach should be used. The major emphasis is on allowing students to think of alternatives to drug use.

TEACHING SUGGESTIONS FOR UNIT SIX ACTIVITY: CLASSIFYING DRUGS

This activity can be used as a pretest or as a culminating activity, or both. The answers to the student activity are as follows:

DEPRESSANT	NARCOTIC	HALLUCINOGEN	STIMULANT
1. tranquilizer	1. heroin	1. PCP	1. caffeine
2. barbiturate	2. methadone	2. marijuana	2. amphetamine
3. whiskey	3. morphine	3. mescaline	3. methamphetamine
4. beer	4. codeine	4. LSD	4. cocaine
5. anti-anxiety	5. opiate	5. hashish	5. nicotine

TEACHING SUGGESTIONS FOR UNIT SIX ACTIVITY: THE CIGARETTE HABIT

After the results of student surveys have been examined and discussed, present the following additional information on cigarette smoking to the class for comments and further discussion.

1. Cigarette advertising usually consists of the following four basic themes: satisfying taste and smoking enjoyment; low tar content; identifying with an appealing, attractive personal image; unique characteristic of the brand (package, style, filter, or length). Most brands have one of these themes or promises as their primary selling feature.
2. A cigarette is considered a "low-tar cigarette" if it contains 15 milligrams or less of tar and 1.5 milligrams or less of nicotine.
3. At least twenty-seven states have laws that limit smoking in one way or another in public places. Minnesota's Clean Indoor Air Act is considered to be the most comprehensive state antismoking law. It has served as a model for other states. As stated in the text of the law, the purpose of the law is "to protect the public health, comfort, and environment by prohibiting smoking in public places and at public meetings, except in designated smoking areas." A person who violates the law is guilty of a petty misdemeanor.
4. Smoking in prohibited areas is a misdemeanor in the following states: Arizona, Kansas, Michigan, Minnesota, Ohio, South Dakota, Texas, and Utah.
5. Penalties for violating smoking regulations vary from city to city and from state to state. A state penalty is likely to consist of a fine, ranging from $10 to $100, or a few days in jail. Local governments tend to issue more severe penalties than do state governments. For example, according to

226

one local ordinance, a person who smokes in a restaurant posted with no-smoking signs can be arrested and fined up to $500, or sent to jail for six months.

TEACHING SUGGESTIONS FOR UNIT SEVEN ACTIVITY: CONTROL OF COMMUNICABLE DISEASES

Precede this activity with a class discussion about communicable diseases. Ask the students, "What do you know about communicable diseases?" During the discussion, record on the chalkboard pertinent vocabulary that the students use. This class discussion will

1. assist the students in recalling information they already know;
2. assist the teacher in determining what the students need to learn;
3. introduce the difficult vocabulary found in Unit Seven in a written form that will help the students read the text with more ease.

Then, allow the students to fill in the activity chart as they study this unit and learn more about the diseases listed on the chart.

TEACHING SUGGESTIONS FOR UNIT SEVEN ACTIVITY: PERSONAL HEALTH RECORD

This activity could also be used in conjunction with Unit Four: Environment and Heredity.

Additional Information. The term "environmental" when used by health experts in reference to cancer-causing factors is used in two different ways. One usage means factors that exist in air, food, and water over which the individual has no control. The second usage means everything other than heredity. In the latter meaning, personal habits such as cigarette smoking are considered "environmental factors."

TEACHING SUGGESTIONS FOR UNIT SEVEN ACTIVITY: WHAT DO YOU KNOW ABOUT SEXUALLY TRANSMITTED DISEASES?

This activity can be used as an introduction to the chapter on sexually transmitted diseases. As a pretest, you can find out what the students know about STDs and in what areas you will need to go into more detail. Students who are normally reserved can participate in small groups to determine which statements are true and what makes the false statements incorrect.

ANSWERS:

+ 1.	○ 6.	○ 11.	○ 16.	○ 21.
+ 2.	+ 7.	○ 12.	○ 17.	+ 22.
+ 3.	○ 8.	+ 13.	○ 18.	○ 23.
+ 4.	○ 9.	○ 14.	○ 19.	+ 24.
○ 5.	+ 10.	○ 15.	○ 20.	+ 25.

TEACHING SUGGESTIONS FOR UNIT EIGHT ACTIVITY: NUTRITION INVENTORY TEST

The nutrition inventory test evaluates the students' habits rather than their factual knowledge. It can be used as a pretest. After students complete the nutrition unit, this inventory can serve as a posttest to compare any habit changes.

TEACHING SUGGESTIONS FOR UNIT EIGHT ACTIVITY: HOW MANY CALORIES DO YOU BURN IN ONE DAY? HOW MANY CALORIES DO YOU CONSUME IN ONE DAY?

Many students want to know how many calories they need each day. The need will depend on how much they use. Have the students calculate the approximate number of calories they use in one day by multiplying the number of calories burned per hour times the number of hours spent in the activities times their individual body weight. (For this activity do not use metric weight.) If the time spent in an activity is a fraction of an hour, the students may choose to use the number of calories burned per minute times the number of minutes spent in the activity times their individual body weight.

After computing the number of calories burned in 24 hours, have the students determine the approximate number of calories they consume in one day. Tell the students to use the "Count Your Calories" sheet to determine the number of calories in foods eaten for breakfast, lunch, dinner, and snacks. The size of the portion of foods should be carefully examined, multiplied by the number of calories listed, and recorded on the work sheet. Remind the students to record all calories consumed in one day, including those in gums, candies, and soft drinks.

TEACHING SUGGESTIONS FOR UNIT EIGHT ACTIVITY: HOW DO DRY CEREALS DIFFER?

This activity can be used to compare the many cereals sold in supermarkets. Have students bring in empty cereal boxes. After collecting enough for the entire class, have several students read off the information from the boxes. In this way the students will know where to look for the important information. The cost of the cereals should also be taken into consideration.

NAME: _____ DATE: _____

WELLNESS INVENTORY   UNIT ONE: ACTIVE BODY

Use the following point method: If you *always* do what is stated below   score 3 points.
                                         If you do it *most of the time*   score 2 points.
                                         If you do it *some of the time*   score 1 point.
                                         If you *never* do it   score 0.

_____ 1. I am aware when my body becomes tense during a stressful situation.
_____ 2. I am aware of the events which are likely to produce stress in me.
_____ 3. When I am under pressure, I usually take time out to relax.
_____ 4. I practice some form of relaxation each day.
_____ 5. I can handle most stresses without getting upset.
_____ 6. I fall asleep easily at bedtime.
_____ 7. I don't spend a lot of time worrying about problems that are beyond my control.
_____ 8. Each day, I do things to keep my wellness level high.
_____ 9. Even when I am ill, I know that I am in control of my body.
_____ 10. I accept responsibility for my state of health.
_____ 11. I feel comfortable with my body and the way I look.
_____ 12. I make time to interact with my family each day.
_____ 13. I exercise aerobically for 20 minutes at least three times each week.
_____ 14. I think about the reasons for the symptoms during an illness.
_____ 15. In general, I consider myself healthy.
_____ 16. I make it a practice to be nice to people if at all possible.
_____ 17. I am happy with the role I play in my family.
_____ 18. I reward myself when I achieve a goal.
_____ 19. I seek help from friends or professional people if needed.
_____ 20. I am happy most of the time.
_____ 21. I feel my health education is adequate.
_____ 22. I make sure my immunizations are up to date.
_____ 23. When I am angry, I know why I am angry.
_____ 24. I think positively and try to make things happen the way I want them to.
_____ 25. I see my dentist twice a year.

_____ TOTAL   70–75   Excellent
                                         65–69   Very Good
                                         60–64   Good
                                         55–59   Fair

Name:_____**Month**_____**Year**_____**Age**_____

DAILY HEALTH INVENTORY

			1	2	3	4	5	6	7	8	9	10	11	12	13	14	15	16	17	18	19	20	21	22	23	24	25	26	27	28	29	30	31
MOOD AND FEELINGS:	very happy	10 9																																
What are your general feelings and mood today? Are you very happy, very sad, or in between the two?	very sad	8 7 6 5 4 3 2 1																																
REST AND SLEEP:	well rested	10 9																																
Did you sleep well last night? Did you have time to relax during the day?	lacking sleep	8 7 6 5 4 3 2 1																																
NUTRITION:	very nutritious	10 9																																
Did you eat balanced meals and snacks that were within an ideal caloric range?	empty calories	8 7 6 5 4 3 2 1																																
EXERCISE:	intense workout	10 9																																
Did you participate in any vigorous recreational or sports activities?	little movement	8 7 6 5 4 3 2 1																																
	all going well	10 9																																
Combine the scores from above and divide the total by four. You now have the average wellness for the day. Record it in the proper column.	missed something	8 7 6 5 4 3 2 1																																

Other observations: The effects of certain food, medicine, weather, pain, friends, parents, or spiritual influence. Record the observations on the back of the chart and indicate the date.

230

SELF-INVENTORY   UNIT ONE: ACTIVE BODY

1. Using your best "artistic talent," draw a stick figure of yourself representing how you feel today.

2. On the stick figure drawing, place an *X* on the part of the body that is experiencing pain now or that experienced the last pain you had.

3. Place the letter *C* on any part of the drawing of your body that you would like to change for the better.

4. Place the letter *E* on the body part that is responsible for your decisions when emotion is involved.

5. What is the best one-word description someone could give of you?

   _____ .

6. What is the worst one-word description someone could give of you?

   _____ .

7. On a value scale of one (low) to ten (high), rate the following about yourself:
   physical health _____
   social health _____
   mental health _____
   total health _____

8. In terms of money, how much do you think you are worth? _____

   _____

9. List two things that you do that other people consider terrific.

   _____

   _____

10. List two personal achievements which made you very proud.

   _____

   _____

WHICH ACTIVITY IS BEST FOR YOU?   UNIT ONE: ACTIVE BODY

ACTIVITIES	FLEX	COORD	EQUIL	AGIL	SPEED	STRENGTH	ENDUR	TOTAL
Badminton								
Ballet Dance								
Baseball								
Basketball								
Bicycling								
Bowling								
Boxing								
Calisthenics								
Canoeing								
Diving								
Fencing								
Figure Skating								
Fishing								
Football								
Frisbee								
Golf								
Gymnastics								
Handball								
Hiking								
Hockey								
Horseback								
Jogging								
Judo								
Jumping Rope								
Karate								
Lacrosse								
Mt. Climbing								
Pool/Billards								
Racquetball								
Rowing								
Scuba								
Skateboarding								
Skiing								
Soccer								
Softball								
Square Dancing								
Swimming								
Table Tennis								
Tennis								
Track and Field								
Water Skiing								
Weight Lifting								
Wrestling								
Yoga								

From the above list of activities, select three sports or recreational activities in which you enjoy being involved. Then decide if the seven skills listed across the top are: (5) very important, (3) important, (1) somewhat important, or (0) not important at all for each activity you select. Add all the points across and place the sum in the total column. Compare the totals for the three activities.

NAME: _____ DATE: _____

WHO IS BETTER?   *UNIT ONE: ACTIVE BODY*

Laboratory on Agility, Dexterity, Endurance, and Strength

ANSWER ALL QUESTIONS THOROUGHLY

Part I: Dexterity: When your instructor gives you the signal, you will remove one bead at a time from the container and thread as many as you can in 1 minute. Answer the first two questions before you begin.
  1. Predict who will win, you or your opponent. _____
  2. List two reasons for your prediction. _____

After 1 minute is up, count the beads and record the results on the data sheet. Now it is your opponent's turn.   3. Who won?_____ 4. Was your prediction correct? _____ 5. Describe your feeling, whether you won or lost the contest. _____

Part II: Agility and Endurance: When your instructor gives you the signal, you will begin to jump laterally over a marker back and forth. Count the number of times your feet touch the floor. Again, before you start you must answer the following questions:
  6. Predict who will win: _____ 7. List two reasons why you think you or your opponent will win. _____

  8. Who won?_____ 9. Was your prediction correct?_____
10. Other than the fact that you are exhausted, how do you feel about who won?_____

Part III: Strength: Compare your arm length with your opponent's arm length. If the arms are uneven, place some books underneath the elbow of the shorter arm to adjust for the difference. Answer the following questions before the signal is given to start.
11. Who will win this contest?_____ 12. What is your reason for this prediction?_____

13. Who won?_____ 14. Was your prediction correct?_____
15. What is your feeling about losing, winning, or tieing your opponent?_____

16. According to the class data, who has more dexterity, males or females?_____
17–18. Is the male or the female considered to be more dextrous in our society?_____
      Why?_____

19. Does the class data in any way contradict the assumptions made by our society?_____
      How? _____

20. According to the class data in Part II, who is more agile, males or females?_____

DATA:

CLASS RESULTS

PART I:

DEXTERITY   Number of beads: Me: _____ Opponent:_____ Males ___ Females ___

PART II:

AGILITY/ENDURANCE Number of jumps: Me: _____ Opponent:_____ Males ___ Females ___

PART III:

STRENGTH   Right/left arms: Me: R L Opponent: R L Males ___ Females ___

NAME: _____ DATE: _____

WHAT DO YOU KNOW ABOUT EXERCISING?

UNIT ONE: ACTIVE BODY

Many common beliefs about exercise are either not true or only partially true. Use (+) for True and (O) for False.

_____ 1. During competition, you should not swallow liquids but just rinse your mouth.
_____ 2. Potassium loss is greater than sodium loss during exercise in hot weather.
_____ 3. Drinking lots of water is no protection against heat cramps.
_____ 4. Eating a candy bar before a game will give you extra energy and strength.
_____ 5. Everyone should participate in a vigorous exercise program.
_____ 6. Women should avoid weight lifting because their muscles will become bulky.
_____ 7. A football player can lose as much as 10 pounds during a game.
_____ 8. The faster you run or jog the more calories you will use.
_____ 9. Jogging can weaken the support structures of a woman's reproductive organs.
_____ 10. Certain kinds of muscle pulls are common to certain sports.
_____ 11. A good way to lose weight is by sweating.
_____ 12. High-protein food, such as steak, eaten before competition will give you strength.
_____ 13. Fast walking and jogging are good forms of exercising.
_____ 14. You need to develop large muscles to develop strength.
_____ 15. You can achieve cardiovascular fitness by exercising a few minutes a week.
_____ 16. When you exercise, you need additional vitamins and minerals.
_____ 17. Exercise uses so few calories that it is not helpful in preventing obesity.
_____ 18. You have to exercise vigorously to get any benefits from it.
_____ 19. To avoid discomfort associated with menstruation, women should not exercise during their periods.
_____ 20. A good way to get rid of unwanted fat on the hips, buttocks, and thighs is to exercise those areas.
_____ 21. Within two weeks of inactivity, the muscles of a superstar can lose strength.
_____ 22. If you are physically active and in good condition, you do not need to stretch or to do stretch exercises.
_____ 23. Exercising makes the heart more efficient.
_____ 24. Amphetamines (speed) taken prior to competition improves physical stamina.
_____ 25. A person should feel tired and hurt a little before an exercise can be considered beneficial.

_____ TOTAL

23–25   Excellent
20–22   Very Good
15–19   Good
11–14   Fair

LIFE GOALS

How long do you plan to enjoy good health? What kind of a life-style would you like to have 5 years from now? 10 years? 20 years? Where would you like to live? What kind of a job would you like to have during your working years? At what age would you like to retire from your job? What would you like to do with your leisure time after retirement? Think about these and other things and then fill in the chart below.

Goal	Desired age to achieve goal	Activities that could help you reach goal	Activities that could keep you from reaching your goal
1.			
2.			
3.			
4.			
5.			

You may want to rank your goals according to their importance to you.

NAME: _____ DATE: _____

STRESS EVALUATION FOR HIGH SCHOOL STUDENTS

UNIT TWO: UNDERSTANDING YOURSELF

RANK	EVENTS OCCURRING DURING ONE SCHOOL YEAR	VALUE		OCCURRENCE		SCORE
1.	Death of mother or father	100	x	_____	=	_____
2.	Divorce of parents	95	x	_____	=	_____
3.	Separation of parents	90	x	_____	=	_____
4.	Death of close family member	90	x	_____	=	_____
5.	Death of a close friend	85	x	_____	=	_____
6.	Personal injuries or illness	80	x	_____	=	_____
7.	Pregnancy	80	x	_____	=	_____
8.	Marriage	75	x	_____	=	_____
9.	Break up with boy/girl friend	70	x	_____	=	_____
10.	Change in health of family member	65	x	_____	=	_____
11.	Final exams	60	x	_____	=	_____
12.	Argument with parents	55	x	_____	=	_____
13.	In trouble with the law	50	x	_____	=	_____
14.	Argument with teacher	45	x	_____	=	_____
15.	Argument with close friend	40	x	_____	=	_____
16.	Failing of one or more classes	40	x	_____	=	_____
17.	Caught cheating on test	35	x	_____	=	_____
18.	Making decisions about college	35	x	_____	=	_____
19.	Peer pressure to drink alcohol or use other drugs	35	x	_____	=	_____
20.	Not being able to graduate with class	30	x	_____	=	_____
21.	Prejudice in school	25	x	_____	=	_____
22.	Being left out of group activities	25	x	_____	=	_____
23.	Rejection by teammates	25	x	_____	=	_____
24.	Older brother or sister leaving home	20	x	_____	=	_____
25.	Ridiculed for being overweight	20	x	_____	=	_____
26.	Fired at work	20	x	_____	=	_____
27.	Making future plans	15	x	_____	=	_____
28.	Buying and maintaining car	15	x	_____	=	_____
29.	Failing a test	15	x	_____	=	_____
30.	Involved in fight at school	15	x	_____	=	_____
31.	Homework assignment forgotten	10	x	_____	=	_____
32.	Elected officer of student council or club	10	x	_____	=	_____
33.	Doctor/dentist appointments	5	x	_____	=	_____
34.	Getting driver's license	5	x	_____	=	_____
35.	Class too difficult	5	x	_____	=	_____
36.	Change in school	5	x	_____	=	_____

TOTAL _____

Multiply the value by the number of times it has occurred in the past school year and put the result in the score column. Then add all the scores together and put on total line.

The events are ranked in descending (lessening) order. The higher the value, the greater the amount of stress that event seems to cause.

Researchers are finding that ongoing stress may have more effects on the body than the common stress symptoms show. New research is underway to find out how stress over a long period of time is responsible for damage and diseases of major body systems.

A total between 400 and 600:   likely to have more colds and minor illnesses than a person with less than 400 points

A total greater than 600:   will have greater chances of illness due to too much stress.

THE YEAR YOU WERE BORN

UNIT THREE: HUMAN SEXUALITY

How much do you know about the year you were born? You can learn a great deal by talking with your parents, grandparents, or other adults. Reading newspapers and magazines produced that year can be a help. Watching movies or television reruns that were popular then could be another way.

Try to find the answers to the questions below. Add other information that you know about that year. Then, on the back of this paper, write a short story that tells about the year you were born.

- When were you born?

- Who was the president of the United States?

- What were some of the popular fads?

- What kind of music was popular? What was the latest style of dancing?

- Where was your family living?

- What kinds of jobs did members of your family have?

- What was happening in the news?

- What was happening in your family?

- What had not yet been discovered in the world of medicine?

- Which television program was the most popular?

- What fast food was most popular?

FAMILY SERVICES

UNIT THREE: HUMAN SEXUALITY

Do you know what kind of family services are available in your community? Would you know where to go for help if you had a serious family problem?

In the first column, list 3 possible family problems. In the second column, list the resources available in your community for a family member to get help with each of the problems. In the last column, list the services that are provided by the resource person, organization, or agency.

PROBLEM	RESOURCE	SERVICE
1.		
2.		
3.		

Rate your community according to the family services that are offered. Circle the appropriate word:
GOOD   SATISFACTORY   NEEDS IMPROVEMENT

NAME: _____ DATE: _____

I AM DIFFERENT, I AM UNIQUE   *UNIT FOUR: ENVIRONMENT*
AND HEREDITY

What are some genetic traits that make you unique? What have you inherited?
1. Do you have dimples? _____
2. Do you have a gap between your two front teeth? _____
3. Do you wear glasses or contact lenses for nearsightedness? _____
4. Are you farsighted? _____
5. Is your little finger slightly bent when you place your hands flat on the table with palms down? _____
6. Are you right-handed? _____
7. Are you left-handed? _____
8. When you fold your hands together, does the right thumb appear on top? _____
9. Will your thumb bend back to form a 90-degree angle? _____
10. Can you roll your tongue into a cigar shape? _____
11. Do you have widow's peak? _____
12. What is your blood type? _____
13. Is your hair whorled in a clockwise or a counter-clockwise direction? _____
14. Are you female or male? _____
15. Is your hair straight or is it curly? _____
16. Are your irises pigmented? _____
17. Is your right eye dominant or is your left eye dominant? _____
18. Do you have any hairs growing on the second segment of your fingers? _____
19. Are your earlobes dangling free, attached, or intermediate? _____
20. Do you have freckles? _____

After completing the inventory of genetic traits, everyone will stand. Then one person will volunteer to read the traits that he or she has inherited. Those students who have the same traits will remain standing while others who do not will sit. The person will continue to call out his or her traits until only one other person remains standing.
1. When it was your turn, how many traits did you have to call out in order to have all but one person sit down? _____
2. Would you have selected the last person(s) standing as being most similar to you? _____
3. What are some of the differences between you and the last person(s) standing?

   _____
4. What are some of the similarities between you and the last person(s) standing?

   _____
5. Check the same traits in this exercise with your sister, brother, or parents to see what similarities and differences there are between you and other members of your family.
6. Repeat the procedure several more times with different people calling out their traits.

WORK SHEET FOR INHERITANCE OF DOMINANT TRAIT

UNIT FOUR: ENVIRONMENT AND HEREDITY

HUNTINGTON'S DISEASE This disease affects the brain. It generally appears between the ages of 30 and 45. Mental and physical decay occurs over a period of 15 years, followed by complete inability to function and death.

PROBLEM The father has Huntington's disease and the mother is normal. What are their children's chances of inheriting the disease? Gene H = Huntington's disease. Gene h = normal.

The father has inherited the dominant *H* gene from one parent and the recessive *h* gene from the other. The mother has inherited normal genes from both her parents. Father is *Hh*. Mother is *hh*.

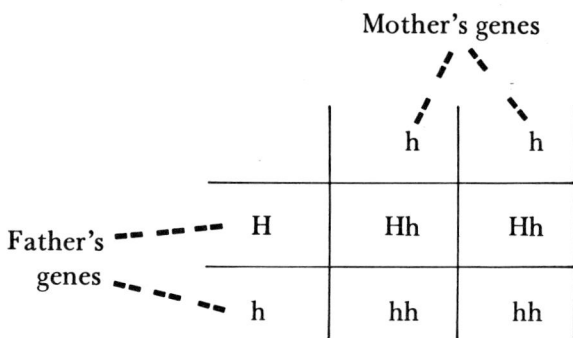

Mother's genes

	h	h
Father's genes H	Hh	Hh
h	hh	hh

Each child born to the couple has a 50/50 chance of inheriting the disease *Hh*, and a 50/50 chance of inheriting all normal genes *hh*.

If the father received the *H* gene from both parents, then he would be *HH*. What would be the children's chances of inheriting Huntington's disease? Fill in the parentheses:

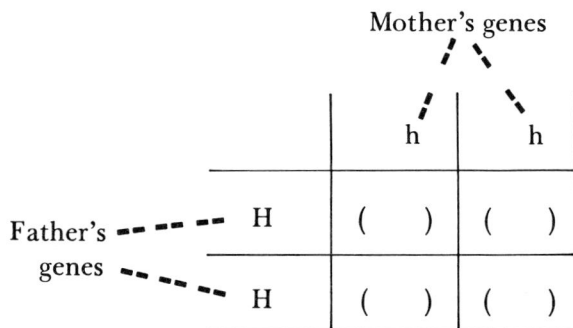

Mother's genes

	h	h
Father's genes H	( )	( )
H	( )	( )

Each child born to the couple has a _____ chance of inheriting the disease, and a _____ chance of inheriting all normal genes.

NOW YOU FURNISH THE DETAILS

POLYDACTYLISM _____

PROBLEM The mother has polydactylism and the father is normal. Gene D = Polydactylism. Gene d = normal.

The mother has inherited a gene for polydactylism from one parent and a normal gene from the other parent. The father has received two normal genes from both his parents. Father is _____.
Mother is _____ .

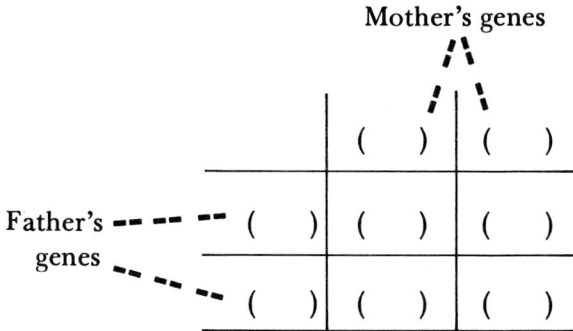

Mother's genes

	( )	( )
( )	( )	( )
( )	( )	( )

Father's genes

Each child born to the couple has a _____ chance of inheriting the disease, and a _____ chance of inheriting all normal genes.

WORK SHEET FOR INHERITANCE OF RECESSIVE TRAIT

UNIT FOUR: ENVIRONMENT AND HEREDITY

PHENYLKETONURIA (PKU) This disease is due to a lack of the enzyme phenylalanine hydroxylase. Phenylalanine cannot be changed into the amino acid tyrosine. Too much phenylalanine in the blood can cause mental retardation.

PROBLEM If both parents are carriers of PKU, what are their children's chances of inheriting the metabolic disease? Gene P = normal. Gene p = phenylketonuria.

Both father and mother have inherited one dominant normal gene from one parent and one recessive phenylketonuria gene from the other parent. Father is *Pp*. Mother is *Pp*.

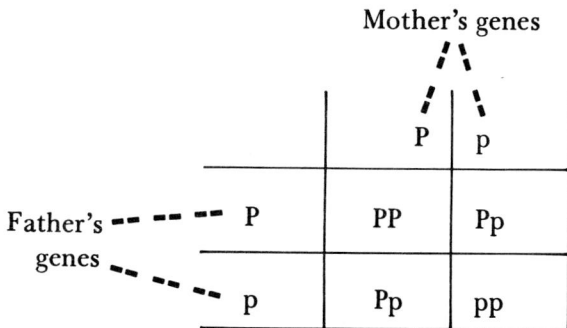

Mother's genes

	P	p
P	PP	Pp
p	Pp	pp

Father's genes

Each child born to the couple has a 25 percent chance of inheriting only the normal genes *PP*. Each child will have a 50 percent chance of inheriting one normal gene and one abnormal gene to be a carrier, *Pp*. Each child will have a 25 percent chance of inheriting the phenylketonuria genes (pp) from both parents.

If the father has inherited the PKU genes from both of his parents and the mother is a carrier, what would be each child's chance of inheriting the disease? Fill in the parentheses:

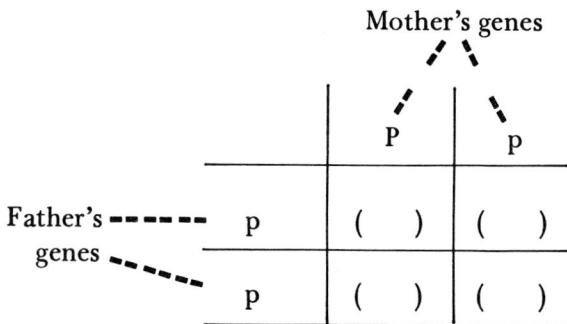

Mother's genes

	P	p
p	( )	( )
p	( )	( )

Father's genes

Each child born to the couple has a _____ chance of inheriting the disease.

NOW YOU FURNISH THE DETAILS

CYSTIC FIBROSIS _____

PROBLEM Both the father and the mother are carriers for cystic fibrosis. Gene C = normal. Gene c = cystic fibrosis.

Both father and mother have inherited one dominant normal gene from one parent and one recessive cystic fibrosis gene from the other parent. Father is _____ . Mother is _____ .

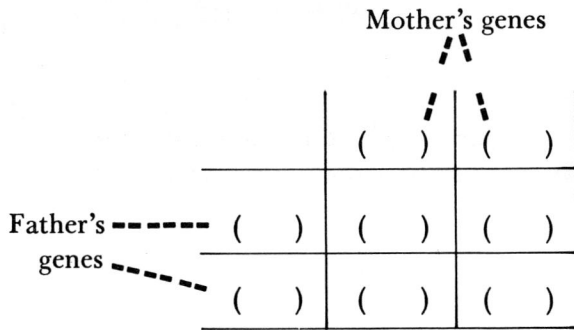

Mother's genes

	( )	( )
Father's ------- ( )	( )	( )
genes ----- ( )	( )	( )

Each child born to the couple has a _____ chance of inheriting the disease.

WORK SHEET FOR INHERITANCE OF SEX-LINKED TRAIT   UNIT FOUR: ENVIRONMENT AND HEREDITY

COLOR-BLINDNESS This is a condition in which a person cannot tell certain colors apart. The red-green color blindness, which is most common, is caused by too few red and green cones of the retina.

PROBLEM The father is normal and the mother is a carrier for color-blindness. What are their children's chances of being color-blind? Gene X^N = normal. Gene X^c = color blind.

The father has inherited gene X^N from his mother and gene Y from his father. The mother has received gene X^N from her mother and gene X^c from her father. Father is $X^N Y$. Mother is $X^N X^c$.

Mother's genes

	X^N	X^c
Father's genes X^N	$X^N X^N$	$X^N X^c$
Y	$X^N Y$	$X^c Y$

Each male child born to the couple has a 50/50 chance of inheriting the defective gene from the mother. If the son receives the defective gene on the X chromosome, he will automatically show the disorder because he does not have another X chromosome that is normal. His Y chromosome will not protect him. Each daughter born to the couple will have a 50/50 chance of being a carrier like her mother and may pass the disorder on to her sons.

If the father is color-blind and the mother is a carrier, what is the chance that their sons and daughters will be color-blind? Fill in the parentheses:

	X^N	X^c
X^c	( )	( )
Y	( )	( )

Each son or daughter born to the couple has a _____ chance of being color-blind.

NOW YOU FURNISH THE DETAILS

HEMOPHILIA _____

_____

PROBLEM The father is a hemophiliac and the mother is normal. What are their children's chances of inheriting the hemophilic genes? Gene X^N = normal. Gene X^h = hemophilic.

The father received a normal gene from his father and inherited the gene for hemophilia from his mother. The mother received normal genes from both of her parents. Father is _____. Mother is _____.

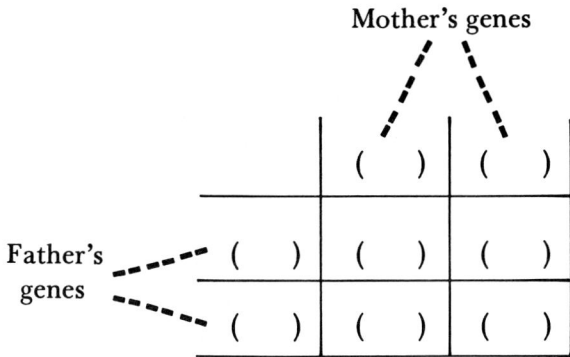

Mother's genes

In this generation, each son and daughter born to the couple has a _____ chance of being a hemophaliac.

Father's genes

( ) ( )
( ) ( ) ( )
( ) ( ) ( )

NAME: _____ DATE: _____

ENVIRONMENTAL RISKS INVENTORY

UNIT FOUR: ENVIRONMENT AND HEREDITY

Use the following point method:

If you *always* do what is stated below   score 3 points.
If you do it *most of the time*   score 2 points.
If you do it *some of the time*   score 1 point.
If you *never* do it   score 0.

_____ 1. I am aware of the hazards of X rays and avoid unnecessary exposure to them.

_____ 2. I avoid sounds over 90 decibels and prolonged noises.

_____ 3. I limit the time my body is exposed to the sun's direct rays.

_____ 4. When I am out in the sun, I use lotion containing PABA.

_____ 5. I avoid closed areas where people are smoking.

_____ 6. I have fewer than three alcoholic drinks per week.

_____ 7. I use the safety belt whenever I ride in a car.

_____ 8. I avoid riding in a car driven by a person under the influence of alcohol.

_____ 9. I read the labels and warnings on all over-the-counter medication.

_____ 10. I drink plenty of fluids during physical activity to prevent overheating.

_____ 11. I wear sufficient clothing on mountain trips to avoid hypothermia.

_____ 12. Before I take any aspirin or other medication for headaches, I try to find out the origin of the pain and look for alternatives to using medications.

_____ 13. I avoid using recreational drugs or psychoactive drugs.

_____ 14. I avoid swimming in rivers and lakes that appear to be contaminated.

_____ 15. I avoid drinking water from mountain streams and bubbling brooks.

_____ 16. I know exactly what to do in case of a tornado or hurricane.

_____ 17. I know exactly what to do in case I am caught in an electrical storm.

_____ 18. I avoid listening to loud music through earphones.

_____ 19. I avoid people who are carriers of communicable diseases such as flu and colds.

_____ 20. I avoid using any product that contains aerosol fluorocarbons to be used in aerosol sprays.

_____ 21. I avoid any product that warns people that the additive used may be carcinogenic.

_____ 22. At school, I avoid prolonged touching of an animal specimen that has been preserved in formaldehyde.

_____ 23. I am aware of the loud noises made by home appliances such as typewriters, vacuum cleaners, garbage disposers, and hair dryers. I protect my ears by using earplugs.

_____ 24. I avoid eating in restaurants that are unclean.

_____ 25. I avoid walking barefoot outside my home.

_____ TOTAL

70–75   Excellent
65–69   Very Good
60–64   Good
55–59   Fair

THE EFFECTS OF NOISE

UNIT FOUR: ENVIRONMENT AND HEREDITY

Can you concentrate when there is noise around you? Some people can sleep through noise while others are disturbed by the slightest sound. If you are concentrating on a difficult math problem, how does noise affect your speed and accuracy?

This activity will test your ability to concentrate. You will need a partner, an obstacle sheet, a mirror, a pencil, and a sheet of notebook paper.

1. Position the notebook paper in front of you to block the view of the obstacle drawing sheet secured on the table.
2. Have your partner hold the mirror in front of the obstacle sheet so that you can only see the reflection of the drawing.
3. If you are right-handed, pick up the pencil with your left hand. When the signal is given to start, follow the path of the drawing with your pencil. If at any point the pencil mark leaves the pathway, you must start the test over again.
4. Set the time limit at five minutes. During the first round, your teacher will provide loud, irritating noises throughout the test.
5. During the second round, no talking or other noise should be permitted in the room. Compare the results of round one with round two.
6. In round three, your partner will follow the same procedure. However, instead of having loud noise in round three, start with a quiet atmosphere. Then include the noise in round four. Compare the results of round three with round four. Record all data in the space provided below.

TEAM RESULTS

	TIME	CONVERT TO SECONDS
Round one with noise	minutes _____ seconds _____	_____
Round two without noise	minutes _____ seconds _____	_____
Round three without noise	minutes _____ seconds _____	_____
Round four with noise	minutes _____ seconds _____	_____

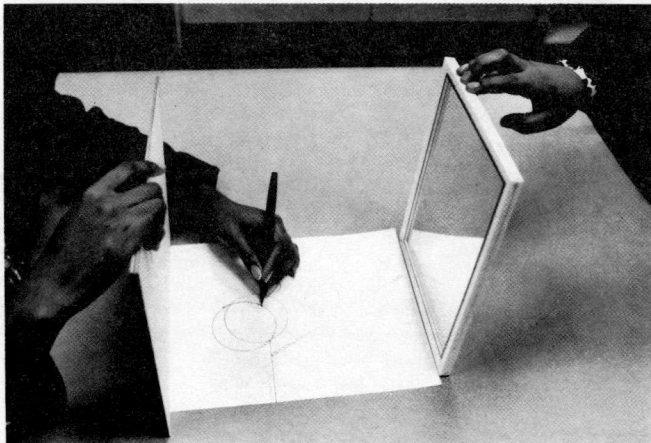

CLASS RESULTS

Round one $\dfrac{\text{Total time in seconds}}{\text{Number of teams}} =$ _____

Round two $\dfrac{\text{Total time in seconds}}{\text{Number of teams}} =$ _____

Round three $\dfrac{\text{Total time in seconds}}{\text{Number of teams}} =$ _____

Round four $\dfrac{\text{Total time in seconds}}{\text{Number of teams}} =$ _____

1. How do the class results of rounds one and four compare with results of rounds two and three?
2. What are some of the problems or errors in the design of this experiment?
3. From the results obtained from the class, decide whether or not noise is a factor in the ability to concentrate. Explain.
4. List some noises or sounds that bother you or interfere with your ability to concentrate.

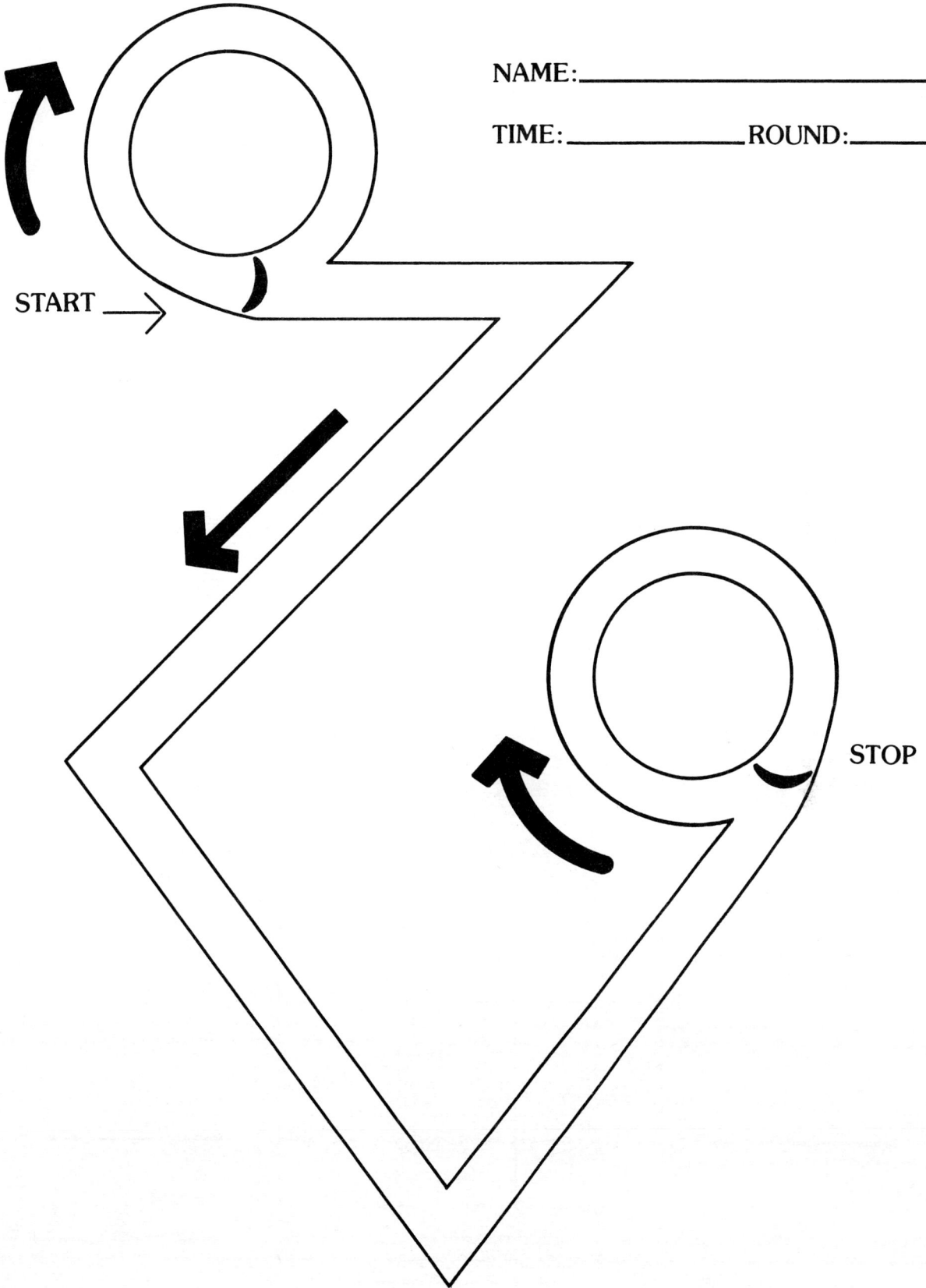

THE EFFECTS OF NOISE

START →

NAME:_____

TIME:_____ ROUND:_____

STOP

EYE ACTIVITIES   UNIT FIVE: FUNCTIONING BODY

I. THE BLIND SPOT

In the innermost layer of the eye (retina), there are many light-sensitive receptors called rods and cones. These receptors join together with neurons which in turn join with ganglion cells. The ganglion cells come together to form the optic nerve. The optic nerve comes out behind the eye at a point called the optic disc. The optic disc does not contain any rods or cones. If an image is focused on the optic disc, no sensation is sent to the brain. Thus, the area called the optic disc is also called the blind spot. The blind spot will not affect normal vision if both eyes are being used.

Find Your Blind Spot:

1. Hold this page at arms' length. Close your left eye and focus your right eye on the letter *B*. You should be able to see both the letter and the black dot.
2. With your right eye fixed on the letter *B*, slowly bring the paper towards you until the dot disappears.
3. Now close your right eye and focus your left eye on the dot. What happens to the *B*?

B   ●

II. HOW FLEXIBLE ARE YOUR LENSES?

1. Have your partner hold a meter stick perpendicular (at right angles) to the bridge of her or his nose.
2. Have your partner close one eye and, with the other eye, watch the letters ZZZ on the bottom of this work sheet as he or she slowly brings the paper close to the eyes.
3. In centimeters, record the distance from the eye to the exact point where the letters become blurred.
4. Repeat the procedures for the other eye.

AGE	NEAR POINT (centimeters)
10	7
15	8
20	9
25	10
30	11
40	17
50	50
60	80 +

ZZZ

VISION TEST

CA

NYOUR

e a d t

H E L A S

t l i n e o

N T H I S

c h a r t ?

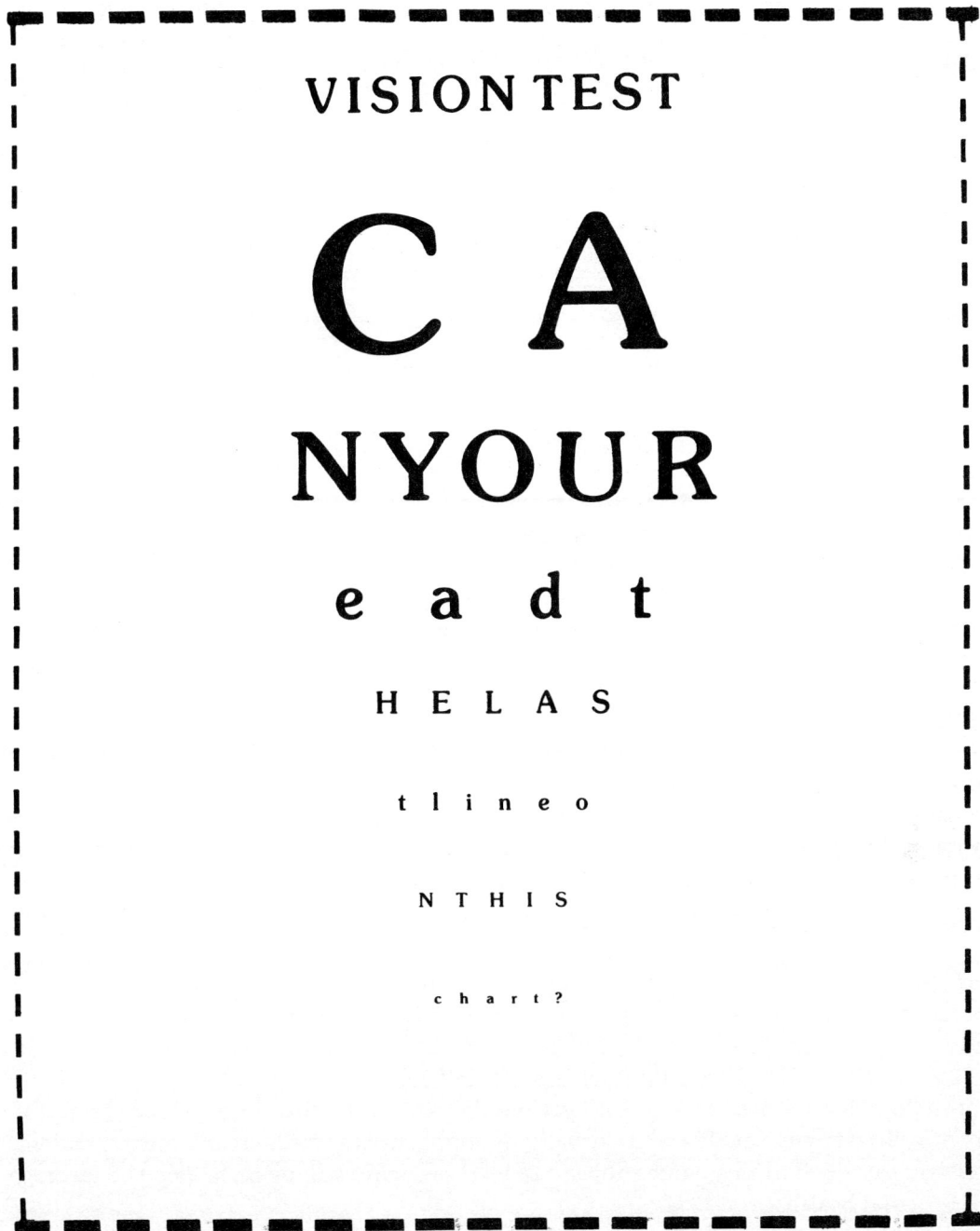

Hold this chart approximately 35 centimeters (14 inches) in front of your right eye. Cover your left eye and see if you can read all the lines. Now check your left eye. This chart cannot test for eye problems such as astigmatism, strabismus, glaucoma, hyperopia, amblyopia, or other eye disorders. If some of the lines are fuzzy, have your eyes examined by an ophthalmologist or an optometrist.

CARDIOVASCULAR RISK FACTORS UNIT FIVE: FUNCTIONING BODY

The purpose of this game is to give you a measure of your chances of suffering heart attack.

The game is played by making squares which—from left to right—represent an increase in your RISK FACTORS. These are medical conditions and habits associated with an increased danger of heart attack.

RULES:
Study each RISK FACTOR AND its row. Find the box that applies to you and circle the large number in it. For example, if you are 13, circle the number in the box labeled 10 to 20.

After checking out all the rows, add the circled numbers. This total—your score—is a measure of your risk.

IF YOU SCORE:

6-11—Risk well below
average
12-17—Risk below
average
18-24—Risk generally
average

25-31—Risk moderate
32-40—Risk at a dangerous
level
41-62—Danger urgent. See
your doctor now.

HEREDITY:
Count parents, grandparents, brothers, and sisters
who have had heart attack and/or stroke.

TOBACCO SMOKING:
If you inhale deeply and smoke a cigarette way down, add one to your classification. Do NOT subtract because you think you do not inhale, or you smoke only a half inch on a cigarette.

EXERCISE:
Lower your score one point if you exercise regularly and often.

CHOLESTEROL OR SATURATED FAT INTAKE LEVEL:
A cholesterol blood level is best. If you can't get one from your doctor, then measure honestly the percentage of solid fats you eat. These are usually of animal origin—lard, cream, butter, and beef and lamb fat. If you eat much of this, your cholesterol level probably will be high. The U.S. average, 40%, is too high for good health.

SEX:
This line takes into account the fact that men have from 6 to 10 times more heart attacks than women of child-bearing age.

This scale only highlights what are the cardiovascular risk factors and what can be done about them. It is not designed to be a medical diagnosis. If you have a number of risk factors, for the sake of your health, ask your doctor to check your medical condition. Then quit your risk factor habits!

NAME:_____ DATE:_____

CARDIOVASCULAR RISK FACTORS

AGE	10 to 20 — 1	21 to 30 — 2	31 to 40 — 3	41 to 50 — 4	51 to 60 — 6	61 to 70 and over — 8
HEREDITY	No known history of heart disease — 1	1 relative with cardiovascular disease over 60 — 2	2 relatives with cardiovascular disease over 60 — 3	1 relative with cardiovascular disease under 60 — 4	2 relatives with cardiovascular disease under 60 — 6	3 relatives with cardiovascular disease under 60 — 7
WEIGHT	More than 5 lbs. below standard weight — 0	−5 to +5 lbs. standard weight — 1	6-20 lbs. over weight — 2	21-35 lbs. over weight — 3	36-50 lbs. over weight — 5	51-65 lbs. over weight — 7
TOBACCO SMOKING	Non-user — 0	Cigar and/or pipe — 1	10 cigarettes or less a day — 2	20 cigarettes a day — 4	30 cigarettes a day — 6	40 cigarettes a day or more — 10
EXERCISE	Intensive occupational and recreational exertion — 1	Moderate occupational and recreational exertion — 2	Sedentary work and intense recreational exertion — 3	Sedentary occupational and moderate recreational exertion — 5	Sedentary work and light recreational exertion — 6	Complete lack of all exercise — 8
CHOLESTEROL OR FAT % IN DIET	Cholesterol below 180 mg.% Diet contains no animal or solid fats — 1	Cholesterol 181-205 mg.% Diet contains 10% animal or solid fats — 2	Cholesterol 206-230 mg.% Diet contains 20% animal or solid fats — 3	Cholesterol 231-255 mg.% Diet contains 30% animal or solid fats — 4	Cholesterol 256-280 mg.% Diet contains 40% animal or solid fats — 5	Cholesterol 281-300 mg.% Diet contains 50% animal or solid fats — 7
BLOOD PRESSURE	100 upper reading — 1	120 upper reading — 2	140 upper reading — 3	160 upper reading — 4	180 upper reading — 6	200 upper reading — 8
SEX	Female under 40 — 1	Female 40-50 — 2	Female over 50 — 3	Male — 5	Stocky male — 6	Bald stocky male — 7

HOW LARGE AND STRONG ARE YOUR LUNGS?

UNIT FIVE: FUNCTIONING BODY

PART 1

Balloon Method of Determining Lung Size (Vital Capacity). Tug on a large balloon until all parts are well stretched. Blow several times into the balloon to test the resistance. Then take a deep breath and blow all you can into the balloon. Pinch off the mouth part and twist to prevent any air from escaping. Using your hand to make the balloon as round as possible, measure the height of the evenly rounded balloon. Use the scale to the right and determine your lung capacity. Repeat the procedure two more times and average. Record the results as shown to the left.

	STUDENT 1	STUDENT 2
Trial 1	cm^3	cm^3
Trial 2	cm^3	cm^3
Trial 3	cm^3	cm^3
Average	cm^3	cm^3

Lung capacity is expressed in cubic centimeter units (cm^3). 1000 cm^3 is a little more than a quart.

PART 2

Huff-and-Puff Method of Determining Strength of Lungs. Lay out several meter sticks end to end on a table. Light a medium-sized candle. Place the candle-holder at one end of the meter stick. Blow from the opposite end and try to blow the candle out. Have your partner move the candle toward you; keep blowing until the flame goes out. Determine the distance between you and the point where the candle went out. Record the information below. Repeat two more times and take the average.

	STUDENT 1	STUDENT 2
Trial 1	cm	cm
Trial 2	cm	cm
Trial 3	cm	cm
Average	cm	cm

BALLOON CONVERSION TABLE

Balloon diameter in centimeters	Lung capacity in cubic centimeters
8	250
9	325
10	500
11	675
12	800
13	1110
14	1300
15	1750
16	2110
17	2600
18	3000
19	3500
20	4000
21	4500
22	5000
23	5500
24	6000

PART 3. Class data for parts 1 and 2.

CLASS AVERAGE

	Males	Females
Part 1	cm^3	cm^3
Part 2	cm	cm

QUESTIONS

1. According to the class data, who has the greater vital capacity? _____

2. Why do you think there is a difference in lung capacity among people? _____ _____

3. Who projects air more forcefully (blowing out the candle), male or female? _____

4. Who would have a greater vital capacity, a tall female or a short male? _____ Why? _____

5. Why would a person with emphysema do poorly in both of the laboratory experiments? _____

6. On the back of the paper, write a paragraph on how you can maintain strong lungs.

NAME: _____ DATE: _____

WHAT DO YOU KNOW ABOUT SKIN PROBLEMS?

UNIT FIVE: FUNCTIONING BODY

There are many myths about acne and other skin problems. Use (+) for True and (○) for False. Put your answers in the left column and your team response in the right column.

MINE TEAM

1. Acne occurs during puberty because young people do not keep their skin clean.
2. The best way to remove acne is to scrub the skin firmly.
3. Acne is one condition which cannot be prevented.
4. Ringworm and athlete's foot are caused by fungi.
5. French fries, chocolate, and starchy foods are causes of acne.
6. A person who is sensitive to poison ivy may become affected without directly touching the plant.
7. Severe forms of acne may be inherited.
8. Bacteria-caused acne is contagious.
9. Acne is not common in people who have dry skin.
10. Controlling daily stresses may help reduce acne problems.
11. Daily exercise is essential for preventing acne.
12. A pimple should not be squeezed until it is fully ripened.
13. Dandruff is made up of clumps of dead cells.
14. Hives can be caused by pollen, chemicals, drugs, or foods.
15. A pimple is a whitehead that has become infected.
16. Boils are skin infections that begin in a hair root. They can be transmitted to other people.
17. Keeping the skin dry by applying alcohol to the face with cotton balls is a good way to fight acne.
18. Vitamins A and B are helpful in preventing acne.
19. People with acne should not use oil-based cosmetics.
20. The skin is the largest organ of the human body.
21. A hair follicle that is plugged with oil and dead skin cells and has an opening on the surface is called a *blackhead*.
22. A mole is always cancerous and should be removed.
23. An increase in hormone production during puberty increases the amount of skin oil called *sebum*.
24. Any over-the-counter (OTC) medication will quickly cure acne.
25. Acne, in most cases, is temporary. With proper care, it can be controlled.

_____ _____ TOTALS

23–25	Excellent
20–22	Very Good
15–19	Good
11–14	Fair

WHAT DO YOU KNOW ABOUT SMOKING?

UNIT SIX: SOCIAL DRUGS

Many common beliefs about smoking are either not true or only partially true. Use (+) for True and (O) for False.

_____ 1. About 20 percent of all cases of emphysema are related to smoking.

_____ 2. Most people start to smoke because they enjoy the smell of smoke.

_____ 3. Adding filters will make smoking safer and will reduce the chance of lung cancer.

_____ 4. Emphysema can be cured if noticed and treated in time.

_____ 5. Arteries of smokers contain more cholesterol than those of nonsmokers.

_____ 6. 60 milligrams of nicotine taken all at once will cause the respiratory system to fail.

_____ 7. The nicotine in smoke causes a temporary increase of sugar in the blood.

_____ 8. A pregnant woman can harm her developing child by smoking.

_____ 9. Nicotine is the drug in the cigarette which acts as a depressant and allows a smoker to relax.

_____ 10. A nonsmoker in a room of smokers often inhales more carbon monoxide than do the smokers.

_____ 11. Carbon monoxide in cigarette smoke damages the heart and blood vessels.

_____ 12. Lung cancer occurs in equal numbers to both smokers and nonsmokers.

_____ 13. The hairlike cilia in the trachea move faster when a person smokes.

_____ 14. The burning zone of a cigarette is 1623 degrees Fahrenheit.

_____ 15. A smoker who gets a physical checkup every year will probably not get lung cancer.

_____ 16. Parents, friends, and advertising may encourage a person to start smoking.

_____ 17. 85 percent of the teenagers who begin smoking will become habitual smokers.

_____ 18. Marijuana contains more tar and known carcinogens than tobacco.

_____ 19. When people start smoking, they never think they will become addicted.

_____ 20. The right to a smoke-free work place is a new legal concept.

_____ 21. Mainstream smoke (smoke inhaled and then exhaled by a smoker) is more dangerous than sidestream smoke (smoke created by burning tobacco in an ashtray).

_____ 22. The overall number of boys and girls aged 12 to 18 who smoke has dropped 25 percent.

_____ 23. Nicotine raises blood pressure and heart rate.

_____ 24. Additives used to enhance the flavor of low-tar cigarettes may themselves cause cancer.

_____ 25. Marijuana does not contain nicotine.

_____ TOTAL

23–25	Excellent
20–22	Very Good
15–19	Good
11–14	Fair

WHAT DO YOU KNOW ABOUT ALCOHOL?   UNIT SIX: SOCIAL DRUGS

Many common beliefs about alcohol are either not true or only partially true. Use (+) for True and (O) for False. Put *your* answers in the left column and your *team* responses in the right column.

MINE TEAM

____ ____ 1. Alcohol is correctly classified as a drug.

____ ____ 2. 50 percent of all first admissions to mental institutions are caused by alcohol.

____ ____ 3. After a cocktail, a person is pepped up because alcohol in a small amount acts as a stimulant.

____ ____ 4. Over 50 percent of all traffic deaths are due to alcohol abuse.

____ ____ 5. Alcohol causes death by overstimulating the nerve cells to exhaustion.

____ ____ 6. Alcohol increases productivity and efficiency.

____ ____ 7. Alcohol is absorbed into the system and digested in the same way as food.

____ ____ 8. Only poor, skid-row men and women become alcoholics.

____ ____ 9. Alcohol has no nutritional value.

____ ____ 10. If you just drink beer, you will not become an alcoholic.

____ ____ 11. Alcohol has caloric value and is used to produce energy just like foods.

____ ____ 12. All alcoholics should be treated by Alcoholics Anonymous.

____ ____ 13. A hangover can be prevented by eating high levels of carbohydrates the night before.

____ ____ 14. A person can sober up faster if black coffee is consumed several hours after a party.

____ ____ 15. One becomes intoxicated faster on rum or gin than on bourbon.

____ ____ 16. Personality disturbance is a basic reason for the development of alcoholism.

____ ____ 17. Social drinking is the first step toward alcoholism.

____ ____ 18. Alcoholics tend to follow a general pattern of behavior on their way to alcoholism.

____ ____ 19. Alcohol is an aphrodisiac.

____ ____ 20. An alcoholic is someone who cannot stop drinking with help.

____ ____ 21. Social drinkers cannot become alcoholics.

____ ____ 22. A developing fetus is never affected by the mother's consumption of alcohol.

____ ____ 23. At a cold football game, it makes sense to drink alcohol because alcohol increases body temperature.

____ ____ 24. Alcohol's direct effect on the liver is the main cause of the high incidence of cirrhosis among alcoholics.

____ ____ 25. Obese individuals should be able to "hold their liquor" better than muscular individuals of the same weight.

____ ____ TOTALS

23–25	Excellent
20–22	Very Good
15–19	Good
11–14	Fair

AN INVENTORY ON DRUGS

UNIT SIX: SOCIAL DRUGS

NAME OF THE DRUG USED	AMOUNT USED	HOW MANY TIMES EACH DAY?	WHAT IS THE COST?	HOW DEPENDENT ARE YOU ON THE DRUG?
Cola Drinks				
Coffee/Tea				
Alcohol				
Cigarettes				
Chewing Tobacco				
Pain Killers				
Tranquilizers				
Aspirin				
Antihistamines				
Sleeping Pills				
Other				
Other				

1. List two reasons why you use the drugs recorded above.
2. List two "benefits" that you get from using the drugs.
3. List two drawbacks to the drugs you use.
4. List two alternatives (nondrug) to using the drugs.
5. How will the drugs you are now using affect your future and the goals you have set?

CLASSIFYING DRUGS

UNIT SIX: SOCIAL DRUGS

There are five words for each of the major drug categories. Place the correct words under the correct headings.

DEPRESSANT	NARCOTIC	HALLUCINOGEN	STIMULANT
1. _____	1. _____	1. _____	1. _____
2. _____	2. _____	2. _____	2. _____
3. _____	3. _____	3. _____	3. _____
4. _____	4. _____	4. _____	4. _____
5. _____	5. _____	5. _____	5. _____

LSD	hashish	barbiturate	heroin
caffeine	whiskey	mescaline	PCP
amphetamine	morphine	nicotine	methadone
marijuana	cocaine	codeine	anti-anxiety
methamphetamine	beer	opiate	tranquilizer

THE CIGARETTE HABIT   UNIT SIX: SOCIAL DRUGS

Using the questions below, conduct a survey among people who smoke cigarettes. Try to get an equal number of responses from individuals under 25 years of age and from those who are over 25. Keep a separate record for each group.

QUESTIONS

1. At what age did you begin to smoke cigarettes?

2. Why did you start to smoke?

3. Do you believe that smoking is dangerous to your health?

4. When you began smoking, did you believe it would become a habit for you?

5. Do you believe that substances released from cigarettes can affect the health of nonsmokers?

Examine the results of your survey. What are your conclusions? Is there much difference between the answers from people under 25 years of age and the answers from those who are over 25? Do you think the results of your survey are typical? Why or why not?

CONTROL OF COMMUNICABLE DISEASES

UNIT SEVEN: PREVENTING COMMUNICABLE DISEASES

Do you know how to keep from getting the most common communicable diseases? If you have had one of the diseases listed below, do you know how you got it?

Fill in the chart below.

Disease	Kind of organism (bacteria, virus)	How the organism may enter the body of the well person	How you can keep from getting the disease
Common cold			
Influenza			
Measles			
Mumps			
Poliomyelitis			
Diphtheria			
Whooping cough			
Tetanus			
Hepatitis			
Mononucleosis			
Gonorrhea			
Syphilis			

NAME: _____ **DATE:** _____

PERSONAL HEALTH RECORD

UNIT SEVEN: PREVENTING COMMUNICABLE DISEASES

Everyone should keep a personal health record. Scientists are learning more about how inherited traits and environmental factors affect the unborn and the newborn. This makes an accurate health record important. Your medical record also will be useful in filling out insurance forms, school records, and travel records.

I. FAMILY HEALTH HISTORY

Information about the health of your family can be helpful. It can aid in early diagnosis and treatment of disease that are known either to be genetic or to happen more often in some families. Make a note of *any* serious or chronic diseases in your family. Give special attention to those listed at the right. It also helps to note the age when the disease first occurred.

Be sure to include:

- Allergies
- Arthritis
- Cancer
- Diabetes
- Epilepsy
- Hearing defects
- Heart defects
- Hypertension
- Mental illness
- Mental retardation
- Obesity
- Tuberculosis
- Visual defects
- Other recurring family diseases

NAME	BIRTH DATE	BLOOD TYPE & Rh	OCCUPATION	DISEASES, ETC.	IF DECEASED, AGE AND CAUSE
Father					
his father					
his mother					
brothers and sisters					
Mother					
her father					
her mother					
brothers and sisters					

Information obtained from the *Family Medical Record. Designed by The National Foundation-March of Dimes in collaboration with the American Medical Association and Woman's Day.*

Permission to reproduce this publication (pages 167-170) has been granted by The National Foundation-March of Dimes as the copyright holder of the original publication.

II. CHILDREN'S BIRTH RECORD (SELF AND BROTHERS AND SISTERS)

NAME	DATE	SEX	WT.	BLOOD TYPE	Rh FACTOR	HOSPITAL, CITY	PHYSICIAN	DETAILS

III. IMMUNIZATION SCHEDULE AND RECORD

The American Academy of Pediatrics recommends that children be immunized and given tuberculin testing according to the immunization schedule below. Vaccine combinations and schedules are improved frequently. Your doctor can recommend what is best for you. Fill in the chart below.

IMMUNIZATION SCHEDULE

2 months — Diphtheria/Tetanus/Pertussis (whooping cough) vaccine, first shot; polio vaccine, first dose

4 months — Polio vaccine, second dose; DTP

6 months — Polio vaccine, completed; DTP

12 months — Tuberculin test

15-18 months — Rubeola (measles) and rubella (German measles) vaccines; polio booster; DTP booster

4-6 years — Polio booster; DTP booster

14-16 years — Tetanus/diphtheria toxoid (adult form)

Thereafter — Tetanus/diphtheria toxoid every 10 years.

IMMUNIZATION RECORD

IMMUNIZATIONS	MONTH	YEAR
DTP completed		
boosters		
polio completed		
boosters		
tuberculin test		
rubeola (measles)		
rubella (German measles)		
mumps		
tetanus/diphtheria		
other		

IV. RECORD OF ACCIDENTS, SURGERY, AND ILLNESSES

List accidents, surgery, and illnesses, including chicken pox, mononucleosis, hepatitis, measles, German measles, mumps, strep throat and whooping cough. If there was surgery, state what was repaired or removed and note X rays taken, medications, and diet.

DATE	NATURE OF ILLNESS, INJURY OR SURGERY	PHYSICIAN	OFFICE, CLINIC, HOSPITAL	TREATMENT

V. PERIODIC PHYSICAL EXAMINATIONS

It is important to keep a record of your physical examinations.

DATE	PHYSICIAN/ CLINIC	HT.	WT.	BLOOD PRESSURE	FINDINGS, ADVICE OR INSTRUCTIONS

VI. SPECIAL PROBLEMS, MEDICATIONS, ALLERGIES

Note any medications that are taken regularly; any substances that must be avoided for medical reasons; and any allergies.

CONDITIONS	SPECIAL INSTRUCTIONS OR MEDICATIONS

WHAT DO YOU KNOW ABOUT SEXUALLY TRANSMITTED DISEASES?

UNIT SEVEN: PREVENTING COMMUNICABLE DISEASES

Many common beliefs about sexually transmitted diseases are either not true or only partially true. Use (+) for True and (O) for False.

_____ 1. Genital herpes has no cure.
_____ 2. The first sign of the primary stage of syphilis is a chancre where the spirochetes entered.
_____ 3. You can have syphilis and not know it.
_____ 4. The second sign during the secondary stage of syphilis includes a rash on the hands and feet.
_____ 5. It is harder for a girl to get syphilis than a boy.
_____ 6. You cannot die from syphilis.
_____ 7. Syphilis is simple to cure during the early stage.
_____ 8. A condom will always prevent syphilis.
_____ 9. You can get syphilis from toilet seats or towels.
_____ 10. During the latent stage of syphilis, mental illness or blindness can occur.
_____ 11. Once you are cured of syphilis, your body develops immunity, and you will not catch any form of STD again.
_____ 12. STDs do not require a doctor's care.
_____ 13. In many cases, females do not show any sign of having gonorrhea.
_____ 14. Currently, you can get an OTC medication called Gonojel, which can be applied directly to the penis to kill the gonococcus on contact.
_____ 15. If gonorrhea is not treated, it will lead to the secondary stage of syphilis.
_____ 16. Once you have gonorrhea you cannot get it again. The penicillin level will remain high as long as the bacteria is present.
_____ 17. A discharge from the penis or vagina always means gonorrhea.
_____ 18. Gonorrhea, but not syphilis, can be contracted from a swimming pool.
_____ 19. Genital herpes can be cured if penicillin is given early.
_____ 20. Zovirax is an ointment currently used by physicians to help a patient's management of genital herpes.
_____ 21. Crabs are always transmitted by sexual contact.
_____ 22. Gonorrhea is twice as prevalent among those 25 years old and younger.
_____ 23. Under the microscope, the gonorrhea and syphilis bacteria look very much alike.
_____ 24. Genital herpes is not like gonorrhea and syphilis. It is a virus.
_____ 25. Embarrassment is one reason that people do not seek help when they acquire an STD.

_____ TOTAL

23–25	Excellent
20–22	Very Good
15–19	Good
11–14	Fair

NAME: _____ **DATE:** _____

NUTRITION INVENTORY

_____	1.	When I eat at fast-food stores or restaurants, I am aware of how the food is prepared and the cleanliness of the kitchen.
_____	2.	I am aware of the possibility of food poisoning at picnics and avoid foods that appear to be spoiled or have been exposed too long.
_____	3.	I drink plenty of liquids each day.
_____	4.	I avoid arguments and tension during meals.
_____	5.	I wash my hands thoroughly before preparing a meal or eating.
_____	6.	I include foods that are high in fibers in my diet each day.
_____	7.	I am aware of how many calories I take in and how many I use up each day.
_____	8.	The snacks I eat between meals are nutritious and low in calories.
_____	9.	I avoid fad diets and seek help from my physician when I need to lose weight.
_____	10.	I read the nutrition labels on most foods I buy.
_____	11.	I follow the Recommended Daily Allowances (RDA) of all nutrients.
_____	12.	I have good appetite at all meals.
_____	13.	I avoid foods that contain large amounts of additives.
_____	14.	I avoid junk foods.
_____	15.	I first taste my food before adding any salt.
_____	16.	I do not drink more than 5 soft drinks per week.
_____	17.	I use the unit pricing on the grocery shelves to compare costs of food per unit of weight.
_____	18.	I eat breakfast every morning.
_____	19.	I enjoy eating with other people.
_____	20.	I eat fruits or cooked or fresh vegetables with each meal.
_____	21.	I check for open dating to buy the freshest food.
_____	22.	I avoid foods that contain large amounts of sugar.
_____	23.	I chew my food well and take my time eating.
_____	24.	I include foods from all four basic food groups in each meal.
_____	25.	I avoid taking unnecessary vitamins, medications, and other chemicals that may harm my systems.

TOTAL

RATING: ALWAYS . . . . 3 POINTS   TOTAL SCORE: 70–75 = EXCELLENT
MOST OF THE TIME . 2 POINTS   65–69 = VERY GOOD
SOME OF THE TIME . 1 POINT   60–64 = GOOD
NEVER . . . . 0 POINTS   55–59 = FAIR

NAME: _____ **MONTH:** _____

LOOKING AT WHAT YOU EAT

	DATE

BREAD AND CEREALS
All breads, grits, rice, macaroni, oats, cornmeal, and noodles

4 servings

100%
90%
80%
70%
60%
50%
40%
30%
20%
10%

FRUITS AND VEGETABLES
Vegetables and fruits high in vitamins *A* and *C*

4 servings

MILK OR DAIRY PRODUCTS
Milk, cheese, ice cream, and yogurt

4 servings

MEAT
Beef, veal, lamb, pork, poultry, beans, peas, fish, peanut butter, and shellfish

2 servings

SNACKS
Indicate:
   empty calorie = x
   nutritious   = n
   snacks

Record how many servings you eat from each of the four basic food groups every day for one month. Find out if you have a well-balanced nutrient intake. For example, if you ate one bowl of cereal for breakfast, one cheese sandwich for lunch, and one dish of spaghetti for dinner, you satisfied three of the four servings of the bread and cereal group required for the day. The bar graph would be shaded up to the 75% mark.

270

HOW DO DRY CEREALS DIFFER?   UNIT EIGHT: FOOD, DIET, AND DIGESTION

CEREAL NAME	COMPANY	LIST FIRST 3 INGREDIENTS	PROTEIN (gm)	SUCROSE	SPECIAL OFFERS AND OTHERS

1. Which cereal has the most sugar per serving? _____
2. Which cereal has the most protein (gm) per serving? _____
3. Which company produces the greatest variety of cereals? _____
4. Which cereal has the least amount of sugar per serving? _____
5. Which cereals have sugar listed first under ingredients? _____
6. Which cereals have sugar listed after the third ingredient? _____
7. Compare the similar cereals produced by each company and examine the sugar content.

HOW MANY CALORIES DO YOU BURN IN ONE DAY?

UNIT EIGHT: FOOD, DIET, AND DIGESTION

ACTIVITIES	I CALORIES BURNED PER MINUTE OR HOUR	II MINUTES OR HOURS SPENT IN ACTIVITY	III YOUR WEIGHT	NUMBER OF CALORIES YOU BURN IS DETERMINED BY MULTIPLYING I, II, III	TOTAL CALORIES
Sleep Nap	.0075/min. .45/hour			(.0075) x (time) x (weight) =	
Sitting and Reading Watching Television Sitting and Eating Listening to Lecture Taking Notes	.0108/min. .64/hour			( ) x ( ) x ( ) =	
Cooking Washing and Dressing Showering Driving Car Ironing	.015/min. .90/hour			( ) x ( ) x ( ) =	
Light House Work Walking to Class Laboratory Work Wood Shop	.0308/min. 1.84/hour			( ) x ( ) x ( ) =	
Gym Class Bowling Bicycling to School Leisure Jogging Disco Dancing Jumproping	.0395/min. 2.37/hour			( ) x ( ) x ( ) =	
Competitive: Swimming, Tennis Basketball, Judo Wrestling, Karate Climbing Stairs	.0483/min. 2.9/hour			( ) x ( ) x ( ) =	

CALORIES BURNED IN 24 HOURS

HOW MANY CALORIES DO YOU CONSUME IN ONE DAY?

UNIT EIGHT: FOOD, DIET, AND DIGESTION

Check Your Nutrient Intake And Compare With Daily Requirement.

NUTRIENTS	BREAKFAST	LUNCH	DINNER	SNACKS	TOTAL	DAILY REQUIREMENTS (AGES 14-18)
Calories						2800-3000 males/2100-2400 females
Fats						Requirements not set
Carbohydrates						Requirements not set
Proteins						44-54 males/44-48 females
Vitamin A						5000 IU males/4000 IU females
Vitamin C						45 mg males and females
Vitamin B_1						1.4-1.5 mg males/1.1-1.2 females
Vitamin B_2						1.5-1.8 mg males/1.3-1.4 females
Niacin						18-20 mg males/14-16 mg females
Vitamin D						400 IU males and females
Calcium						1200 mg males and females
Iron						18 mg males and females

CALORIES CONSUMED _____

CALORIES BURNED _____

COUNT YOUR CALORIES

UNIT EIGHT: FOOD, DIET, AND DIGESTION

This chart will help you figure out how many calories you consume each day.

TYPE OF FOOD	SIZE OF PORTION		CALORIES
DAIRY FOODS			
Cheese, American	1	oz.	104
Cheese, cottage	½	cup	120
Cheese, Swiss	1	oz.	103
Ice cream, vanilla	½	cup	138
Milk, skim	1	glass (8 oz.)	77
Milk, whole	1	glass (8 oz.)	150
Yogurt, strawberry	1	cup	225
MEAT AND OTHER PROTEIN-RICH FOODS			
Bacon	1½	oz.	92
Bologna	1	oz.	86
Chicken, fried	3	oz.	201
Egg, hard-cooked	1	large	82
Meat patty	3	oz.	186
Peanut butter	2	tbsp.	186
Tuna, canned	3	oz.	168
POPULAR MAIN DISHES			
Macaroni and cheese	½	cup	215
Pizza, cheese	¼	of 14″ pie	354
Spaghetti, meat balls and tomato sauce	1	cup	332
FRUITS			
Apple	1	medium	80
Cantaloupe	¼	medium	29
Orange	1	medium	65
Orange juice	½	cup	56
Peaches	½	cup	39
VEGETABLES			
Beans, green	½	cup	16
Broccoli	½	cup	20
Carrot sticks	5″	carrot, raw	21
Coleslaw	½	cup	82
Corn	½	cup	70
Lettuce	⅙	head, ½ cup	10
Peas, green	½	cup	54
Potato	1	large, baked	132
BREAD AND CEREAL			
Bread, whole wheat	1	slice	55
Corn flakes	¾	cup	72
Pancake	4″	diameter	61
Rice	½	cup	112
Roll, hard	1	roll	156
CAKES AND DESSERTS			
Cake, devil's food	¹⁄₁₆	of 9″ cake	234
Cookie, sugar	3″	diameter	89
Doughnut, cake type	1	doughnut	125
Pie, apple	⅙	of 9″ pie	403
Roll, Danish pastry	1	roll	274
SNACKS			
Bar, milk chocolate	1	oz.	147
Frankfurter, including bun	1	medium	291
Hamburger, including bun	1	medium	305
Milkshake, chocolate	1½	cups	391
Popcorn, plain	1	cup	23
Potato chips	10	chips	114
Sherbet, orange	½	cup	129
Soft drink, cola	1	cup	96
Soup, cream of tomato	1	cup	173
Taco, beef	1	medium	216
COUNT THESE, TOO			
Butter	1	tsp.	36
Chocolate syrup	2	tbsp.	93
French dressing	1	tbsp.	66
Jelly, currant	1	tbsp.	49
Mayonnaise	1	tbsp.	101
Sugar	1	tsp.	14

Source: Comparison Cards, Comprehensive List of Foods, National Dairy Council

NAME: _____ DATE: _____

CHECK UP ON THE SAFETY IN YOUR HOME

How safe are you in your own home? Check your home for possible safety hazards. Use this checklist to help you.

For every question that applies to you, write "yes" or "no" to the left of the question on the list. Then add up all the "no" answers. If the total is more than 2, you need to pay immediate attention to improving the safety in your home. This is your chance to possibly prevent a serious accident from happening in your home!

_____ 1.Are stairways lit well and kept clear of toys and other objects?

_____ 2.Are ice and snow cleaned off of porches, steps, and sidewalks during the winter?

_____ 3.Do family members know to be careful when walking on waxed floors or loose rugs?

_____ 4.Are electric appliances and cords in good condition?

_____ 5.Do family members know not to use electrical appliances where they may be dangerous?

_____ 6.Are knives, garden tools, boiling water, matches, and medicines kept from children?

_____ 7.Are poisons kept in plainly marked containers and out of the reach of children?

_____ 8.Do family members know not to use gasoline or flammable cleaning fluids indoors?

_____ 9.Are guns unloaded and out of the reach of children?

_____ 10.Do family members know how to arrange bedclothes so that a baby cannot smother?

_____ 11.Do family members know to keep plastic bags out of the reach of children?

_____ 12.Do family members know to keep small objects that might be swallowed away from babies?

_____ 13.Are family members who use power tools careful when using them?

_____ 14.Do family members know not to leave small children alone, even for a few minutes?

_____ 15.Is gasoline stored in well-marked containers out of the reach of children?

_____ 16.Does everyone know what to do during a hurricane, an earthquake, or a tornado?

_____ 17.Is at least one member of the family trained in first aid and in CPR?

_____ 18.Are there skid strips in the tub or shower?

_____ 19.Are handles on pots and pans turned inward when in use?

_____ 20.Is there a fire extinguisher in the kitchen?

_____ 21.Are the fire department and ambulance phone numbers close to the phone?

_____ 22.Is there a smoke alarm system in your home?

_____ 23.Does your family have a "no smoking in bed" rule?

_____ 24.Do all family members know what to do if fire starts?

_____ 25.Has the family practiced the fire escape plan during the past year?

HOW DOES YOUR RESTAURANT RATE?

UNIT TEN: HEALTH CAREERS AND SERVICES

Do you worry about how your food is prepared and served? How can you reduce the chance of experiencing stomach cramps, diarrhea, and other discomforts that are related to possible unsanitary conditions of restaurants?

The best prevention is not to eat in a restaurant that has a poor rating. Use the following rating sheet to decide which restaurants to avoid.

On a scale from one to ten (extremely poor = 1, excellent = 10),

HOW CLEAN IS THE FOLLOWING:		NOTES/COMMENTS
1. counter	_____	_____
2. kitchen	_____	_____
3. floor	_____	_____
4. seat	_____	_____
5. table	_____	_____
6. entrance	_____	_____
7. utensils	_____	_____
8. plates/glasses	_____	_____
9. trash receptacle	_____	_____
10. restroom	_____	_____
SUBTOTAL	_____	

Subtract 15 points if the person who handles your food also handles your money.

Subtract 15 points if people who are serving or preparing foods have cuts, sores, or bandages on their hands. Also, if they are coughing, sneezing, or have a runny nose, subtract the same number of points.

Subtract 10 points if there are insects crawling or flying about.

Subtract 10 points if the food is not cooked properly or is served cold.

Subtract 5 points if utensils or straws are not wrapped and are exposed to handling by other customers.

TOTAL POINTS   _____

100—90	Safe enough to return
89—80	Possible contamination; return at own risk
79—70	Definitely stay away
69—0	Report them to the local health department

NAME OF RESTAURANT _____

_____

RESOURCE SECTION

In this section are resource sheets for
optional use in the classroom or with individual
students. The following materials are included:

SUICIDE
Some background information for the teacher

Why teach about suicide?

Every year half a million adolescents attempt suicide; 5,000 succeed. The incidence of suicide in this age group has tripled in the past 20 years. Ranked as the ninth leading cause of death for all ages in the United States, suicide is one of the top three causes of death among young people between 15 and 24. This rate in the United States is approximately 12 per 100,000. Most of these young people want desperately to live. Since suicide is a leading cause of death among young people, many of those who attempt to kill themselves will be in the high school age group. A number will try again and succeed.

There has been a great deal of speculation and discussion by experts, community and school leaders, and parents about the reasons for this tragic phenomenon. Among the possible causes suggested are the loss of strong, stable support systems due to the breakup of the nuclear family, the decline of religion, and the increase in geographic mobility. Also mentioned frequently are the strong, competitive social pressures adolescents face at school, especially as they enter a new community. Education alone cannot solve the problem of suicide. Too much about how to reduce the suicide mortality rate still remains unknown. However, even in the absence of a more complete understanding of suicide, important steps can be taken. The U.S. Department of Health and Human Services report, *Promoting Health-Preventing Disease: Objectives For the Nation*, recommends education and information measures including: inclusion of stress recognition and management in school health curricula, public awareness of indicators of possible suicide, and awareness in the population over the age of 15 of community agencies that assist in coping with stressful situations.

Individual approaches to suicide education will necessarily vary depending on the information students may have already received and on your school's educational philosophy. The material presented here can serve as a supplement to the chapters on stress and mental health. Emphasis throughout the time allotted for this topic should be on promoting the necessary life skills to prevent suicide. Helping teenagers become aware of the importance of handling stress in their own lives, or of indicators that a friend or relative may be contemplating suicide and how to cope with such a situation, may save the lives of many young people. Although dealing with the sudden tragedy of the loss of a friend, brother, or sister is not the best way for an adolescent to be introduced to the phenomenon of suicide, you may find that a suicide within your school community makes class coverage appropriate as a way of helping students cope with what has happened.

It is important to be sensitive to the feelings of all students. Discretion must be exercised when leading classroom discussion to insure that it does not become too painful for any student. Students may wish to reveal stresses in their own lives but should be discouraged from citing specific or detailed examples. Privacy should be respected in all group discussions.

Student Reading

Two student resource readings—"Suicide: A Look at the Problem" and "Facts and Fables on Suicide"—are included for use with your class. They may be duplicated for distribution and begin on page 280.

The *Readers' Guide to Periodical Literature* is the best source for real-life case studies of adolescent suicides should you decide that this approach is appropriate.

Suggested Activities

1. Possible Discussion Questions
   - What is the difference between feeling lonely and being alone?
   - What are the benefits of spending time alone?
   - What are some activities that can be enjoyed alone?
   - Do you think teenagers tend to need more or less time to be alone than people of other ages? Why?
   - What advice should you give to someone who is feeling lonely?
   - How is self-concept formed?
   - What effect does self-concept have on a person's interpretation of experiences? What effect does it have on relationships with others?
   - Do you think most people look at themselves realistically? Why, or why not?
   - Why are some people better able to handle a stressful situation than others?
   - Using only one word to answer, what do you think would make someone want to commit suicide?

2. Have a class discussion on the topic of stress, emphasizing the following points:
   - the definition of stress,
   - the physical signals of stress,
   - possible positive and negative outcomes of experiencing stress.

3. Have the students, individually or in small groups, compose a list of healthy ways to relax. Have them share their lists with the entire class. Then ask each student to try a new way to relax for one week. At the end of the week, have the students share their experiences.

4. Ask each student to list three "Do's" and/or "Don'ts" for dealing with everyday problems. Discuss the lists. What were the three most frequently listed "Do's" and "Don'ts"?

5. Have the students write a statement explaining their philosophy for dealing with everyday problems. Have students share their philosophies.

6. Have the students, as a class, make up a list of stressful situations that teenagers may face; e.g., breaking up a relationship with a boyfriend or girlfriend, parents getting a divorce, having a family member who is an alcoholic, failing a course in school. Divide the students into small groups. Have each group list negative and positive actions that can be taken in each situation. As a follow-up, have the groups discuss the reasons why a person may choose a negative action over a positive action or vice versa. This activity is geared to helping teenagers realize the many options available in any given situation.

7. Have the students develop a list of resource agencies in your community that are prepared to assist in coping with one or more kinds of stressful situations. Include telephone numbers for the agencies as well as "hotlines." Ask the students to transfer this list onto poster board or some other attractive form for displaying the information in an appropriate location in your school. You might also have them publish the list in the school or local newspaper.

8. Invite one or more experts to the class to discuss teenage suicide. Suggestions for guests might include: a representative from a local mental health association or suicide prevention center, a member of the clergy, counselor, therapist, or crisis-intervention expert. Have the students prepare questions. If possible, send the questions to the speaker before the scheduled class session.

9. You may also have students review Chapter 5 in connection with a discussion of problems that occur when family or friends commit suicide.

FACTS AND FABLES ON SUICIDE

FABLE: People who talk about suicide don't commit suicide.

FACT: Of any ten persons who will kill themselves, eight have given definite warnings of their suicidal intentions.

FABLE: Suicide happens without warning.

FACT: Studies reveal that suicidal people give many clues and warnings regarding their suicidal intentions.

FABLE: Suicidal people are fully intent on dying.

FACT: Most suicidal people are undecided about living or dying, and they "gamble with death," leaving it to others to save them. Almost no one commits suicide without letting others know how he or she is feeling.

FABLE: Once suicidal, a person is suicidal forever.

FACT: Individuals who wish to kill themselves are "suicidal" only for a limited period of time.

FABLE: Improvement following a suicidal crisis means that the suicidal risk is over.

FACT: Most suicides occur within about 3 months following the beginning of "improvement," when the individual has the energy to put morbid thoughts and feelings into effect.

FABLE: Suicide strikes much more often among the rich—or, conversely, it occurs almost exclusively among the poor.

FACT: Suicide is neither a rich person's nor a poor person's disease. Suicide is very "democratic" and is represented proportionately among all levels of society.

FABLE: All suicidal individuals are mentally ill, and suicide is always the act of a psychotic person.

FACT: Studies of hundreds of genuine suicide notes indicate that although the suicidal person is extremely unhappy, he or she is not necessarily mentally ill.

Adapted from *Some Facts about Suicide* by E. S. Shneidman and N. L. Farberow, Washington, D.C., PHS Publication No. 852, U.S. Government Printing Office.

SUICIDE: A LOOK AT THE PROBLEM

Suicide is the willful act of bringing an end to one's life. It is also one of the leading causes of death among young people between the ages of 15 and 24.

Why do young people commit suicide? Teenagers who attempt suicide often feel worthless, helpless, hopeless, and overwhelmed. The most frequent stressful situations that seem to bring about these feelings are

- the loss of an important relationship with a boyfriend, girl friend, or parent;
- conflicts or problems they feel cannot be solved;
- living conditions they see as unbearable;
- being under the influence of a drug.

According to a recent government report, some people appear to be especially prone to suicide because of "stress overload." These people include adolescents, the elderly, the unemployed, and workers in certain occupations. However, whether or not stress becomes a problem for a person depends on a combination of things unique to that individual. Also, a person's feelings of stress and his or her reaction to it may change with time, circumstance, and environmental factors.

It is normal for teens to be depressed at times or to experience feelings of loneliness or of being overwhelmed. At one time or another, many people think about suicide as a possible solution. But these thoughts should pass quickly as the person realizes there are better ways to solve the problem. It is cause for concern when depression lasts and the person is not getting help.

What are some clues that a person might be a likely candidate for suicide? Mental health experts suggest the following:

- withdrawing socially
- daredevil behavior
- extreme ups and downs in mood
- giving away treasured possessions
- previous threat or attempt at suicide
- change in work or school performance

- talking, reading, or writing (letters or poems) about death
- increase in smoking; use of alcohol or other drugs
- talk of martyrdom or extreme desire to punish another person

How Can You Help?

How can you help a friend who may be in trouble? First, keep yourself in a high state of wellness. Then you will be better equipped to help. Why? Recent studies show that you are better able to manage stress if your life includes the following:

- happiness in your school or job life
- time for yourself
- enough sleep
- people who care about you and are willing to help you

- sense of belonging to a group
- physical fitness
- freedom from disease

If you suspect that a friend might be thinking about suicide, here are some things you can do to help:

- Listen. Even if you cannot solve the problem, listening will let your friend know his or her well-being is important to you.
- Be supportive. It is a mistake to call someone's problems or feelings unimportant. It is also a mistake not to take suicide threats seriously.
- Never leave a suicidal person alone.

- Take action. Try to get the person to come with you to a teacher, counselor, his or her parents, your parents, a doctor, an emergency room, or an adult who can provide help. By going with your friend, you are making sure the person gets help. You are also showing that you care. Even if your friend won't come with you, don't carry the load alone. Tell someone that you think your friend might harm him or herself and that you need help.
- You will find more helpful information in Chapter 5.

DEATH AND DYING
Some background information for the teacher

If health and life are antitheses to illness and death, is it ironic to include the subjects of dying and death in a health class? Why discuss dying and death when most students are maturing, developing, and in good health?

Researchers are finding that young people have less fear and anxiety about the subject when they discover that death is a natural part of the human life cycle. Also, students who study the stages of dying feel more comfortable and willing to talk with a terminally ill person. Therefore, the rationale for inclusion of dying and death in a health class is to help students to deal early with emotions that are inevitable.

Elisabeth Kübler-Ross, a physician specializing in psychiatry, interviewed many people with terminal illnesses. She wrote a book called *Death and Dying*, which summarized her findings about how people feel and the emotions that arise while awaiting death. She organized the feelings of the dying into the five stages described in the student reading on page 285.

Student Handouts

Before giving the students the background information, "The Life Cycle," have them read and discuss "Something to Think About."

Students can be introduced to the five stages of dying by applying the stages to other life crises, such as failing a class, having something of value stolen, or losing a job that provided money for school expenses. Allow the students to explore the subject of dying and death openly.

Possible Student Activities

The student-activity questions that follow provide content and are open-ended. There are no incorrect answers. Use the questions to facilitate a class discussion.

1. Thinking or talking about death is difficult for many people, and yet the subject of dying and death fills our newspapers and television programs. On an average day, the theme of death may appear dozens of times from the headlines to the comic section of a newspaper. So why is it difficult to comprehend death? Maybe the news media, while competing for ratings and audiences, show too many vivid scenes of violence, war, and accidental death. Perhaps we cannot separate, in our minds, what is real and what is entertainment. Or perhaps we know the difference, but we are saturated and bored by the subject.

    Write a paragraph expressing your views. Do you agree or disagree with the above comments? Explain.
2. Birth, growth, maturation, aging, and death complete the life cycle of a human being. At what stage in the cycle do you think death is most feared? Why?
3. Life expectancy for the average American has changed over the years. Why do you think the average life span has increased from 45 to 75 in the past 200 years? What will life expectancy be in the year 2000? Why?
4. Why are cosmetics, health spas, vitamins, face lifts, aerobics, and jogging called the "modern-day Fountain of Youth?" How will this "Fountain of Youth" affect the first stage of dying?
5. What are some ways for a person to help a terminally ill patient who is going through the five stages of dying?

SOMETHING TO THINK ABOUT

Have you ever failed an exam or a course? If so, you might have gone through one or more of the five stages of emotional change that are described below.

Let us assume that a student fails a course. His first reaction would be one of *surprise* and *shock*. He might *deny* failing, reexamine the grades posted on the board, or confront the teacher. His *denial* of failing might cause him to say, *"No, not me."*

He will think of all the reasons why the teacher failed him. He will be *angry* at the teacher and the school. He might say, "Why me?"

After calming down, the student may plead with the teacher to give him *another chance*. He will try to *bargain* with the teacher by smiling and promising to turn in a special project. During this stage, the student still feels that he can pass the course.

Eventually, the student realizes that he cannot bargain with the teacher. He becomes depressed. Soon his parents will learn about his failure. He may retreat to his room and pout about the failure.

Finally, after a period of time, he may *accept* the fact that he has failed the course. He is no longer angry at the teacher and is at *peace* with himself.

The five emotional stages that this student went through can be summarized in the stages shown below:

Stage 1: Denial and shock
Stage 2: Anger and bitterness
Stage 3: Bargain and compromise
Stage 4: Depression and sorrow
Stage 5: Acceptance and peace

The five stages can be applied to many other life conflicts. Using the five stages, write a scenario involving one of the following:

- an adult who is cut from her job after working for a company for 20 years,
- a person who has lost something of great value,
- a high school student who is informed by her physician that she has a terminal illness and will die within 3 months.

THE LIFE CYCLE

When you were young, your idea of death was probably similar to that of many children. Children view death as simply a temporary vacation or a long sleep. They do not see it as a permanent condition. As children grow older, they begin to see death as something that could affect them. By the time they reach 10 years of age, many children see themselves as a part of a life cycle. They learn that living things grow, mature, age, and then die.

As young adults, you are able to understand that the length of the life cycle is influenced by heredity and environment. Also, you are better prepared to accept and to deal with the biological process that we call death. The fears we have about dying and death can be better understood if we allow ourselves to be open-minded and to talk freely with others. There are certain recognizable steps that occur emotionally when we are faced with death. They are as follows:

Stage 1: Denial and Shock

When patients are told that they will soon die, many go into temporary shock. Often they react by saying, "No, that's not possible," or "It can't be me." Some patients will go from one doctor to another, hoping that at least one will make a different diagnosis.

Stage 2: Anger and Bitterness

When the patients finally accept the fact that they will die, they enter the second stage. The patients are usually angry with everyone. The doctor, nurse, family member, or friend will be the target of the patients' anger. They ask the question, "Why me?" The patients try to hide behind masks, because they are not sure how they should react to the terminal illness. After the rage is over, they enter the third stage.

Stage 3: Bargaining and Compromise

During this stage, the patients try in many ways to extend life. Some will look for a "doctor" who has a miracle cure. Others will attend religious services more often to make promises that they will be better people. They attempt, in as many ways as possible, to prevent death or at least to postpone it for a little while longer. But finally, the patients realize that they have no control over death.

Stage 4: Depression and Sorrow

By now, the dying patients are showing more signs of tiring. The disease has spread to many parts of the body or a vital organ is not working properly. The reality that they will not be able to fulfill promises and goals brings on depression. The fact that they will lose many friends and loved ones becomes unbearable.

Stage 5: Acceptance and Peace

The final stage is one of understanding. The dying patients accept their illness and are at peace with the world. They prefer to be in a quiet environment, and visitors are generally limited to several close relatives and friends.

While the stages described above are helpful to understanding the changes that dying patients may go through, not everyone will follow the stages in this exact order. Some patients may go back and forth from one stage to another, while others may not go through all of the stages. Relatives and close friends can be very helpful to the patient during all five stages. They must understand and anticipate the changes. Most importantly, they must provide support and empathy.

Knowing the five stages of dying can help you to understand the fears and anxieties that may occur at the end of life. Although an understanding of the emotional changes and a knowledge of the life cycle of humans are very important, we must focus our attention on the part of the life cycle called "here and now." Rather than living a daily struggle against the end of life, we can use our knowledge of death to enliven and enrich life's present moments. Knowing that tomorrow may be our last day can motivate us to see that some growth takes place within us now. Compassion, tolerance of others, and love are just a few of the qualities that enrich all experience. As we acquire more of such qualities each day, life becomes more meaningful and lasting in value. In other words, after biological death, the influence we have had on our families, friends, and world will continue.

TOXIC SHOCK SYNDROME
Some questions and answers

What Is Toxic Shock Syndrome?

Toxic shock syndrome (TSS) is a recently recognized, life-threatening disease that occurs mainly in women under the age of 25, particularly those using tampons. It usually occurs during or just after the menstrual period.

What Are the Symptoms of TSS?

The symptoms of TSS are quite specific, although not all symptoms appear in every case. The usual symptoms are fever over 102° F; vomiting and diarrhea; fainting or feeling faint when standing up; pale, cold skin and red eyes; blue hands and feet; and a sunburnlike rash, followed by peeling. Anyone with TSS symptoms should see a doctor at once.

Do People Die from It?

Yes. Approximately 10 percent of the cases reported to the Centers for Disease Control (CDC) have resulted in death.

How Long Does TSS Last?

Duration of illness is usually 4 to 5 days in the acute phase followed by 1 to 2 weeks of convalescence. Most deaths occur within a week.

What Causes TSS?

Scientists at the National Centers For Disease Control have found that TSS is caused by bacteria that make a toxin, or poison. The bacteria are called Staphylococcus Aureus (S. Aureus). These bacteria live in the lining of some people's noses, and in some women's vaginas. If they get into a sore on a person's body, they can enter the blood stream and cause toxic shock. The bacteria are spread by touching and by sneezing. About 2 percent of people have them. But not all these people are susceptible to TSS. Those who develop the disease lack the antibodies that can protect them. Patients with some antibodies experience milder cases.

What Is the Relationship between TSS and Tampons?

Tampons play a contributing role in the development of TSS but do not cause the syndrome. Studies are underway to better define the role of both S. Aureus and tampons. There are two reasons that using tampons increases the risk of getting toxic shock. One reason is that tampons, especially super-absorbent tampons, dry out the lining of the vagina. Then irritation can lead to a sore that lets bacteria into the blood stream. Another reason is that bacteria find it easy to live and grow in the menstrual blood on the tampon. Any woman should consider the risk of TSS before deciding to use tampons. Changing tampons regularly can decrease the risk, and so can switching between tampons and menstrual pads.

How Common Is Toxic Shock Syndrome?

TSS is a rare disease. One study showed that TSS occurred at the rate of 6 per 100,000 menstruating women per year; another study found the rate to be 15 per 100,000 menstruating women per year.

Is It Possible To Have TSS More Than Once?

Yes. Current studies suggest that there is a 30% chance of recurrence.

Is There a Treatment for TSS?

In the acute phase, patients frequently need to be hospitalized in intensive care units where they can be given large volumes of intravenous fluids and medications to help raise the blood pressure. Some doctors may use certain antibiotics to treat patients after taking appropriate cultures—vaginal, cervical, blood, nose, urine, and stool. It has not been documented that these drugs cure the disease or improve outcomes, but they do appear to prevent recurrences.

Is There a Test I Should Take To See If I Can Develop TSS?

Visit your doctor or clinic to determine whether testing for S. Aureus is appropriate for you.

Does TSS Occur Only in Women?

The vast majority of reported cases have been in menstruating women who were using tampons. However, there have been cases reported in men, children, and nonmenstruating women. In these cases the bacterium, S. Aureus, was isolated from a wound on the body. This presumably caused the illness.